UNDER FIRE AND SUN

The Third Book in the Tom Archer Series

By

Richard A. Basquill

UNDER FIRE AND SUN

 This is a work of historical fiction. While inspired by real events, locations, and figures from the Second World War, the narrative, characters, and dialogue have been fictionalised for dramatic purposes. Some characters and incidents are products of the author's imagination. Any resemblance to actual people, living or dead, outside of clearly referenced historical figures, is entirely coincidental.

ISBN: 978-1-0681502-1-0

Copyediting and proofreading by Sage Proofreading and Copyediting Services - info@sageproof.co.uk

First Edition

Published by Basquill Books through Kindle Direct Publishing

ACKNOWLEDGEMENTS

By the time you reach a third book, you begin to understand that writing is not a solitary pursuit at all. What started as an idea has become something far bigger than I ever expected, shaped not just by me, but by the people who have supported it along the way. To my friends and family, thank you for continuing to stand behind me as this journey has grown. Your encouragement, patience, and steady belief have carried me further than I could have managed alone. To my friends, thank you for your support, your encouragement, and for parting with your hard-earned money to read these stories. That means more to me than you might realise. Knowing you've backed this from the start, not just in words but in action, has been a constant source of motivation. To Sue, my wonderful wife, thank you for everything you give to this process. Your patience with the long evenings, your humour when it's needed most, and your constant support mean more than I can properly express. You've been there from the very first page to this one, and I would not be here without you. To my editor, Lorraine Sage of Sage Proofreading and Copyediting Services, thank you once again for your honesty, your precision, and your commitment to making each book better than the last. Your input continues to shape not just the work, but the way I approach writing itself. And to the readers. The continued support for this series has been both humbling and motivating in equal measure. With over 1,400 copies sold and more than 1.1 million pages read on Kindle Unlimited, I remain genuinely grateful that so many of you have chosen to follow this story. Every review, whether generous or critical, plays its part in pushing me to improve and to do justice to the trust you place in these books. This story continues because you are reading it. Thank you for that.

MAP

North Africa 1941
Mediterranean Sea
N
Benghazi
Al Marj
Al Bayda
Derna
Timimi
Gazala
Mechili
Tobruk
El Adem
Bardia
Capuzzo
Sollum
Sidi Barrani
Sofafi
Nibeiwa
Matruh
Msus
Soluch
Beda Fomm
Ajdabiyah
C Y R E N A I C A
L I B Y A
E G Y P T
0
50
100 miles

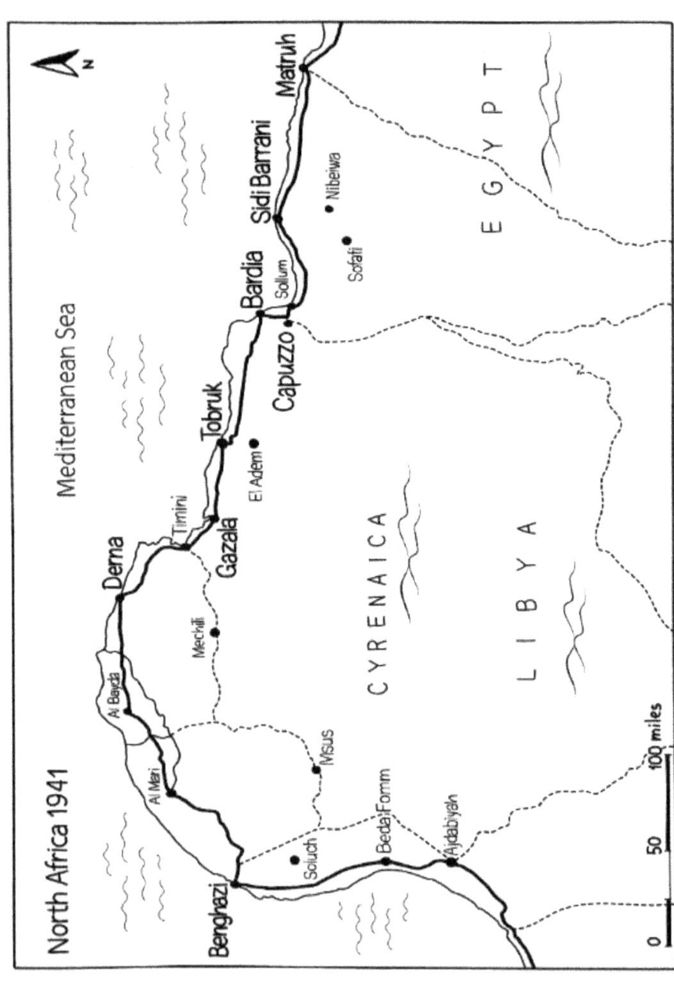

PROLOGUE

The ship's engines thrummed a steady rhythm beneath Archer's boots, a low, constant heartbeat that seemed to pulse through the deck and out into the endless, heaving darkness of the sea. The whole vessel felt alive with its dull, vibrating presence that never ceased, as though the ship itself strained towards the horizon, dragging them inexorably forwards into whatever lay ahead. He stood at the rail, the cold iron biting into his palms, slick with salt and dew. The metal smelt of rust, oil, and the sour tang of the sea: familiar scents were now edged with a strange foreboding. The wind cut across the deck, sharp and damp against his skin, carrying the briny breath of the ocean and the faint, acrid hint of the ship's funnels coughing into the night. Somewhere out there, far ahead, though no one could yet see it, lay land. North Africa. Heat and sand and a new war waiting to swallow them whole. Around them, the convoy of ships ploughed on through the night, forming a line of dark shapes moving slow and steady across the swells while their engines hummed beneath the sea wind.

The war was waiting. And they were heading straight for it. Around Archer, the ship murmured: low voices, boots on steel, the clank of machinery below. Men moved like shadows, hunched against the cold with their breath steaming in the damp air. Somewhere, a canvas flap snapped, and a mess tin clanged before being swallowed by the sea's endless whisper. Without thinking, his grip tightened on the rail, the salt and cold biting into his skin. He reached into his pocket, pulled out the battered silver flask, and slowly unscrewed the cap. Lifting it to his lips, he took a slow, steady swig and felt the liquid warm and raw across his tongue. As he pulled the flask away, he stared at it for a moment, the worn metal catching the faint light. A warmth stirred in him, not from the drink, but from the memory it carried. It had been

Pembroke's flask, a gift, a token, a reminder of the man's unflappable grin and sharp, steady voice. And, more than anything, a reminder of the moment they had found each other again after the chaos of the retreat, when Archer had thought him lost for good.

He lifted the flask to his lips again, the taste lingering, and his mind drifted back to a different memory in Colchester. He'd been sat in the lounge at The George Hotel on the High Street with Pembroke, Mallory, Evans, and Pritchard. The others who had made it back crowded in around them, all clean and starched in new uniforms. It had been the first chance they'd had to gather for a drink, the first moment to breathe after the horrors of the last month, a chance to reflect on lost friends. Pembroke, glass in hand, had held court. his voice had been steady but low as if speaking too loudly might make it all too real. He told them how his party had fled through the backroads and fields of France, keeping to the hedgerows, diving into ditches when aircraft roared overhead and crawling through mud and brambles in the dark. How they'd swum across black, oily canals, boots slung round their necks, packs half-sunk in the water, rifles held high above their heads, and their breath always coming in ragged gasps as tracer fire stitched the banks. He'd spoken of slipping past German patrols in the night, of clinging to the shadows as tanks rumbled down the roads, of the sharp crack of rifle fire in the distance, and the thud of boots on broken cobbles when they'd run. He recounted stealing eggs from a farmyard in the dark, cooking them over a fire so small it barely flickered, and the shells still stuck with dirt and feathers.

Twisting the flask in his hands, Archer remembered how Pembroke had become almost mournful as he told how they'd reached Dunkirk, *the beach*: a wasteland of shattered trucks and burnt-out lorries, bodies half-buried in the sand, and the air thick with the stench of smoke and fuel. They'd huddled there for days, packed tight with thousands of others, stomachs hollow, throats raw, and each hour stretching into the next under the shriek of dive bombers and the roar of distant guns. Pembroke had described the sound of the Luftwaffe's engines, the rising whine, the moment of dreadful pause, and then the earthshaking crash as bombs fell among the men, tearing holes in the sand, in the ranks, in their minds.

As they'd sat in The George, all the men had relived those moments with Pembroke as he'd retold the long, endless wait in the freezing water, boots and kit waterlogged, fingers numb, bodies shrinking in on themselves as the tide pulled at their legs, and the surf slapped against their chests. Queueing for rescue, but rescue hadn't come. Not that day. Not the next.

Until the little boat, the *Susan*. A pleasure craft, Pembroke called her, barely bigger than a fishing launch, her paintwork scuffed, her deck smeared with oil and blood. She had come chugging through the grey chop, a dogged thing, making trip after trip across the heaving water, plucking men from the waves and ferrying them to the larger ships waiting further out. Fourteen, sixteen men at a time, packed in tight, shivering, soaked through, teeth chattering, boots sloshing. The *Susan*'s engine coughed and rattled, and the deck creaked under the weight of desperate men, but each time she turned back for another load, stubborn and steady. "Little boat, big heart," Pembroke had said with a crooked grin, and the others had laughed, low, tired laughs that spoke more of relief than humour, and echoed with their shared experience. Archer had listened silently, letting Pembroke's words settle like an ache on his chest. It wasn't just luck that had got them back, he thought. It was grit and stubbornness, and something else: a refusal to let go even when the odds had been against them. They'd clawed their way back from the jaws of hell. There had been a pause then, the clink of glasses and the low murmur of the bar filling the space. Mallory had leant back in his chair, a fresh pint in hand, his face shadowed in the dim light, and he'd spoken quietly, his voice low but sharp-edged. "Finch. Poor bastard was wounded in the woods, lying there waiting for help and they just shot him. In the head. No mercy. No warning. Just killed him. No quarter."

Evans had let out a bitter snort, shaking his head. "Didn't even give him a chance. Lying there, unarmed, bleeding...and they just pulled the trigger. Bastards didn't even stop to check." The raw words had hung in the air, heavy and raw. Around the table, jaws tightened, eyes darkened. Even the clink of glasses from the rest of the pub had seemed to fade as if the weight of it all pressed in, thick and suffocating them. The anger had simmered, spreading like a slow fire among the men at the table. Pritchard had stared into his drink and clenched his hands tightly around the glass. Jacks sat stiff, eyes narrowed, his usual swagger gone.

Webb glanced down, jaw working, while Wilson's gaze fixed on some distant point beyond the pub wall, lips pressed tight. For a moment, no one had spoken. The room seemed to pulse with quiet fury, a low, shared burn of hatred that no drink could wash away. The memories were too fresh, the loss too deep, the injustice too sharp.

Archer had sat among them, the glass feeling heavy in his hand as the silence settled. The battalion had been battered to the bone, men lost, men scattered but the flame still burnt. That stubborn, bloody-minded flame. And that, more than anything, was what they had left. The young officer could feel the mood sinking, the weight of their reflections dragging at the room. He had glanced at the men, then raised his glass in a slow, deliberate gesture towards Pritchard, a glint of knowing menace in his eyes. "Pritchard... tell the lads how you got out."

Pritchard leant in, a sly grin tugging at the corner of his mouth. "Well, while you lot were legging it across France, I had my own bit of luck," Pritchard had said, swirling the half of his pint. "After that little scrap with the guns, I made my way round to the east and ended up on the outskirts of some village, middle of nowhere, Jerry all over it. Bugger, I thought. That's me done for!" He paused, letting his story breathe, the corners of his mouth twitching. "So, I'm trying to make an alternative route, right? Picking my way through the hedgerows, and what do I do? Stumble straight into a French farmhouse. Thought it was empty." He shook his head, grinning now.

"Turns out, there's an old couple sitting at the table, eating, like it's bloody peacetime! They looked up at me, eyes wide, jaws on the floor, must've thought I was the Angel of Death himself. And fair enough, I must've been a sight, filthy, stinking, boots covered in mud and shit." The table had burst into laughter, Evans nearly spilling his pint, Jacks slapping the table with the flat of his hand. Pritchard had raised his voice, acting it out, hands gesturing wildly. "So, there's me, trying to wave them off, 'Non, non! Le Bosch! Le Bosch! Waving my arms like a bloody windmill. And what do they do? The old man's up, ushering me to the table, and the old lady, God bless her, grabs a plate and starts setting me a place!" He had leant back, shaking his head in disbelief, the grin still fixed on his face. "Next thing I know, Jerry's a hundred yards down the road, and I'm sat there tucking into onion soup and bread. I tell you, it was bloody marvellous." Saunders, a long grin across his face, looked at Pritchard. "And...?" Pritchard dropped his voice low, leaning in.

The whole room was hanging on his every word. "Well." He let the pause drag, milking it, then carried on. "No sooner had the old boy poured me a cognac, the missus comes back, arms full of clothes, and starts motioning at me to get my kit off. I'm like, Ay up! I ain't got time to play dress-up!" The men burst out laughing, Evans nearly choking on his drink.

Pritchard kept going, hands gesturing wide, voice half outraged, half amused. "I'm standing there, pushing her away, *Non! Non!* and she's pulling at my battledress, tugging like a bloody terrier! And the room's full of French words, some I'd heard before, some I hadn't!" He paused, grinning, letting the men laugh. They were leaning in now, caught in the story.

"Well," he said, shaking his head. "The old woman's a tough old bird, and next thing I know, I'm stood there in the middle of this little room, I kid you not, head scarf, blouse, and a full-blown red skirt!" The place had erupted, disbelief, hoots, men banging on the tables.

Jacks shouted over the din, "Piss off, Pritchard!"

Evans called out, "You're full of it, mate!"

But Pritchard held up a hand, mock serious. "No, seriously, as Mr Archer is sitting there!" He pointed at Archer, his grin wide, defiant. Archer had replied with a massive smile and a gentle nod of approval. Pritchard had barely been able to keep the grin off his face, seeing the men in stitches around him. He raised his almost empty pint, half in salute, and carried on, his voice steady but pitched just loud enough to fill the room. "That's not even the best bit. So, after the old girl's finished dressing me up like a bloody music hall act, the old boy claps me on the back, points to his wagon outside, and motions for me to get on board. So, there I was, sitting there bold as brass in the back, right on top of a stack of turnips, with my gear stashed under it all."

The men leant in closer, laughter bubbling under the surface. "So, there I am," Pritchard went on, waving a hand in disbelief. "Trundling through this little French village on this bloody horse-drawn cart, head scarf flapping in the breeze, red skirt flapping over my knees, blouse buttoned tight and, on my feet, the scruffiest, mud-caked pair of hobnailed boots you've ever seen!" The room had exploded. Jacks let out a bellowing laugh, nearly toppling his pint, Evans wiped tears from his eyes, and even Mallory shook his head with a grin that crept across his face. "And the best part?" Pritchard added, leaning in conspiratorially. "Jerry's everywhere, lorries, bikes, foot patrols and they're too bloody preoccupied to notice me. Too busy pulling the town apart, looking for God knows what. They never even glanced at the old farmer's cart. Just a little old French girl, sitting on top of the turnips." The laughter had risen again, louder, freer this time an absurd story in the middle of an absurd war. Pritchard sat back, raising his pint with a grin. "And that, gentlemen, is how I made it to Dunkirk."

The laughter had rung out long into that night at The George, filling the corners of the old pub. The clink of glasses and the soft crackle of the fire had been the only sounds to follow. They had sat there as comrades, the lines between ranks softened by shared survival and the sharp, bitter edge of the memories they carried. For a while, the war had felt distant, just a story traded over pints, a stress shared among friends.

Now, standing on the deck of the ship, Archer could still hear the echoes of that laughter, the warmth of it, the sharp edges that had been dulled by distance and time. The cold wind continued to cut across the deck, snapping at the hem of his greatcoat, and once again, he felt the sea's endless motion beneath his boots, pulling him away from England, away from home, away from the men who hadn't made it back. Archer unscrewed the flask again, took a slow, measured sip, and let the burn settle in his chest. He thought of the men of Jacks, Webb, Pritchard, Wilson, Saunders. Of Mallory and Evans. Of Pembroke. The ones who had made it through. And he thought, too, of Charlotte, her face framed by the soft light of a London streetlamp, the warmth of her hand in his, the memory of her smile lingering in the quiet spaces of his mind.

The war wasn't over. Not yet.

He capped the flask, slid it into his pocket, and turned to face the sea. Somewhere ahead, the coast of North Africa waited, a faint smudge on the horizon beneath a sky wide and endless. He would be ready.

CHAPTER 1

The desert was too quiet. Too still. Tom Archer scanned the ridgeline through his binoculars, the glass briefly fogging with the heat of his breath. The sun was just dragging itself above the horizon, a red eye opening over a sea of dust. Long, blade-sharp shadows spilt across the wadi below. No birdsong. No wind. Just the tick of cooling metal and the slow, shallow breaths of three men lying motionless in the sand. A fine mist of grit clung to his lips. The world was all silence, sun-bleached sand, and the faint tang of engine oil. "Still think this is a good idea, Sir?" Jacks muttered beside him, his voice low and dry as parchment. He'd taken over as platoon sergeant after Mallory was promoted to company sergeant major during the reconstitution of the 9th Battalion. "Ten days out of Alexandria, and they've already got us poking our noses where they don't want us."

Archer didn't reply. His stomach was tight... not with fear, but with something colder. Doubt. The kind he couldn't afford to show. He shifted, careful to stay below the dune's crest. Sand scratched between cloth and skin, worming into every seam, boots, sleeves, the curve of his spine. It was inescapable. The desert didn't fight fair. It just wore you down.

Behind them, Pritchard let out a dry cough, one hand resting across his Lee Enfield. To no one in particular, he muttered, "Don't like ground you can't hide in." They were out on a reconnaissance patrol southwest of Fort Capuzzo, skirting the edge of Italian-held territory near El Adem. Officially, their mission was to confirm intelligence reports ahead of the planned bombardment. Unofficially, Archer suspected it was a test—a quiet appraisal of the new arrivals. A chance for the 7th Battalion to see what the "Dunkirk boys" were really made of. But the air between the seasoned hands of the 7th Greenmoors and the battered survivors from Archer's outfit—the decimated 9th Battalion—had been stiff with unease since the moment they'd come ashore. Not among the men. The enlisted ranks had found easy ground in shared routines: fixing kit, filling sandbags, grumbling about rations and the heat. You didn't need to know a man's name to share a cigarette.

It was the officers who trod warily around Archer—a lieutenant already awarded the Military Cross, his record the quiet envy of regulars who had spent the past year stationed in the forlorn desert, guarding forts, rail crossings, and other mindless outposts.

A few weeks before, his twentieth birthday had been spent aboard the Durban Castle, somewhere south of Crete. He felt older than the number suggested as though the year behind him counted for more than all of those before it. There had been tinned fruit and a tot of rum passed along the mess, nothing more. He hadn't mentioned the occasion, and no one had asked. Voices carried along the steel passageways, and a wind that smelt faintly of salt and diesel worked its way in wherever it could. The men had swapped smokes, played cards in narrow bunks, and tried not to think too hard about where they were headed. Archer had kept the day to himself. A quiet marker, nothing worth announcing.

Archer remembered standing alone on the deck that night, a tin mug of lukewarm tea in his hand, staring out over black water. The little parcel had sat in the bottom of his kit for weeks, tucked inside an old gas mask case he now used as a personal bag. The khaki canvas casing was faded, the original markings long worn away, and a leather strap had been added by a farrier of the Essex Yeomanry back in Colchester—for the costly sum of half a bottle of Napoleon brandy that Archer had swiped from the mess one drunken night. He wore it slung across his chest and over his webbing, so it rested comfortably on his thigh... a quiet constant amid the weight of official gear.

Inside, he kept his captured binoculars from the German officer at the bridge, some six months ago. There was also a folding travel clock that ticked silently; a battered shaving kit; and a small picture frame, containing the image of his beloved Charlotte wrapped in cloth to stop the glass from breaking. Two pairs of thick socks. A set of brown leather gloves, softening with wear. A new, although already bent, notebook that still smelt faintly of paper and ink. Folded among it all was the letter he'd been handed in Colchester, informing him he had been awarded the Military Cross for his actions at Cassel. He hadn't looked at it since. Then, at the very bottom of the case was the small, battered metal flask... Pembroke's given to Archer on the first day he'd joined the battalion in France, in what seemed a lifetime ago.

He'd promised Charlotte he wouldn't open her parcel until Christmas. Yet standing beneath a foreign sky with only the creak of steel and the wind for company, it had felt like the right time. Archer had untied the twine, careful not to tear the paper. Inside was a small, square dark-green box, the lid embossed in faded gold leaf: "F.H. Steer & Co. Jewellers of St James'."

He'd opened it. Nestled inside was a wristwatch, an Omega, understated and elegant, with a black dial, luminous hands, and a chestnut leather strap fitted with a stitched leather cap to protect the face. The kind worn in the field... not for fashion, but for function.

He'd turned the watch with a slow and methodical inspection the cap open. On the back, engraved in small italics, were five words: *Stay safe, my love... Charlie.* As he'd stood on the deck that night, he ran his thumb over the words, then slipped the watch onto his wrist, the strap snug and reassuring against his skin. For a long moment, he had stood at the rail with the box open in his hand, the wind tugging at his collar, and the sea stretching away into the night. Then he'd closed the box gently and tucked it back into his satchel. The thought of Charlotte engraved deep in his mind and heart. As he hunched below the dune's crest, Archer lifted the leather cap on his watch, holding the bezel between the thumb and forefinger of his right hand. For a fleeting moment, the thought of Charlotte crossed his mind the memory of her light hazel eyes set shallow in her pale, smiling face. Just a moment, and then it passed, carried away by the dry whisper of the desert wind.

Jacks' hand nudged his boot. "Sir. Movement... two o'clock. Just dust for now, but it's coming fast."

Archer's mind cleared, and he swung his glasses towards the ridge. The sun caught on something metallic—a glint, then two. A pair of trucks, maybe more, shrouded in the rising haze. Italian? Hard to say. The light bent everything out here. Even time.

"Down," he ordered. "Stay low. If they pass—good. If they stop... we wait, then move." Behind him, Pritchard whispered a clipped prayer into the sand. Jacks checked his rifle, bolt sliding forwards with a quiet finality. Archer steadied his breathing.

The trucks slowed on the track below the ridge, their outlines sharpening through the heat shimmer as they crawled along the hard-packed ground at its base. One of them hissed as it halted, tyres grinding against loose stone. Archer lowered the binoculars just enough to see Jacks' jaw tighten. "They've stopped," Jacks murmured. "That's never good." Through the haze, shapes began to shift dark blotches against the burnt gold of the landscape. At least half a dozen men dismounted from the lead vehicle. Another figure clambered out from the second truck and moved towards the front, gesturing in wide, sweeping arcs. Officers, maybe. Whatever they were saying, it wasn't casual.

The soldiers began to fan out, rifles cradled, their movements deliberate. They weren't just stretching their legs, they were sweeping the ground. Archer's gut clenched.

"They're coming this way," Pritchard whispered. "Bloody hell... they're sweeping the bloody wadi."

Archer lifted his glasses again. No mistaking it now...

Italian infantry, sun helmets glinting, spread in a shallow arc across the scrub. They moved with a purpose, eyes scanning the ground ahead of them, boots treading in a lazy zigzag.

"Did we leave anything?" Archer asked, voice barely audible.

"No," Jacks said, curt. "But the sand's soft here. Could be tracks. Pritchard?"

"I wiped 'em best I could on the way in," Pritchard said, not taking his eyes off the Bren. "But they've got a dog, or a scout, or just a lucky bastard. I don't like how close they are."

Archer ran the options through his head. If they stayed, they'd be overrun. If they moved too early, they'd give themselves away.

One of the Italians paused. He squatted, examined something on the ground, then turned and called back to his officer.

"Shit," Jacks muttered. "That's us."

Archer's hand moved to his rifle without thinking. The desert didn't echo like the woods of France. Here, sound stuck to the ground heavy, close. But the silence now was a kind Archer knew too well. It was the moment before everything falls apart.

"We go back. Quietly," Archer said. "No noise unless it gets noisy first. Pritchard, cover the rear. Jacks, you're with me." He shifted backwards in the sand, keeping low, motioning the others to do the same. Their carrier was maybe two hundred yards back... just over a small ridge, partially camouflaged beneath a net. Too far if the enemy started shooting.

As Archer moved, a sudden glint caught his eye. The sun bounced off Pritchard's Bren gun's metal receiver–just a flicker, but enough.

The nearest Italian stopped dead and pointed.

Then he shouted.

"Run," Archer hissed. "Back to the carrier now!"

The wadi exploded with noise. A rifle cracked. Sand spat up near Archer's boot. Pritchard swore and wheeled around with the Bren, firing short, sharp bursts to suppress the Italians. Archer didn't look back. The desert flat, hot, and suddenly deafening swallowed everything else. Jacks turned and dropped to a knee, delivering steady, aimed shots. Archer was already shouting to Saunders and Webb. "Get the netting off the carrier, get it started!"

The Italian fire was sporadic, undisciplined, but it was coming in the right direction. Sand kicked up in sharp puffs around them, each round hitting the ground with brutal force. The carrier loomed ahead, squat and half-shrouded beneath the camouflage netting. Webb and Saunders were already tugging it free, Webb scrambling up into the driver's seat as the engine coughed, sputtered, then caught with a reluctant roar. Then all hell broke loose again—from the other side of the carrier. A crack of rifle and machine-gun fire from the rocks to their right. Close. Too close. A second Italian patrol, smaller, unnoticed and waiting. The trap hadn't been perfect, but it was close enough.

Archer ducked instinctively as rounds whistled past.

"To the right!" he shouted, diving behind the carrier's side plate. Webb flinched behind the wheel. The engine stuttered but kept running. Jacks spun mid-stride and fired two clean shots into the scrub: one was followed by a strangled scream.

Pritchard dropped flat and raked the rocks with the Bren, dust and blood spraying into the air. Another Italian tried to run for cover—didn't make it three steps. Archer, crouched low, turned to Webb and Saunders. "Give covering fire!"

Webb, having got the carrier started, leapt into the back in an awkward crouch and began firing his Lee-Enfield. Saunders dropped to one knee behind the carrier, braced against its rear, working the bolt smoothly between each shot. He fired steadily, breathing slow. One of his targets spun clockwise, a fountain of blood arcing from the man's throat.

Behind them, more rifle cracks. Closer now.

Archer twisted to look. Jacks and Pritchard were still fifty yards out, bounding forwards in bursts. Jacks fired on the run, his

rounds snapping toward the ridge. Pritchard paused just long enough to fire a burst from the Bren, pivoting left to catch movement on their rear flank. "They're trying to cut us off," Archer muttered, heart thudding. "Come on! Some on..."
A shout in Italian echoed through the rocks.
More fire from the left, wild but closing.
Jacks dropped into cover behind a scrub bush, shouted something Archer didn't catch, then dashed again, crouched low. Pritchard fired from his shoulder, leaning into the Bren, the weapon chattering as he laid down a rough curtain of lead.

Archer raised his rifle, sighted a flash of movement on the left ridge and squeezed the trigger. A figure dropped. Pritchard reached the carrier first, diving behind the armour plate with a gasp. Jacks followed a second later, blood on his sleeve, not hit, just cut. His expression was pure fury.

"They're thinning out," Jacks growled. "Push back hard now and they'll fold." Archer didn't hesitate. He turned to the front of the carrier. "Webb! Straight at them!" Webb was already clambering back into the driver's seat. As soon as he was in, he gunned the engine. The carrier surged forwards, treads biting deep into the sand. "Pritchard, let them have it!" Archer shouted, as he was trying to settle himself after being dragged into the carrier by Saunders.

Pritchard didn't need telling twice. He clambered forwards, crouching beside Webb, and jammed the Bren up over the carrier's front glacis plate. The barrel swung into position, his stance solid. Then he opened up. The gun roared beside Webb's head, deafening and relentless. He let out a strangled yelp, half curse, half survival instinct... as he flinched behind the wheel.
"Bloody hell, Pritchard!"
But Pritchard was already laughing over the rattle of the gun, eyes narrowed against the spray of dust and grit. The stream of rounds tore into the scrub ahead. Dust and screams followed. The

Italians scattered, some dropping their rifles, others diving for cover they no longer trusted.

The carrier ploughed through, engine roaring and metal groaning over loose rock and sand. One Italian rose to fire and was cut down instantly. Another bolted, diving for a small cluster of rocks.

Inside, it was chaos made functional. Jacks braced himself against the side and pulled the pin on a Mills bomb. "Grenade!" he shouted, lobbing it into a cluster of scrambling figures near a shallow depression in the sand. The explosion came half a second later, tearing up a geyser of sand and shrapnel, the blast echoing off the rocks like a thunderclap. Saunders was firing fast, his rifle pressed against his shoulder, bolt working smooth and quick. Archer sitting beside him, twisted and lined up his shots, each one clean and controlled. He caught a glimpse of an Italian officer running for cover and dropped him with a single round to the back. Webb ducked lower behind the wheel, flinching as another burst from Pritchard's Bren tore past his ear. Pritchard was grinning as he sent short bursts stuttering from the gun, sweeping the rocks and shadows to the left.

"Don't stop! Don't stop!" he bellowed between bursts, the heat of the barrel rising around him like desert breath.

The Italians were breaking, scattering in twos and threes, their fire now wild and panicked. Archer gritted his teeth, crouched low behind the armour as the carrier punched through the last of the Italian's position. A grenade went off behind them—late, wide, useless. Just one more sound in the echoing storm.

Then, just like that, it was over. The carrier roared clear, past the smoke and wreckage, out into open desert. The gunfire faded. The dust began to settle, and the desert fell silent. Only the low, steady hum of the engine remained, low as the bitter sting of sweat crept into Archer's eyes. He blinked against the dryness, against the sting. Grit clung to his lashes. The wind had picked up, curling faint ribbons of sand across the sun-beaten plain. He glanced around. Pritchard was still hunched over the Bren, scanning the horizon. Saunders sat slumped against the side plate, face streaked with dust, reloading with calm, practised movements. Jacks was already checking their ammunition with that quiet efficiency of his, blood drying on the sleeve - an injury he hadn't bothered to mention.

The scenery might've changed, but the lads hadn't. Archer let out a slow breath. They were still solid. The desert might try to strip a man down to bone and instinct, but these men, his men, had held. Their first taste of combat in the sand, and not one of them had folded. But pride gave way to a quiet unease. This had been a reconnaissance patrol. Eyes and ears, not bayonets and Bren guns. And they'd made contact. Opened fire. Left bodies behind. He could already hear the voice of his new CO cool, clipped, unimpressed.

"Reconnaissance, Lieutenant. Not a bloody cavalry charge!"

Archer rubbed at his temple, feeling the grit and sweat loitering. He didn't regret the call. He'd do it again. But that didn't mean the brass would see it the same way. In the stillness, the weight of command pressed in again. A little heavier this time round. The carrier bucked and jolted as it hammered its way back towards the lines, treads chewing through loose sand and bone-dry ruts. The sun was fully up now, high, hard, and merciless. Light bounced off the sand in every direction, turning the world into a blinding sheet of white-gold glare. Dust poured in from every gap in the armour. It clung to sweat-slick skin to sneak its way into throats and ears and eyes. The men cursed through cracked lips, trying to shield their faces with whatever they could find. Webb, the only one with proper goggles, hunched over the controls, his knuckles white on the wheel. "When we get back, we need to get some goggles," Pritchard muttered, blinking furiously as another gust sent a sting of grit across his face.

"Should've brought a bloody scarf," Jacks growled, pulling his shirt collar higher with little effect. "Feels like someone's rubbing salt and broken glass into my eyes."

They were veterans, Archer reminded himself. Solid soldiers. Pritchard and Jacks had both done time in Palestine... but not like this. Not bouncing across the desert in a metal box, choking on sand with the sun trying to boil your brain. They'd marched, camped, fought but back then, everything was slower. Closer. Less... endless. This was different. This was relentless.

Archer squinted against the brightness, eyes watering. The sand felt like it had worked its way into the very seams of his body—his sleeves, his boots, even his teeth. And they were still less than two weeks into their time with the battalion.

What the hell had they been doing out there? It was madness. They hadn't acclimatised. Hadn't drilled with the 7th. Hadn't learned a damn thing from the men who'd been living and fighting this war in heat and dust for months. Instead, they'd been thrown straight into the deep end, told to scout enemy lines like they knew the terrain, the tactics, the bloody sun. He clenched his jaw, feeling the grit between his molars. Even at his age, he wasn't naïve enough to miss the point: this patrol had been a test. Was he up to it? If he got lost, well, hell, it wouldn't matter much. If he pulled it off, they'd find something to tear into him for anyway. There had to be more experienced officers in the battalion who could have done this.

It wasn't the men.

They'd held.

Done everything he'd asked of them. And more.

No... it was on him now.

He wouldn't let it happen again.

No more stumbling through unfamiliar country like blind men in a sandstorm. They'd learn. Adapt. Turn every slip in the sand into a lesson drilled deep. Talk to the men who'd lived this war before them. Strip the desert of its secrets, one blister and mistake at a time. He'd take whatever dressing-down was coming his way. Maybe he'd even deserve it. But he'd wear it every sharp word, every ounce of doubt from the senior officers. Because what mattered now was what came next.

They needed to adapt. Fast. First thing when they were back, he'd get Jacks and Pritchard to find one of the Indian or Aussie NCOs he'd seen around camp. Hard bastards, the lot of them, men who'd been out here since the start. He wanted to know how they moved, how they wrapped their rifles against the grit, how they found cover in a landscape that looked like nothing but stone and heat. He wanted to learn what they knew. And if someone above him had a problem with that, fine. Let them. If he was going to be challenged, he wouldn't step back. That wasn't in him. In his own stubborn way, he'd face it and run straight through it.

The camp rose into view like a mirage that refused to disappear... low canvas tents staked tight against the wind, scattered supply crates, and the hard silhouettes of watchful men behind sandbagged walls. Archer's carrier rattled into the perimeter, grinding to a halt in a haze of engine heat and dust.

Throughout the perimeter of the tents, a series of rifle pits had been scraped into the sand... neat, narrow, and reinforced with rocks and timber where they could get it. Closer in, sandbagged machine-gun nests flanked the approaches, their Vickers guns covered with canvas. Just past the main trench line sat a 6-pounder anti-tank gun, squat and ugly, its barrel wrapped in a weather-stained tarpaulin and tilted up slightly, as if still waiting for a fight. The shield was scorched from earlier use, the breech scratched and oily.

No cheering. No reception. Just a few heads turning. A couple of nods. Most just watched, silent.

Archer climbed down slowly, boots hitting the ground with a thud that jarred all the way up his spine. He rolled his shoulders, dust cracking in the folds of his uniform. Behind him, Saunders muttered something about water. Pritchard was still wiping grit from his eyes, grumbling about "bloody goggles" and "sodding sun." Jacks said nothing... just slung his rifle and stared towards the Company CP. A corporal approached young, clipboard in hand, too clean by half.

"Lieutenant Archer?" he asked.

"That's right."

"Captain Wetherby wants you in the tent. Now." His tone wasn't rude, but it wasn't friendly either.

Archer stared at the corporal, feeling Jacks' eyes lock onto the lad like twin bayonets. Then Archer, voice low and even, asked, "Now?" He paused, just long enough to make the moment uncomfortable.

The corporal looked between Archer and Jacks, uncertainty flickering then, like a lightning bolt, it dawned on him. His spine snapped straight. "Sir!"

Archer nodded, the edge of a smile tugging at one corner of his mouth. He turned toward the carrier. "Pritchard, see to the men. They need water and a dust-off." The tent was a squat square canvas reinforced with spare netting and anchored with fuel cans and rocks. It looked temporary. Everything here did. Inside, it was hot and close. No chairs. Just a map table, a kerosene lamp, and Captain Wetherby balding, lean, and standing like he'd been waiting for this moment all day.

Archer stood to attention. "Sir."

Wetherby didn't look up straight away. He was staring at the map. The pause went on just long enough to sting.

Captain Wetherby leaned over the map table, his eyes flicking to Archer. "Well, Lieutenant? Let's have it."

Archer straightened, dust still clinging to his uniform. "Italian forward positions along the ridge, Sir. Dug in with overlapping arcs at least four machine-gun nests, a mortar pit with four mortars behind them. Regular patrols, battalion strength infantry, well-spaced. Discipline looked tight."

He took a breath and pressed on, voice steady. "We got as close to the wire as we could... about two hundred yards. Used a dried-up wadi for cover. Watched them most of the day. No tracked vehicles in sight, just a few lorries well back under netting. The position's clearly defensive. Saw them working on the fortifications–hauling sandbags, reinforcing dugouts. They're not planning to move anywhere soon." He produced a folded page from his satchel and laid it on the table. "Made a rough sketch, shows layout, rough patrol timings, sentry posts. I think it gives us a decent picture of the area."

Captain Wetherby nodded slowly, picking up the sketch and turning the paper in one motion. "Artillery?"

"Four pieces, Sir. Forgive me, I didn't recognise type but from the size of the barrels and the way they were dug in, I'd estimate seventy-five or a hundred-millimetre guns. Short-barrelled, field guns, not anti-tank. They were sited to cover both the ridge line and the approach through the wadi. Looked well camouflaged canvas and brush netting." He paused to take a short breath, then added, "They've sited two field guns on the left flank, two further up the slope."

Wetherby narrowed his eyes. "You sure about the number?"

"Yes, sir.

The position's surrounded by barbed wire, thirty yards deep in places. No sign of mines, but I can't rule them out."

Wetherby looked up from the sketch and his own map. "Casualties?"

"Sergeant Jacks' got a scratch to his arm, but nothing serious, Sir. Everything was fine. We watched them come and go from the wadi most of yesterday. Then during the night we crept up to the wire, tried to confirm how deep it ran, whether it was covered by fire, and if there were any gaps or signs of mines. Nothing obvious, but they're thorough."

Wetherby's intrigue was up. "How did Jacks get a scratch?"

"Apologies, Sir. I was getting to that. Around 1100 hours, we had two Italian patrols converge on our position. I can only assume we were spotted earlier in the morning, and they were sent to investigate."

"And?" Wetherby's face was open, waiting for the next instalment. "They opened fire from about 120 yards. Not exactly accurate, but close enough. We returned fire and made our withdrawal. I'd estimate we inflicted at least ten casualties, Sir."
Wetherby gave a long exhale through his nose, fingers tapping lightly on the map table. "Your first patrol with this battalion, and you bring back a detailed sketch, gun positions, patrol timings, and a rough casualty count. Not bad, Lieutenant."
He looked up, eyes steady.
"Truth be told, it's a bloody good report. You've done well, and your men, too. That position will be a hell of a lot easier to crack now we know what's in front of it."
He paused, stepped around the table, then reached into his pocket and offered Archer a cigarette.
"But just so we're clear, you've made an impression," Wetherby said, his tone even. "Word gets around quickly in a battalion like this. Some of your fellow officers have been marching columns, guarding wells, and swatting flies for the better part of a year. You arrive, and within ten days you're dodging bullets!"

The tent flap opened, and Lieutenant McBain ducked inside with a clipboard tucked under one arm. Broad-shouldered, sun-browned, and grinning like a man who'd slept well or hadn't been shot at lately.
"Begging your pardon, Sir," he said to Wetherby, "just dropping off the new ration schedule."
Wetherby waved him through. "We're nearly done."
McBain cast a sidelong glance at Archer and raised a brow.
"Heard you caused a bit of a ruckus out by the wadi. What was it, a few Italians and a mule?"
Archer gave a faint smile. "Not sure I can divulge."
McBain laughed, a short, warm sound. "You know there's a few here who think it's not fair on the rest of us. You can't go hogging the war all to yourself."
Archer met his eye. "If it helps, I didn't go looking for it."

McBain gave Wetherby a quick nod, then backhanded the clipboard onto the table. "Job done. Got some tea brewing when you're finished here, Tom."

As McBain turned to go, Wetherby said under his breath, "I see you're getting on well with McBain. How are you finding the others?"

"Fine, Sir. A couple of early issues, but I'm starting to settle in."

Wetherby leaned in: voice quiet but not unkind. "For a junior officer, you've got a fine record, and the Military Cross doesn't go unnoticed. Some will be impressed. Some... less so. The Colonel doesn't care much for the arrangement that brought you here, and he likes even less the whispers about your men being some kind of untouchable group."

Archer gave a slow nod. "I don't know what strings were pulled or if any were, Sir. All I know is, we were told to report to the 7th Battalion, and it was the Colonel himself who informed me we were to be kept together. Whatever the orders said, they weren't shared with me." He paused, then added, "To be honest, Sir, I started to get a sense of it during our conversation. The way McBain spoke... it was clear he didn't much care for the arrangement. I got the impression he'd already decided we were going to be trouble."

Archer straightened slightly. "But I can assure you, Sir, we're not. Yes, some of us, mainly the NCOs, had it rough and got through it. But we're here to do a job. Same as everyone else."

Wetherby gave a small grunt, somewhere between agreement and thought. "You're not wrong," he said at last. "The Colonel's a by-the-book man. Doesn't take kindly to unusual decisions made above his head, especially when they arrive with citations and clean kit. It's just not proper soldiering" He paused, letting the tension hang for a beat. "But he's not the only voice in the battalion."

He stepped around the table, now more conversational than confrontational. "Some of the lads are glad you're here, whether they say it or not. There's pride in having men here who have held up the standards and traditions of the Greenmoor Light Infantry among us. It matters. Your actions made many of us very proud of the GLI."

Wetherby glanced towards the tent flap, then back at Archer. "But pride's a fickle thing, Lieutenant. For every man who's proud, there's another watching, wondering if the medals mean you think you're better than them. Even if you don't." He offered a faint smile. "Me? I admire what you've done. You brought your men back across France and held them together. That counts.

But I've seen good officers sink in this sand, not just from bullets, but from quiet envy and loud mistakes." He clasped his hands behind his back and straightened slightly, voice shifting with a touch more formality. "You're off to a strong start. Just make sure you finish the same way." Wetherby paused, then added, "While you're with this company, you've got my support and the company's. We look after our own here, Lieutenant. Medals or none." He reached for the clipboard McBain had left behind, the moment already folding back into routine. "Now, go get your tea before he drinks it all."

CHAPTER 2

Despite the shelter of the tent, the map fluttered on the table, its corners pinned down with stones, a bayonet, and a mess tin filled with tepid tea. Thin red lines marked the proposed axes of advance pencilled curves sweeping towards the coast like someone planning a holiday rather than a war. Archer stood in the semi-circle of officers inside the company HQ tent, squinting as Wetherby tapped the map with the end of a two-foot bamboo cane. "As you've no doubt noticed between the move and the sudden appearance of half the Western Desert Force's armour we've been officially attached to 7th Armoured, effective immediately."

He paused, letting the words land.

"There's a forward movement planned to begin in earnest within the week. Exact timings are still sealed, but you can assume we'll be on the move soon."

Wetherby gave them a moment, then continued.

"Each of you can see McBain. He's holding your orders for the next 48 hours. Mostly lectures and demonstrations...working alongside armour, clearing routes, and the sort of tasks we're likely to be handed when things kick off."

Wetherby stopped his briefing as another figure stepped in from behind the tent flaps, casting a long shadow across the group. Captain Wetherby called them to attention as Blackstone entered no barked order, just a sharp word and a shift in stance. The tent stiffened. Lieutenant Colonel Richard Blackstone wore his uniform like it had been tailored yesterday, creases sharp, boots buffed to a quiet gleam despite the sand. He carried a swagger stick tucked under one arm and looked across the assembled junior officers as though evaluating a row of imperfect paintings.

Lieutenant Colonel Richard Blackstone took his time approaching the map table, his boots whispering against the canvas floor. He didn't acknowledge the gesture... didn't release them, either. He let the silence settle, heavy as a dropped sandbag. "I've briefed your company commanders," he said, voice clipped with importance. He paced once along the edge of the table, hands clasped neatly behind his back, swagger stick held horizontal like a yardstick of judgement.

"My concern is not the details of the advance. That's for your commanding officers to handle. My concern is how this battalion will *appear* and *conduct itself* in front of 7th Armoured." His eyes swept the line of junior officers, taking in their scuffed boots, sun-reddened necks, and the posture of men shaped more by distance marched than by drill square turns.

"They are fast, sharp, and proud, some of the oldest regiments in the British Army are here and they will be watching us. I expect a standard that reflects this battalion's name."

He paused again, letting his gaze settle on the collar of Archer's dusty shirt, then ran down the rest of him slowly, as if inspecting something unpleasant. "Turn-out and personal equipment will be brought up to standard immediately. All officers will present themselves for inspection at 0600 hours. You will then inspect your men at 0700." A moment of silence followed. Archer's eyes shifted across the line, catching a similar flicker of disbelief from McBain and one or two others. Surely this wasn't serious. They were about to march with tanks across open desert and the Colonel wanted boot polish and parade-ground posture?

As quickly as he'd arrived, Blackstone was gone... likely off to deliver the same sermon to another company.

"At ease, gentlemen," Wetherby said, releasing them from their rigid postures. Shoulders relaxed, a few exchanged glances.

Lieutenant Riley broke the silence first. "What..."

"Enough, Riley," Wetherby cut him off before the question had a chance to form. He stepped forward and tapped the bamboo cane against the edge of the map table, marking the shift in tone. "We're to be under 7th Armoured for this push. We know we haven't operated alongside armour before, this will be a crash course. Movements will be fast. This is an armoured spearhead. Shock action. We'll be in support as infantry. Our job will be to deal with whatever the division requires of us." Wetherby took a moment, studying the expressions around him. Some of the officers were still trying to reconcile what this meant, not just for them, but for the men they led. He stepped around the table.
"The battalion's been earmarked for close support. That means staying tight behind the lead squadrons. Our jobs will likely be clearing dugouts, strongpoints, anything so the tanks can roll past. If they meet resistance, we move up and crack it."

He paused, then tapped the map sharply, circling a section with the end of his cane. "We haven't received full operational orders yet, but based on what we've seen of the armour's disposition, we're likely to be operating in the area around Sidi Barrani, Nibeiwa, and Sofafi. Maps covering this area are with McBain. Make sure you and your platoon sergeants and other NCOs familiarise yourselves with the sector maps and local grid references. Focus on key junctions, wadis, and the escarpment routes. Once we're moving, we won't get another chance to study them."

The tent flap rustled again. A dust-covered officer stepped inside, his uniform streaked with oil and sand. Behind him came a stocky, blunt-faced man with the bearing of someone used to shouting over engines or bullets.
Wetherby looked up. "Perfect timing, gentlemen. Gents, this is Captain Corbyn of the 3rd Royal Tank Regiment. And...
CSM Tinsley?"
"Yes, Sir. King's Royal Rifles," the sergeant major replied, his voice low and gravelled.

Wetherby nodded and turned back to the officers.

"As I mentioned earlier, we've been attached to the 7th Armoured Division for the duration of this operation, operating under their Support Group. That puts us alongside the King's Royal Rifle Corps and the Rifle Brigade motorised infantry and practised in working with armour. Our job is to reinforce their efforts and to do that, we've been allocated transport: one Bren gun carrier and three 15-cwt trucks per platoon, which you are all familiar with." Wetherby glanced to his left and gave a short nod. "Captain Corbyn, all yours." Corbyn stepped forwards, removed his beret, and set it down on the edge of the map table. His hair was sweat-matted, and a faint line of oil ran along his collar. He surveyed the gathered officers with a practised eye.

"Right, gents. You've been attached to us to act as close support for the armour. That means you're not marching in after the tanks you're moving *with* us. If we're pushing, you're pushing. If we hit resistance, you're the ones who go in and clear it. Dugouts, strongpoints, anti-tank pits – anything we roll past, you deal with."

He leant over the map briefly, then continued. "You'll be travelling behind our lead squadrons in those carriers and 15-cwts. When we halt to engage, you'll debus, spread, and get to work. Stay off our flanks unless ordered – we don't need to be tripping over each other, and I promise you, the Matilda doesn't stop if it doesn't see you." A few mutters and dry chuckles rippled around the tent.

"Over the next forty-eight hours, you'll be running through basic familiarisation. That means learning how to load and unload under pressure, how to laager up, forming a tight defensive line of vehicles without causing a mess, and how to signal or mark positions so our drivers and gunners know you're not the enemy. We'll also cover what not to do – like bunching up behind armour or silhouetting yourselves on a ridge when we're in contact." He gave a short nod towards Tinsley.

"The CSM will be handling most of the on-the-ground stuff. He's been working with us a few months now, and I'm sure what he has to tell you will be most valuable for the next few days or weeks."

Tinsley stepped forwards with the deliberate air of a man who didn't waste words or time. His boots sank faintly in the canvas floor as he surveyed the officers with eyes that had clearly measured men before – and likely found a few wanting.

"Each platoon will rotate through drills with the carriers and trucks. We'll run through mounted approaches, infantry cover tactics, and emergency action if the armour gets hit or bogged down. You'll also get time with one of our drivers to go over mechanical checks – nothing fancy, just enough to stop you breaking the damn things the first time you take a corner too hard." His eyes flicked to Archer's side of the tent. "And before anyone asks – yes, you'll be running it again if it's not sharp. The tanks won't wait for you to catch up, and we don't do passengers in this brigade."

A few of the junior officers shifted uncomfortably. Tinsley either didn't notice or didn't care. "Questions will be taken at the end. You'll receive your drill timings this afternoon. Get your NCOs briefed and your men ready to move. First light tomorrow, we start." Corbyn gave Wetherby a brief nod. "We'll leave you to it, Captain. We'll be at the west end of the vehicle line if anything comes up."

"Appreciated," Wetherby replied.

Tinsley gave a final glance around the tent – no fanfare, no farewell – then followed Corbyn out into the sunlight.

The officers began to shift, murmuring among themselves as the tension ebbed. Some bent back over the map, others reached for canteens or notes. Wetherby gave the officers a final look, voice firm but even. "You've got your orders, you've met your counterparts, and you've heard what's coming. This isn't a ceremonial role – we've been attached to the 7th Armoured because someone up the chain believes we can keep pace with the best mobile force in the desert. Make sure that belief isn't misplaced." He glanced at the map, then back at his officers. "Drill timings will be posted within the hour. I expect every platoon to be on the ball."

With that, Wetherby gave a nod to dismiss them. The officers began to filter out – some lingering by the table, others already muttering about the heat. Archer waited until the tent cleared, then stepped outside into the hard, glaring light. The sun had climbed, casting the vehicle lines in harsh contrast – shadows tucked beneath wheels and open bonnets, crews already elbow-deep in grease or kit inspections. He spotted Tinsley near the second row of trucks, crouched beside a Bren carrier with his sleeves rolled up, inspecting the wheel hubs with a mechanic's eye. Oil-streaked and dust-caked, he looked like part of the machinery – blunt-edged and functional.

Archer crossed to him, boots slipping softly through the sand. Tinsley stood as he approached, upending a petrol can with a rag over the spout. He soaked the rag, then began wiping his oil-stained arms and hands, his expression unreadable. He straightened slightly as Archer drew near.

"Lieutenant."

Archer returned the nod. "As you were, CSM. Mind if I have a word?"

Tinsley caught the tone – something in it made him pause. Still cleaning himself, he nodded. "Petrol, Sir. More abundant than water."

Archer gave a faint, dry smile. "That's part of the reason I came to find you, Sergeant Major."

Now it was Tinsley's turn to look curious. "Go on."

Archer hesitated a beat. "I want more than the drills. For the men. And for me."

Tinsley raised an eyebrow. "That right?"

"We're not green," Archer said carefully, "but this isn't France. Several of us were there, and the lads have grit – I've seen it. They held the line when it mattered. But out here..." He exhaled through his nose. "Out here, there's a fair few things trying to kill you before the Italians ever get a chance. Sunstroke, thirst, getting lost – just to name a few."

Tinsley stopped wiping his arms, now listening more closely.

Archer went on. "We've done one patrol. We ran into an Italian unit, and we got out of it – more by luck than judgement. I don't want the next time to be like that. I don't want it to be luck. I want you to train them – hard. Not just on the carriers. On all of it. Kit, water, how to find cover when there's nothing but shadows. Anything you think matters."

He paused, then added, "Jacks served in Palestine before the war. Says he's used to the heat, the dust, the way things move out here. But that was years ago. Policing actions. This isn't that. It's armour, aircraft, open desert. It's going to be faster, harsher. I don't want to rely on half-memories and hand-me-down tricks."

There was a long silence, broken only by the ticking of the engine cooling beside them. Tinsley folded the rag slowly, methodically.

"Most officers wouldn't ask that."

"I'm not most officers, Sergeant Major."

"So I heard." He gave a small nod.

"Truth is, Sir, we're all still learning out here. In my opinion, we're still geared to fight the last war. But I'm happy to share what we've picked up so far. We can fit it in around the motor unit familiarisation."

Archer gave a quiet smile. "That's fine. See you in the morning."

Archer watched him go, the canvas flap settling behind him. For a moment, he stood where he was, turning the conversation over in his mind. A test, perhaps. Or simply the way things were done out here.

He made his way back through the lines as the light began to fade. The camp was settling into its usual low murmur of voices and movement. Somewhere a lorry engine ticked over. Beyond that, nothing but the open desert and the weight of what lay ahead. He slept lightly.

The next morning, under a bleached sky and rising heat, Archer's platoon gathered beside a row of Bedford OY trucks and Bren gun carriers parked just outside the company lines. The Bedford's loomed like beasts of burden – their long snouts pointed into the wind, square cabs stiff as saddles, and rounded mudguards bulging like knees. Their open backs were canvas tilts that drooped like blankets already rubbed pale with dust, and their olive-drab paint was sun-faded and chipped at the edges. The white service markings were barely legible beneath the grime. Each of the Bedfords sat high on thick tyres, their beds still empty but waiting – soon to be crammed with kit, men, and whatever else could be made to fit inside. Simple, rugged, and built for purpose. Not that anyone knew it yet, but the trucks would become the battalion's lifeline – not glamorous, but reliable.

The canvas tilts flapped gently in the morning breeze, and a fine layer of dust clung to every surface, already settling in corners and seams despite the trucks having barely moved. As Archer and his men stood waiting, the camp had stirred into life around them – cooks stoking stoves, men scrubbing out mess tins, NCOs calling out the day's duties. Company Sergeant Major Tinsley stood by the first lorry in the row with his sleeves rolled high, and a clipboard tucked under one arm. He didn't raise his voice. He didn't need to. The platoon straightened the moment he looked their way. He called the men to gather round. Tinsley let the last of the men settle into a loose semi-circle beside the lead truck before speaking. His voice was measured but carried easily over the distant chug of an engine somewhere deeper in camp.

"Listen in," he said, tapping the side of the Bedford with his knuckles. "Most of you have never worked as a motorised unit. Heck, until recently I hadn't. It's a relatively new concept to the

British Army. So I'll start with the basics, and how we are to be lined up – because if you don't understand the layout, you'll end up in the wrong place at the wrong time."

He paused, letting the words hang for a moment.

"Each platoon gets three Bedford's – one per section," Tinsley began, rapping the tailboard of the nearest truck. "The sections ride together, all their kit with them. You'll stow your gear under the benches or along the sides, lashed down tight. Corporals, you're responsible for loading, lashing, and making damn sure your men can get in and out without tying themselves in knots."

He swept a hand along the truck's interior. "Rifles held, nothing loose. You'll have your ammo in your pouches, but there'll be spare crates, water tins, maybe a few tools in here too. They all go under the benches or lashed along the sides. You don't want anyone tripping over a shovel or getting their boot caught in a rolled-up greatcoat when it's time to move. Keep it tidy. Keep it out the way."

"She's no Bessie, is she?" Archer said quietly, fondly recalling the battered old farm truck they'd used during the bridge job at Pont de la Lys before the stand at Cassel.

Jacks smirked. "No – this one might actually make it to the fight."

"Oi, she may've been a temperamental old gal, but she got the job done," Matthews shot back – he was the one who'd found the wreck in the first place.

"Temperamental?" Evans snorted in his Scouse drawl. "She was bloody frigid!"

That earned a proper laugh from Archer, Saunders, and Webb. The newer lads looked confused, but no one explained. The Company Sergeant Major gave the small group a stare – the kind only long-serving senior ranks could deliver, honed over years of making men jump with just a look.

"Apologies, Company Sergeant Major," Archer said quickly, realising they'd become a distraction from the task at hand. "Gentlemen."

"Your platoon commander, sergeant, signaller and runner will typically take the lead as HQ Section. Sir, that's your little command post on wheels. If you're lucky, you might even get a working radio, but they're in very short supply out here."

He stepped aside, motioning towards the row of vehicles stretching into the distance. "Now, in between the platoons, you'll see Bren gun carriers - not many, as always- just enough. They're used for fire support and fast scouting, or when we need to get someone forwards in a hurry. Each company has a few, but they're usually under the company commander's hand. You'll also find carriers in the battalion's support company. Those lads handle the heavier kit – mortars, anti-tank guns, Vickers. They're under battalion control, same as always."

Tinsley turned slightly and continued his lecture.

"Company headquarters and a couple more Bedford's carrying stores are usually sitting between the lead and centre platoons. They're close enough to support either side if things go sideways."

He pointed down the line, towards where the vehicles thinned out and the camp opened into open desert.

"The battalion HQ and reserve elements – transport, cooks, medics, quartermaster – they'll be strung out behind, out of direct fire but not out of reach. Whole thing moves like a column when we're on the road – trucks spaced out, dust rising, everyone watching for air cover. First contact, we halt, debus, and form up on either side of the road or track, depending on where the threat's coming from."

He turned back to the platoon, expression firm.

"Right then," he said, eyes sweeping over the assembled men. "This isn't a route march across Kent. This is motorised

warfare in the desert – fast, exposed, and bloody uncomfortable. Although, be grateful you're not marching to point."
He nodded to the trucks. "Alright, first things first. Stowage."

Archer watched as Tinsley led the men to the rear of the truck. The canvas flap was already rolled up, revealing benches running down either side and a narrow centre strip littered with sand and last night's grit. A few battered tins of petrol were lashed to the frame behind the cab and rolled-up tarpaulins hung from the curved metal struts that supported the canvas roof – the so-called tilt supports.

"As I said, each section is assigned a vehicle. So, everything you've got will be collected and kept in here – greatcoats, spare webbing, any additional ammo crates – they go under the benches, tight and secure. Whenever possible, strap it down. You want to avoid anything rolling loose. If we hit a bump or brake hard, you don't want a No. 36 grenade rolling underfoot. Or worse – dropping over the side and losing it."

Corporal Pritchard stepped up, inspecting under the benches and noting the hooks fixed to the underside. He gave a small grunt of approval. "Hooks'll hold," he muttered, then glanced around the cramped space. "Still – a section per lorry and all their kit? It's gonna be close in here. Sweaty, loud, and probably half of 'em stepping on each other."

He continued his inspection, sliding a hand along the timber boards as he made his way towards the cab. It wasn't the first time he'd seen a Bedford OY, but it was the first time he was being told to make it his home. He stopped by the passenger door, peered through the window, then turned to Archer and Jacks. "Reckon we can fit two in the cab, seven in the back. Sir." There was a murmur of agreement, but it was short-lived. Tinsley climbed up into the bed of the truck and faced them from the back, speaking now to the full group.

"When we debus – that's get off for you slow learners – it needs to be clean and fast. No arsing about looking for rifles or sorting kit. You go over the tailboard, form up facing outwards, and take up a fire-ready position by section. Nearest man to the rear steps out first. No jumping. Climb, land, move. You jump off and twist your knee, you're an immediate problem for your mates."

Archer watched his men nod – some more confidently than others. He caught sight of Webb near the back, brow furrowed, mentally sketching every detail. Good. They'd need men who paid attention when things went loud.

Tinsley continued, turning to Archer, "Sir, if you could allocate your sections to each vehicle, we can run through the drill of getting out and forming up."

Archer immediately called out each section in order and allocated them to a lorry. He took a moment watching the men form up behind each vehicle as he and Sergeant Jacks made it towards the fourth lorry in line.

"Mount up!" came the call from Tinsley.

With some confusion and awkwardness, each section clambered into the back of their assigned vehicles.

Almost immediately Tinsley raised his voice just enough to cut through the ambient noise. "Stop! Get down! Jesus Christ! This isn't just about climbing in and out. You'll do it fast, in order, and without turning it into a bloody music hall routine. Each of you has an assigned place – same place every time. No shuffling about, no swapping. Corporals, that's on you to enforce."

He tapped the truck's tailboard.

"Front section boards first, rear section last. Same coming out – nearest the tailboard debusses first. You move clean, you move silent, you form up in fire-ready formation." There was a brief pause as the words settled.

"Alright, section commanders – assign seating. Then we'll run it again. Keep it smooth this time."

At the order, each corporal turned to his men, pointing to the benches and calling out names. Almost without needing

instruction, the men began sorting themselves into position, falling into the order they'd need to board and disembark.
Tinsley glanced at his watch, then raised his voice.
"Mount up!"

The command was brisk, practiced and the men moved. One by one, they clambered into their assigned places, the nearest pair swinging into the cab, the rest hauling themselves up over the tailboard and onto the benches. Boots thudded on timber, canvas flapped, and the truck creaked faintly under the weight. "Hold!" Tinsley called, watching the last man settle. "Now! Debus!"

The truck emptied just as quickly. Men dismounted in reverse order, dropping down one by one, rifles in hand, fanning out to either side just as they'd drilled. A few were smooth, most were not. Someone clipped their shin. Someone else landed sideways. But no one hesitated.
They reset. And again.
"Mount up!"
"Debus!"
"Mount up!"
Voices muttered.
Gear jangled.
Dust kicked up around the wheels.

The drivers sat in their cabs, arms folded, watching the chaos with mild amusement. Archer stepped in, catching the drivers' smirks as the men reset for another run.

"Listen in," he called. "You'll each rotate through the cab and the rear, driver, co-driver, tailboard. Get a feel for every position, how fast you can move, what gets in your way. No passengers in this unit. You might have to switch under contact."

Jacks gave Archer a knowing look. It wasn't about moving fast, but because someone might go down. The men nodded, a few groans, but no arguments. They knew Archer expected excellence. So, they went again.

Over the next hours, the process was repeated: board, stow, brace, dismount. Rotate roles. Webb took a turn behind the wheel. Saunders in the passenger seat. Pritchard supervised a rear exit drill, barking when someone tangled a boot in their rifle sling.

Tinsley stalked the line, clipboard in hand, checking timing, pointing out faults, correcting posture. "You wait too long to drop, you're a bloody speedbump. Move." By the sixth run, the rhythm had started to form, still awkward but improving. The trucks moved forwards a few lengths each time, drivers grinding gears with varying degrees of embarrassment. The rear groups hopped down faster now, weapons ready, forming up like they meant it.

Not perfect. Not polished. But getting there.

The Bren carriers came next, sleek, low slung, and noisy as hell. Their open tops exposed the crew positions while engine covers sat slightly ajar to help with cooling in the desert heat.

"Same principle," Tinsley said, tapping the metal flank. "You dismount over the sides or out the rear, depending on who's driving and where we've stopped."

He walked them around the vehicle, showing how blankets and greatcoats could be strapped behind the front seats or bundled into the carrier's limited rear stowage. There was barely space for crew, weapons and water tins, let alone comforts.

Webb was inspecting the carrier with a knowing look. Saunders tapped the rear plate and turned to Matthews, who ran a practised hand over the hull.

Jacks stood in front of the vehicle. "Several of the lads are familiar with these ladies." The men who knew glanced at him, each recalling the assault they had made against the guns back in France.

Jacks continued, "How many of these do we get per platoon?"

"One would be ideal," Tinsley replied, not terse, but sharp. "But at present, it's one per company. We may get more, but no word on when."

Tinsley stood by the carrier, voice steady as the men gathered around. "Right, listen in. Each vehicle carries a few 4-gallon petrol tins and a couple of 2-gallon water cans. That's enough for immediate needs, but it won't go far. The bulk of fuel, water, rations, and spares stays with the trucks in the transport column. Allocations come down from battalion, same as always.

But here, it's tighter. Petrol for at least 200 miles. Water's rationed as per standing orders. One gallon per man per day, and it's strictly enforced. That's fine while we're sat here in camp, but you'll need to watch it when we're on the move. So, pack what you can, but remember, there's never enough. You'll fight dry before you fight hungry in this place."

Archer listened, letting Tinsley's words settle. The heat pressed down, shimmering off the hard metal of the carrier and blurring the horizon into a haze of yellow and white. Around him, the men shuffled their feet, kicking up little clouds of dust that hung in the still air. There was a faint, metallic tang of engine oil that lingered, carried on a breath of hot air that did little more than shift the dust.

Archer adjusted his cap, feeling the sweat sticky on his neck, and watched the men start to move again, checking ties and straps, their faces set. Tinsley's warning had landed. There wasn't a man here who didn't understand the stakes.

By late afternoon, shirts were clinging with sweat, and most of the men had a fine layer of sand pasted to their faces. Archer ran a hand over his brow, watching as the platoon repeated the drill again. It had become better, cleaner, tighter. The trucks pulled up in staggered formation, engines idling, and within seconds the men were out, spread in two arcs on either side, weapons braced.

Tinsley crossed his arms. "Still not pretty, but no one died. We'll take that for now." He turned to Archer, voice low. "After grub up, we'll meet back here, and we'll run them through it but digging in. It'll be cooler then."

Archer nodded. "Appreciate it. I'd rather they swear at us now than scream later."

Tinsley allowed the ghost of a smile. "Exactly."

The men began drifting away in search of tea, dust had drawn pale streaks across their faces, and their uniforms hung on them, darkened and pasted to their backs with sweat. The desert sun still blazed overhead, but the day's work wasn't done, not yet.

CHAPTER 3

The heat hung heavy, thick and stifling as the men clustered around a patch of desert in two rows, the front kneeling, the rest standing behind. Dust clung to every surface, filling the air with a faint, gritty haze. Tinsley stood square at the front, flanked by two privates gripping entrenching tools, his hands resting on his hips. "Right, listen in," Tinsley began, his voice steady but carrying over the shuffling of boots and the low clink of shovels. "This isn't Blighty or France. The ground here's no good for much, nothing grows in it." He let that settle a moment, then motioned to the sand at his feet. "But one thing we do have, same as at home, is the ground itself. And like in any war, the ground is our friend."

"After last night's efforts, I thought we'd better return to basics." Tinsley paused, his gaze sharp as it swept the group. Then he turned to the men at his side. "Crack on, Murphy." The two privates, clearly the targets of the RSM's displeasure, stepped forward. Without waiting for turns, they began driving their shovels into the sand.

Tinsley picked up his lecture. "Shell scrapes first. Quick and dirty. Twelve to eighteen inches deep, wide enough to lie flat. If the sand's soft, pack the sides down as you go, use your boot, your bayonet, whatever you've got. If it's rocky, wedge stones in to keep the walls from crumbling. And don't waste time trying to dig deep straight away. Go wide first, get a proper shape, then deepen it. Otherwise, it'll just cave in on you."

He looked out at the faces, sweat-darkened collars, sunburnt skin, a few still half-listening, half-daydreaming in the oppressive heat.

"That scrape's what keeps you alive when the Stukas come calling. One man, one tool. You don't stop till you've got a hole big enough to hide your arse in." Jacks, standing off to one side, chipped in, his voice quieter, matter of fact.

"And when you've dug in, cover the spoil. Break up the outline. Blanket, greatcoat, rocks, if you can find any. You'll be surprised by the differences in ground we'll come across. Don't think it's all soft sand out here. Some places, the ground's like concrete, baked hard by the sun, packed solid. You'll be hacking at it with your bayonet just to scratch the surface. Other times, it's loose as flour, collapses in on itself as soon as you cut into it. And then there's the gravel patches, small stones, dry as a bone, all shifting under your boots. Dig too deep and it'll cave. Go too shallow, and you're just waiting for the first round to find you." He paused, glancing at the sand around their boots.

"Sometimes you'll get lucky, hit a patch near a wadi where the soil holds. But don't count on it. Most of the time, it's sand, stone, or worse, salt flats. Try digging in those, you'll be there all day and still get nowhere." Taking a moment to wipe a bead of sweat from his cheek, "Ok lads, spread out and get digging."

Pritchard crouched down and ran a hand across the loose grains. "Dig shallow, dig wide. Don't make a neat little grave for yourself."

A few of the men shifted, muttering under their breath. Saunders, standing with his shovel upright and resting against his shoulder, gave a half-smile and murmured, "Bloody hell, thought we'd done this drill a hundred times already."

Evans, flicking dust off his sleeves, chimed in with a grin, "Yeah, but never in a bloody sandpit."

Jacks cut across the low rumble, voice even but firm. "Well, if you've done it that many times, I'd expect you to get it right."

That earned a few disgruntled looks. The grumbling faded, though not entirely, understood this as part of a soldier's lot. The men settled in, shoving and driving their shovels down, scooping up mounds of sand and carefully piling it to the side of the holes they made.

Archer stooped to lift a spare shovel. The handle was already warm, polished soft by use and sun. He moved to an untouched patch of sand and began to dig with slow, steady strokes, the blade biting in and sending up arcs of powdery grit. Around him, the men stole glances. No speech. Just their officer, sweating beside them, shovel in hand. That spoke louder than any parade-ground talk. He glanced up, and for a brief moment, the men's efforts slowed, their eyes drawn to the quiet example.

But just as quickly, they turned back to their tasks, the pause dissolving like mist. Archer caught sight of Private Joyce, a large man whose every swing shifted a tremendous weight of sand, stone, and grit, only for it to collapse back in on itself.

"Remember what Mr Tinsley said, Joyce. Dig wide, not deep," Archer said quietly, pausing just long enough to gesture towards the crumbling sides. Joyce gave a grunt of acknowledgment, brushing sweat from his brow. "Sir. Didn't think I'd miss mud, but this stuff's bloody treacherous."

Evans, half-buried in a neighbouring scrape, flicked a clump of sand over his shoulder. "At least with mud, it doesn't try to fill the hole back in while you're still in it."

Archer glanced up as a shadow fell across the pit. Tinsley stood at the edge, arms folded, eyes narrowing with faint approval.

"Not bad, Sir," the Company Sergeant Major said, eyeing the shape of Archer's trench. "Angle's good. Spoil's placed right. You've done this before."

"Once or twice," Archer replied, brushing grit from his brow. "Figured if I'm asking the men to dig in, I'd best show willing."

Tinsley gave a curt nod. "They noticed. That sort of thing sticks." He stepped closer, voice dropping slightly. "While you're up, would you mind accompanying? Let's see how the rest are getting on."

Archer wiped his hands and passed the shovel to a nearby private, then followed Tinsley along the loose line of shallow scrapes and half-finished pits. They stopped first at Section One. Lance Corporal Webb was down on one knee, muttering to Private Beckett who'd managed to collapse one side of his trench wall into the scrape.

"Try widening the base," Webb said to himself, glancing up as Archer approached. "You're digging a grave, not a well."

Archer crouched beside them. "Webb, I know it *feels* like a grave, but let's not say it out loud. Gives me the willies, God knows what the rest might think."

Webb, who had served with Archer in France, caught the tone instantly. "Sorry, Sir. It won't happen again."

"Good man, Corporal. Pass the word," Archer said, his voice soft but firm.

Webb gave a sheepish nod. "Yes, Sir."

As the two men walked along, dust clung to sweat-slick skin. Around them, the men worked their shovels and picks with weary rhythm. Archer, beside Tinsley, was carefully inspecting the line of trenches - or what passed for them so far. Shallow scrapes, loose spoil heaps, and a few determined pits stretched unevenly across the sand.

They stopped near a pair of men working in silence. One was lean and wiry, bent low and moving with precise, deliberate strokes. The other - broader, with a boxy frame and a look of quiet focus - was reinforcing the spoil edge with small stones.
"Those two seem to have the right idea," Archer murmured.

Tinsley raised an eyebrow but said nothing. A few yards on, another man hacked away with brute energy, sweat running down his neck. His shovel strikes were wide and clumsy, more force than finesse, and the sides of his trench were already caving in.

"Good effort," Archer said, crouching beside him, "but it's all going back in on you. Try angling your cut. Keep it wide at the base."

The private blinked, then gave a nod. "Yes, Sir."

Nearby, a group of three were clustered around a half-dug trench. One older, thick-set man was delivering a monologue on the virtues of dry tea leaves over wet socks. "Tea keeps you sane," he declared in a broad accent. "Wet socks'll rot your feet before Jerry gets the chance."

Beside him, the younger soldier beside him nodded along, eager or just trying to keep up. The third man said nothing, digging steadily with the dull rhythm of someone tuning out the noise.

Archer approached with a raised brow. "Are they solving the war?" Tinsley replied, "Bit of foot care advice. Not sure how his socks'll get wet in this bloody sandpit though."

They moved on. At the next pit, a pair of men worked side-by-side, one fast-talking and laughing under his breath, the other clearly trying to ignore him. The talker wore his helmet tipped back and kept glancing around like he was waiting for someone to argue with him, pausing now and then to swipe irritably at the flies gathering at the corners of his mouth.

Further along, a scrawny man was shifting spoil like it was currency, fast, light scoops, always looking up between strokes, blinking hard as the flies latched onto the sweat around his eyes. Behind him, a burly figure dropped a full load of sand outside of his scrape with a grunt and started again, his breath loud and steady.

A little further on, a few of the men had finished digging and were now sat in their own trench, passing around a smoke. One leant back against the shallow wall, eyes half-lidded, the cigarette glowing faintly between his fingers. Nearby, another man had abandoned his shovel altogether and was sketching something on a scrap of card, the tool propped behind him and forgotten.

As they passed, Archer turned to Tinsley. "They look like they've cracked it." The CSM glanced down at the men who were clearly taking a breather, and with a grudging flicker of admiration muttered, "It appears so, Sir." He'd emphasised the "Sir" just enough to catch the soldiers' attention. A ripple of panic stirred from inside their trenches as the men scrambled upright.

"As you were," Archer said calmly, a small chuckle escaping as he watched Pritchard and Hale stumble into action. He took a knee beside the improvised hole in the earth.

"How are you finding it, Pritchard?" he asked, his tone familiar and light.

Pritchard wiped a forearm across his brow. "Well, Sir, it's not as easy as mud, but you can get through it with some effort. The lads are learning. Slowly like, but they'll get there."

They'd reached the far edge of the platoon line. Looking back, both Archer and Tinsley seemed satisfied with the men's progress. With a little more practice in different types of sand, they'd have it nailed down. Tinsley turned as a gust kicked up loose sand, swirling it across the line like smoke. Archer felt it too, squinting into the glare, his eyes scanning the horizon.

"Not sure I like that," Tinsley muttered.

Across the scrubby rise, the men were still scattered in their pits, shoulders hunched, heads low. The occasional shout rang out, but most had settled into a rhythm, spooling out sand and rock from their individual holes. Then the light changed. Subtly at first, a shift in the angle, the sun dulled behind a thickening veil. It wasn't just Archer and Tinsley who had noticed the change in atmosphere. Each man had suddenly paused in their actions. Archer stood still, trying to make sense of it.

The wind carried a hiss now, like dry breath scraping across the dunes. It wasn't loud, more suggestion than sound, but it threaded through the air with a strange persistence, tugging at any loose fabric, lifting the edges of blankets and kit rolls. Grains of sand began to dance across surfaces, skipping and swirling in low, restless eddies. The horizon, once harsh and sharp, was beginning to blur, the line between earth and sky softening, smeared by the dust creeping in. Archer narrowed his eyes. The air had weight to it now, not just heat but pressure. A tension you felt more than heard.

Tinsley tensed. He turned a half step into the growing wind, eyes narrowing at the smear crawling across the horizon. At first, it looked like heat haze, a blur against the baked skyline, but it didn't shimmer. It rolled. Thick and low, stretching across the desert like a stain. What started as a smudge deep in the distance was swelling, darkening, lifting. The colour was wrong. It wasn't the pale gold of dune dust, but a dirty, churning brown, like soot mixed with smoke. He watched a moment longer. The movement wasn't fast, but it was relentless – crawling forwards like a wave without water. A line of grit and sky-blindness that would eat everything in its path. A heavier gust swirled grit around his boots, pulling at his shirt. He didn't need a second guess.

"Storm," he muttered. "Bloody hell, sandstorm. Sir!"

Even as he spoke, the light dimmed further, the sun vanishing behind a fast-advancing curtain of dust. Archer saw it too, a dirty brown wall stretching across the desert, rising like smoke to the low clouds. All the men were still, unsure of what they were witnessing.

Tinsley stepped forward, voice rising without shouting.

"Sir! Get the word round. Cover up. Get low. Blankets, greatcoats, whatever they've got. Jump in their scrapes and get under cover as best they can. Now!"

Archer turned and repeated the order. For a split second, the platoon hesitated, then the spell broke. Men bolted. Bare legs flashing, boots skidding. They sprinted across the sand towards the waiting trucks where their gear was stowed. A few shouted warnings or names as they ran, weaving between scrapes and spoil heaps. Canvas covers were flung back, webbing sets yanked from beneath benches. A mess of belts, rifles, and folded groundsheets spilled into the open. Someone tripped, rolled, and scrambled up again, teeth gritted against the rising wind. Another hauled a greatcoat free with both hands, cursing as it snagged on the leg of the lorries bench.

The air was thickening fast now, wind howling, sand swirling low. The first proper gust tore through the line like a slap. It rattled the trucks and sent a wash of grit through the air like a bucket of dust being hurled. Jacks was moving between the men, boots churning up grit as he broke into a jog, shouting, "Get back to your scrape! Get down! Cover yourselves! Just stay in your holes!"

Shouts cut through the rising wind. A blanket unfurled like a sail. Someone fumbled with a kitbag, pulling loose straps and dragging it back towards the trenches. A groundsheet flapped wildly in another's grip, refusing to be held. The ripple of urgency spread quickly. Men scrambled, diving into their scrapes, grabbing for kit. One hauled a ground sheet up and over his head like a sail. Another crouched, wrapping a scarf around his mouth with shaking hands.

Archer quickly looked around. "Evans! Saunders! Get down and covered!" he called, his voice sharp with command. "Foster, into cover. Now!"

Around them, the air thickened. Fine dust whipped past, swirling into eyes and mouths. A groaning wind began to rise, low and steady: a deadly, living creature. Tinsley dropped beside a trench, yanking a soldier down with him.

He bellowed out, "Head down! Breathe through cloth if you've got it. Don't bloody move unless you have to!"

Archer reached the trucks just ahead of the worst of it. He grabbed his webbing, the 1937 pattern haversack already clipped in place on the shoulder straps. His folded groundsheet was packed in front, half exposed and tucked under the securing straps. As he stumbled along in an attempt to run, he wrestled with it, shifting the pack side to side, trying to work the sheet loose without undoing the buckles. The air had teeth now. Hot and coarse. It sliced his face like sandpaper. Around him, men were scattering, some diving into pits, others still fumbling with belts and rifles. Then the light shifted again, a deep, unnatural brown washing over the desert like floodwater.

Time was running out. Archer dropped to the ground beside the nearest shallow scrape and was about to throw himself in when a voice cut through the rising wind.

"Sir! In here!" Jacks was already hunkered down, waving a hand from the edge of his trench. "Sir! Get in here!"

Archer didn't argue.

He scrambled in, half-tumbled, and landed hard against the side wall, bouncing off Jacks.

"Bloody hell, Sir!" Jacks grunted, his voice muffled but unmistakable. "If I thought you were coming in swinging, I'd never have invited you!"

Archer, having won the fight with his groundsheet, began wrapping himself in it. He turned slightly and, in his best toff's accent, muttered, "Apologies, good chap. Now shift over." Jacks, whose grin could light up an entire room, gave a low chuckle and shifted to make room as the officer hauled the sheet over his head, tucked it beneath his legs, and curled tight. He locked his arms across his chest, holding the sheet shut against the rising storm.

The wind hit like a freight train. The first blast sucked the breath from Archer's lungs, slamming into the groundsheet like a hound. It thrashed and snapped around him, tugging the corners with violent strength, trying to tear it free.

Archer gritted his teeth and pulled his sheet tighter, curling inwards, knees drawn up, chin tucked low as he fought the pressure.

Beside him, Jacks was doing the same. Both of them curled tight in the narrow scrape, shoulders jammed together, sharing the delicate safety of their shelter.

The noise of the beast was staggering, not a howl but a roar, constant and shapeless, its breath a steady rasp of sand against the cloth. Sand was everywhere. It slipped beneath the edges of the sheet, snuffling into the tiniest seams, and working its way in – down the collar, into the boots, behind the eyes. It scratched, scoured, and stung like ash from a fire.

Archer shifted slightly, just enough to ease the tension in his arms, already burning with the effort of keeping the sheet sealed. His knuckles ached. Every muscle was taut, braced against the power of the wind. Still, it didn't stop. The scrape offered no room to move, no comfort, just a shallow hollow in an unforgiving land. The ground beneath him was scorching hot, the sand piled against his side like the inside of a furnace. Sweat soaked his shirt. Grit ground between his teeth. A shape moved beside him.

Jacks, voice low, tight with effort, "How you doin' Sir!"

Archer didn't answer. He couldn't. His lips were dry, throat full of dust, and he was too busy holding on – not just to the groundsheet, but to the belief that this would end. Eventually. Seconds stretched. Minutes dragged. The wind never let up. It hammered and screamed and scraped, like the whole desert was trying to get in. It wailed like a living thing, not steady, not one note, but rose and fell in angry surges that tore at the sheet with menacing claws. Archer's fists were locked tight beneath his ribs, every muscle burning from the effort of staying small, clasping at the groundsheet trying to stay covered. Beside him, Jacks shifted slightly, his boot nudging Archer's leg. No words passed between them. Jacks felt the movement and took it as a sign his officer was still breathing. The storm wasn't fading. Not yet tired. It was still building, louder, hotter, closer.

The sand came in harsh waves. It slammed the sheet and hissed as it slid off before returning harder, faster, a million tiny, relentless impacts like a rabid dog. At some point, it found its way in. Fine grains worked through the smallest gaps in the groundsheet, riding the wind like smoke. They clung to the sweat on Archer's skin, turning slick dampness into scratching grit. It coated his arms and the back of his neck, and it pooled behind his knees. The heat inside the sheet became stifling. It wasn't just desert heat, but a thick and breathless shroud, sealing around him like a coffin. Sweat ran unchecked, soaking his shirt. The fabric of his uniform, sodden and sagging, scraped across raw skin with every twitch of muscle. He could feel it. The sand wedged into seams, gathering at the cuffs, settling under the collar like biting teeth. He tried not to move. Tried not to breathe too deeply. He buried his mouth and nose into his sleeve, filtering each low breath through his sleeve. But every shift, no matter how slight, dragged the grit across him like sandpaper.

The wind eased for a second, just a second, and for that moment there was silence. No roaring. No shouting. No rustling kit. Just the thudding of his own pulse in his ears. Then it came again. Louder. Stronger. The groundsheet kicked against his back as if something had smashed against it, and Archer instinctively tightened his grip, curling tighter into himself. His shoulders ached. The cords in his forearms were taut as wire. He wanted to shout at the wind, at the storm, even at the silence inside his own head, but the air was thick with grit, and there was no breath to waste.

He pushed his thoughts towards something better, trying to pull himself clear of the storm's relentless curse. Charlotte's voice came, somewhere distant. The Strand Palace, tucked into London's West End. It hadn't been the Ritz, but it had clean sheets, polished brass, and blackout curtains that slightly muffled the city's hum. The image of a quiet drink with Pembroke in the lounge, their collars open, uniforms creased just enough to suggest leave. That's where he'd first seen her. Charlotte. A clear vision of her seated near the window in an immaculate Wren uniform, waiting for a friend who never arrived. She'd stayed for one drink. Then another. Pembroke, never shy, had noticed her glance at the clock and taken it as permission to stride over and introduce them both. He thought of her half-smile. A laugh that caught Archer off guard. And then, just for a moment, the soft light had caught her face, calm, clear, and utterly unforgettable.

As quickly as it had come, the image of Charlotte slipped away, replaced by the present. The heat. The sweat. The ache.

Sand had begun to collect on top of them. He could feel the weight of it, pressing down in the small of his back. The sheet between him and the prowling wind sagged slightly, not tearing, but pulling, dragging. They were being buried. Jacks grunted softly.

Not a word, just a sound of acknowledgement, or discomfort, or both. Archer clenched his jaw. His lips were coated with grit. He licked them, tasted nothing but dust. His mouth was dry, too dry to swallow, and each breath came through the corner of his arm where a sliver of air could still reach him. Time had lost meaning. Minutes or hours. It could've been either. The storm gave no sign of stopping. It just blew, and howled, and scoured. Every so often, it shifted pitch, rising like a scream, then dropping to a low groan. Like it was thinking of how to make them suffer before taking them. He adjusted slightly, not much, just enough to keep his hands from going numb. The sand piled higher. He could feel it pressing in at his sides now, creeping along the edge of the trench like water seeping under a door. It was heavy. Relentless.

"Still with me?" came Jacks' voice, hoarse and muffled through the layers.

"Just about," Archer managed, his own voice barely a breath.

"Could be worse," Jacks muttered.

"How?"

There was a pause, and for a moment Archer thought he'd imagined the exchange. Then, "Could be snow."

Archer let out something between a laugh and a cough, swallowed it, and closed his eyes.

The storm refused to be done with them.

The wind didn't stop all at once.

It eased in fits, a breath, then a gulp, then a lull that held just long enough to feel strange.

The wind didn't stop all at once. It eased in fits, a breath, then a gulp, then a lull that held just long enough to feel strange. Beneath the battered groundsheet, Archer loosened his grip slightly to ease the cramps in his hands. The fabric was damp from sweat and half-torn from his fists. He risked lifting the edge.

Grit scratched as it slid off the sheet. The world beyond was a strange silence. Not peace, but the stunned aftermath of violence. Light filtered through the dust that hung in the air like a torchlight through gauze. Shapes moved slowly in the haze.

Jacks stirred beside him, lifting his groundsheet and pouring out the inches of sand that had collected. "Still alive, then?"

Archer coughed, spat grit, then uncovered his watch. "I think so. Christ, that has to be the longest three hours I can remember. Can't feel my bloody fingers."

Jacks stood, shook the sheet, dropped it, then began brushing grit from his neck. "That'd be a *Khamsin*, Sir. Or maybe a *Ghibli*, depending on who you ask."

He squinted up at the dull sky, still hazy with dust. "Got caught in one back in '37, down near Beersheba. That bastard's dry, hot, wind lasted all day, sunrise to sunset."

He gave a crooked grin.

"To be fair, that time I was stuck in the guardhouse, not in a scrape with just a sheet. Thought we were going to get flayed alive today!"

As Archer hauled himself upright, sand poured off his sleeves. His joints protested, and the groundsheet trailing behind like shed skin. His boots felt like they were filled with sand, heavy and raw against his ankles. He looked around. It was like crawling out of a burial site. The entire landscape had shifted. Trenches were half-filled and spoil heaps were gone, levelled flat by the wind. The nearest truck was coated in sand from bonnet to tailboard, one side scoured pale where the grit had stripped away paint like acid. Dust clung to every hinge and latch, caked thick at the wheel arches and piled high around the tyres. The canvas tilt roll lashed across its side half unfurled and trailing like a dead limb while a groundsheet hung from the front bumper, shredded and flapping in the residual breeze.

All around them, men were rising from their scrapes, groaning, coughing, blinking against the light. Some moved slowly, like sleepwalkers. Others just sat in their pits, dazed, faces grey with dust, hair matted flat and streaked with grit. Evans emerged dragging a sheet behind him like a forgotten flag. His head was uncovered, and his side cap was gone. His face was pinched beneath a layer of sand so thick it looked like cracked plaster.

"Christ," Evans said, his voice raw. "That was a bit lively."

Saunders stumbled past, shaking out his webbing like a man wringing water from a coat. A stream of sand poured from the pouches and onto the churned earth. Near the vehicle line, Webb was helping Private George "Ginger" Meakin dig out the rear wheel of one of the Bedfords. Ginger Meakin, who was a quick-tempered redhead and already suffering from sunburn, cursed the harsh sand biting at his raw skin. The sand had drifted waist-high in places, banked up like snow against a hedge. One of the carriers had both tracks buried; a shovel blade jutted from the top, half-buried with its handle snapped.

Pritchard came jogging over to Archer, his uniform still streaked with dust and sand despite having brushed himself down. "Sir, the tents stood up well. All weapons and kit are accounted for. Nothing damaged."

True to form, the no-nonsense poacher's first instinct had been to check the gear, not just his own, but everyone's. The quiet efficiency of it snapped Archer back to himself. Whatever they'd just been through, there was still a job to do, and that meant getting the platoon cleaned up, rearmed, and ready.

A moment later, Tinsley approached at a brisk walk, eyes already scanning the men as they began to regroup across the camp. His sleeves were rolled high, and his boots were caked in grit. "Lieutenant," he said with a nod. "Your lot held up well. I'll need to get back to my own, make sure they're squared away and nothing's gone walkabout. You might want to get someone to the quartermaster too. That sand's stripped the paint bare on those trucks."

Archer gave a short nod. "I'll get right to it, Sergeant Major. And thanks for this morning."

He paused, took a breath, and turned. "Jacks."

Without hesitation, Jacks replied, "On it, Sir."

Archer turned, scanning the camp. The men were scattered, shaking out webbing, inspecting the lorries, and even admiring the damage the sandstorm had inflicted on the paintwork.

He called over Wilson, Pritchard, and Corporal Matthews.

Archer's voice was firm. "Right, listen in. Get your sections to sort their kit and clear out the scrapes. If we get another one of those, we'll need them ready. Get the vehicles seen to as well." He paused, taking in the dishevelled state of the men, dust-caked and sunburnt, but upright.

His tone softened. "I want a state of readiness in thirty."

As the corporals turned to carry out Archer's orders, Matthews paused and turned back.

"Sir?" he asked, voice low, almost hesitant.

Archer looked up. "Yes, Corporal?"

Matthews shifted his weight slightly, brushing dust from his sleeves. "Well... I was just thinking. Not so long ago we were blowing bridges and holding the line at Cassel. Now we're out here, cooking like sausages and shifting sand with shovels too short for the job."

Archer gave a dry smile. "You're the one who requested the transfer."

Matthews shrugged. "Didn't feel right, Sir. After France... Dunkirk... everything at Cassel, all that. We crawled out of that together. Me, Webb, Pritchard, Saunders... Jacks... you. I could've been a sergeant in the Engineers by now. But after what we went through...didn't sit right, being away from you lot." He glanced toward the trucks where the men were already moving to their tasks. "You don't meet blokes like this twice. Not in one war."

Archer nodded slowly. "No, I guess you don't."

Matthews gave a faint smile. "Besides, it's all soldiering, whichever way you look at it."

Archer chuckled. "That's true, Corporal."

"Bloody right." Matthews stepped back, the grin fading slightly. "Truth is, I'd rather fight on with this lot than anyone else."

He paused, eyes narrowing slightly as if weighing something unsaid. Then he looked at Archer, more directly this time.

"If you don't mind me asking, Sir... how did this happen?

Us, I mean.

The transfer.

The whole bloody lot of us ending up together out here."

Archer held his gaze, saying nothing for a moment. Nearby, the wind tugged at the edge of a canvas, flicking it with a dry snap. Around them, the men were settling into routine, brushing out scrapes, airing kit, clanking water tins. Life after the storm. He looked down, then back up at Matthews. His voice was quiet.

"Well, to tell you the truth, how the remnants of France are still together? I asked if it would be allowed. If any of you wanted to come along, when they told me I was being sent out here with a reinforcement draft. As for how *you* ended up here..." Archer paused, then added, "That took a string or two. Let's just say, I made a few friends in France – friends who could help."

Matthews gave a small nod, his expression unreadable.

"Well... someone, somewhere must think you're worth the bother and gave you the transfer."

Archer let out a short breath, somewhere between a laugh and a sigh. Matthews turned and walked off, boots crunching in the sand. Archer stayed where he was. The light was fading fast as the desert settled into a quiet pause. He didn't know if it had been luck, loyalty, or something else entirely, but they were still together.

And for now, that was enough.

CHAPTER 4

The wind carried dust in long, lazy curls over the wadi, soft as smoke but sharp enough to sting the eyes. Somewhere behind the rise, a truck backfired, followed by the distant cough of a Vickers being tested. The sun was up and already scorching skin through cloth and sweat, turning sleeves sodden and brows slick. It wasn't just hot. It was the kind of heat that settled into a man's bones and stayed there, patient and unforgiving.

The trench wasn't theirs.

That much was obvious from the way the Indian troops watched over them – quiet, curious, and just detached enough to remind Archer he and his platoon were only passing through.

The dugout itself was shallow, hacked into the hard sand of a dry wadi. Its lip was ringed with a mix of sandbags, empty crates, and sweat-darkened canvas. Someone had stretched a tattered piece of canvas overhead which was weighed down with rocks and tangled in wire, offering more shade than shelter.

Outside the dugout, the faint murmur of idle chatter drifted up from the transport line, mingled with the rattle of tools and the whine of a carrier engine being coaxed back to life.

Inside, there was strict concentration.

Captain Wetherby was stooped over a field map spread across a pair of ammunition boxes; his sleeves were rolled and sweat darkened his shirt collar. A single oil lamp sat on a crate next to the ammunition boxes, unused in the daylight. Wavering shadows from the sun flickered across their figures as the men gathered around the field map.

With his helmet tucked beneath one arm and his uniform streaked with the morning's drive, Archer stood shoulder to shoulder with the other platoon commanders. Lieutenant McBain was stood to Archer's left, tall and steady, arms folded across his chest, his face unreadable beneath the dust etched across it. Second Lieutenant Philip Kingsley was stood to Archer's right, looking clean-shaven despite the heat, his collar still buttoned, posture clipped and precise. Archer marvelled at how this was possible in such suffocating heat. There was also Second Lieutenant Riley, younger than the others, a fresh-faced Yorkshireman with a faint twitch of nervous energy as he glanced at the map..

The dugout felt cramped, but they weren't here for pleasantries. This was business, urgent, final, and likely the last quiet they'd know until the guns opened up.

Wetherby didn't look up. "Orders came down last night. 7th Armoured is pushing on Sofafi - screening the flank and keeping the Italians guessing. The 4th Indian Division is going in against Nibeiwa, and 11th Indian Brigade will be backed by Matilda's from the 7th Royal Tank Regiment. The Infantry and armour will push straight through the position." He paused, then added, almost as an afterthought, "If it works, it will crack the Italians here wide open."

He tapped a point on the map, a rise just west of the wadi where Archer had conducted his reconnaissance days earlier.

"From Lieutenant Archer's reconnaissance the other day, we know the Italians are dug in right on the flank of the main armoured advance toward Sofafi. Division wants them dealt with before the armour rolls through, so..." Wetherby paused, then continued.

"Our orders are simple. We approach, assess the situation, and if they're still there, we call in the artillery, then take the position. Timing's going to be tight. The main assault moves at 0600 hours tomorrow. That means we need to be in position by first light, around 0500. If they're still holding, we engage immediately, destroy the guns, and hold the ground until the armour rolls past." Wetherby took a moment to gauge the reaction around him. Archer shifted slightly, eyes scanning the map briefly, then spoke.

"They're dug in tight. Looked like two rifle companies, maybe more judging by the patrol strength and how many positions we counted along the wire. At least four mortars at the rear and four field guns that I saw. Dug in and camouflaged. No armour, but a couple of lorries under netting."

He tapped the ridge on the map.

"Barbed wire's thick. Thirty yards deep in places. Didn't spot any mines, but we couldn't rule them out. The ground's been worked over, sandbags, trenches, weapon pits, and they've got good lines of sight from the slope."

Archer looked up from the map. "If they're still there in the morning, they'll be able to fire straight down on anything heading west. It's a strong position." He tapped his notebook. "But that was a couple of days ago. For all we know, they've reinforced."

Wetherby sat back on his haunches. "Could be. Doesn't matter. Division wants that position neutralised before the armour go in at Sofafi. And they want it done quickly."

He looked at the cadre of officers around him. "Our company's been given the task." His stare centred on Archer. "I know you're new to the company, but you're the ranking officer and, quite frankly, you've got more combat experience than any of us. You'll serve as my second."

Archer glanced up, surprised.

Wetherby continued. "McBain, your platoon will lead. Kingsley, you'll bring up the rear. I'll move with Riley and the HQ platoon. We've got a Forward Observation Officer joining us shortly, he'll be responsible for calling in the artillery."

"So, it's just us?" Archer asked.

"Just us," Wetherby confirmed. "We go in quiet, confirm the guns are still there, then call in the barrage. Hit fast, clear the ridge, and hold until the armour pushes through. No backup. No second chance." He leant over the map, finger tracing a thin track skirting the wadi. "We move out at 1900. We take the trucks to a staging point here, about three miles short of the objective. From there, we advance on foot. Quiet. No lights. No engines. I want us in position and ready to go by first light."

He looked up, eyes steady. "Any questions?"

No one spoke.

Wetherby gave a quick glance around at his officers.

"Right. Get your men ready."

With that the platoon commanders filed out of the dugout without fuss, each turning the plan in their minds. The sun was just kissing the horizon as Archer moved down the line of vehicles, checking each section in turn. Shadows stretched long across the sand, bleeding into the edges of the trucks' canvas tilts The air was dry, still, and oddly expectant as if the desert was holding its breath.

The trucks were loaded. Water tins topped off. Weapons checked. Dust hazed the low light as boots scraped, and webbing settled. The men didn't speak much now. Not out of fear, that would come later, but from the tight focus that came with routine. Archer stopped by the front lorry and watched as Pritchard tightened the last strap on a petrol tin lashed to the tailboard, giving it a sharp tug before nodding to himself. Wilson and Webb sat side by side in the cab of their lorry, helmets tipped low, watching the light fade beyond the line of vehicles. The engine was cold beneath them, the metal already losing the last of the day's heat. Webb shifted slightly in his seat, rolling his shoulders as if to ease a stiffness that wouldn't quite settle. "Be a long night," he muttered.

Wilson gave a small grunt, eyes still forward. For a while they said nothing. The desert stretched out ahead, empty and colourless now, the last of the sun slipping away behind them. Somewhere further down the line a man laughed. Webb glanced sideways. "You reckon they know we're coming?"

Wilson shook his head once. "Not if this lot's done properly."

He tapped the dashboard lightly with his fingers, more habit than thought, then settled back again.

The light finally drained from the sky, leaving the shapes of the lorries in shadow. Wilson reached up, nudging the brim of his helmet a fraction lower.

“Get your head down while you can,” he said quietly. “Won’t be much chance later.”

Webb didn’t argue.

He shifted again, settling into the seat, though his eyes stayed open a moment longer, fixed on the darkening horizon.

Sergeant Major Sid Rudge moved down the line of trucks with a slow, deliberate gait, his limp, a souvenir from the first war, just noticeable in the fading light. He was all business. No fuss. Just a heavy stare that made men straighten without a word. His presence was enough. Archer caught his eye as he passed, and Rudge gave the faintest nod. Not approval exactly, but acknowledgement. You were either squared away, or you’d hear about it. Sharp and public, regardless of rank.

Archer voice raised. “All platoons mounted?”

“Ready as they’ll ever be,” the sergeant major replied, then tapped his watch. “It’s time we were moving!” His frustration evident to all.

Archer gave a final look up and down the length of the column: twelve Bedford 3-ton trucks and two Bren carriers, one belonging to the Forward Observation Officer, the FOO, and one for his crew. No headlights were on, just blackout shields to obscure their presence. There was the low rumble of idling engines, waiting with bated breath to get moving. At the head of the convoy, Wetherby stood beside the lead lorry, exchanging quiet words with Lieutenants McBain and Kingsley. Riley lingered behind, checking a small satchel one last time. Archer climbed into the truck and settled beside the driver seat. Pritchard was at the wheel with firm hands and boot hovering over the clutch.

Just then Wetherby came over. "Slight change Tom. I'll lead in the carrier with the Sergeant Major."

With that, the Sergeant Major and Captain Wetherby moved to the front of the column, disappearing into the darkening sky, and Archer waited.

Moments later, the first vehicle lurched forwards, tyres grinding through loose sand. One by one, the rest followed. Each truck moved with the restrained momentum of something too heavy to stop once it had started. Archer's lorry jolted into gear and fell in behind the 3-tonner ahead.

"Watch your spacing Pritchard. Try and keep your distance," Archer stated, and Pritchard nodded in acknowledgement. The column moved out into the desert, engines humming low and shadows stretching wider as night approached. They left the forward line without fanfare. No cheers. No salutes. Just the faint clatter of shifting kit, the creak of canvas, and the occasional muttered order from an NCO correcting a man's posture or sling. Within minutes, the fortified line had slipped into the night, first from sight, then from memory.

The desert began to swallow them. Not all at once, but morsel by morsel as if each lorry was slipped under the spell of the night, until all that remained was the constant moan of engines echoing through the vast emptiness. The terrain unfolded in muted tones, low rises, shallow depressions, and the skeletons of old scrub trees turned to brittle charcoal by sun and wind. The column hugged a faint track that curved northwest, skirting the edge of a long wadi. Wetherby had chosen the route to avoid Italian outposts and natural choke points, but the ground was no road. The lead carrier bounced and groaned over patches of stone, its suspension creaking under the load.

In his Bedford, Archer scanned the terrain. His hand drifted to the watch Charlotte had given him, and he lifted the leather cap. The dial glowed faintly in the gloom. 2140 hours. They were making good progress, all things considered. The dips and risers, and the soft sand and hard rock - all of it was unforgiving on the springs beneath the men. By his estimate, they'd already covered around twelve miles He hunched beneath a blanket, giving it a small shake before pulling it tighter around his shoulders, cocooning himself against the night. The fabric rustled softly as he settled, shutting out what little light remained beyond it.

Inside the dim space, he angled the map across his knees and flicked on a small, metal bodied Ever Ready torch. The beam was weak, yellowed, and he cupped a hand over it, then drew the blanket closer still, half-smothering the light to keep it from spilling beyond the folds.

The air beneath the blanket warmed quickly, close and stale, the smell of dust and sweat lingering in the fabric. He adjusted the map again, tracing the route with a finger, committing each turn and contour to memory before the light faded. Beside him, Pritchard was muttering something about the wind dying completely.

"Omen," he added, darkly.

"Just the calm before."

Another half-hour passed.

The last of the light had long drained from the sky, and it had been replaced by a smoky blue-black dome peppered with stars. The convoy slowed naturally as the darkness had deepened. Pritchard kept a respectful distance from the 3-tonner ahead, relying on the faint silhouette of its canvas tilt against the night.

In the lorry just ahead, Jacks sat near the tailboard, rifle across his knees. He exchanged a glance with Corporal Matthews across the bench. "Been a while since we rolled into anything like this," Jacks said quietly.

Matthews nodded. "Yeah...just once I'd like us to have the odds in our favour!" He hesitated, then added, "Also, I'm not so sure about this desert malarkey. It's too open. No cover. No *real* cover anyway."

Jacks gave him a look, then reached over and patted his knee. "Pete, don't let it get to you. When it starts, it'll be no different from what we've done before." The column halted briefly to check bearings and spacing. Sergeant Major Rudge moved up the line on foot, conferring with the drivers and checking that nothing had shaken loose. Archer stepped out of the truck to stretch his legs, and he scanned the low ridge to the west. He saw no lights, no silhouettes, just the endless slope of starlit desert. He paused, tilting his head back to take in the sky. The sheer number, their brilliance, and the quiet wonder of those stars was hard to put into words.

Somewhere, beneath that same sky, Charlotte might be looking up too. His right hand moved instinctively to the watch on his left wrist, thumb brushing the leather cap. The small gesture gave him comfort, a fragile thread of connection in the vastness. Wetherby came walking back down the column, a torch cupped in his hand, its beam not visible.

"We're almost there," he said to Archer. "Another thirty, forty minutes and we'll be at the debus point. Ridge line ahead, then a shallow descent. Jump-off point's just beyond it. We'll dismount there and start the march."

He paused, scanning the track ahead, then added, "There's a patch of ground about 300 yards up that looks rough, broken surface. Might be a wadi cutting across it.

I'll take the carrier forwards with the sergeant major, have a look. Get to the front and hold the column here until you get my signal. No point dragging everyone into a jam if we don't have too."

Archer gave a short nod, then turned to Pritchard. "I'm heading to the front of the column." As he followed Wetherby along the line of trucks, they passed the lorry in front, and he knocked on the tailgate in a quiet firm voice "Jacks on me."

He didn't stop to wait for Jacks but continued at pace to the front of the columns with Jacks in a slow jog behind.

The temperature had dropped dramatically. The heat of the day had bled from the sand and had been replaced by a creeping chill that settled deep in the bones. Archer noticed men unfolding their trench coats, seeking warmth and comfort in the thick, coarse wool. He reached into his shoulder bag, the one he'd fashioned himself back in Colchester, and pulled out his scarf. With a quick adjustment of the knot, he tucked the loose ends down inside his shirt.

As the driver, a lean lance corporal with a cigarette tucked behind his ear, settled into the carrier, its engine coughed once, then settled into a low, purposeful growl. Archer stood at the front of the column, scanning the horizon while Wetherby climbed aboard with Sergeant Major Rudge. The Bren gunner swung in last, his kit already dusted from the trail. No words were exchanged. Just the shuffle of boots, the clink of metal, and the dull thump as the rear flap dropped into place. The carrier eased slowly forwards into the dark, its silhouette quickly swallowed by the folds of night. Dust rose behind it, briefly lit by the tail lamp's faint red glow before it vanished. Archer watched it go, his eyes tracking the shape until it disappeared beyond a shallow rise.

McBain appeared out of the dark like a man walking through fog, hands tucked deep into his trench coat pockets, officer's cap resting on his blondish hair, just enough to show the lines on his brow. "Can't say I like sitting around here," he said quietly, falling in beside Archer. "I've got the lads out on both flanks, watching the perimeter."

Archer didn't look away from the darkness. "Good. Probably pointless to spread the whole company now. We should be on the move again shortly. Wetherby's signal can't be far off."

McBain nodded, slow and thoughtful. "Still not sure why he always has to see for himself." Jacks' voice came from just behind them. "Some officers don't trust maps. They enjoy getting into trouble leading from the front." Archer glanced at him, but Jacks said nothing more, just took a sip from his canteen and kept his eyes focused on the dark. A silence hung between them. It wasn't uncomfortable, just watchful. The kind that came with shared responsibility. McBain tilted his head back, breath curling in the cooling air.

"Hell of a sky tonight," he murmured.

"Makes you forget, for a second, where we are."

Jacks followed his gaze.

The heavens stretched from horizon to horizon: a great vault of black glass pricked with starlight.

Without cloud, smoke, or town glare, the stars shone in impossible numbers. Some were sharp and cold, others soft like dust blown across a lamp. The Milky Way hung overhead like a river of frost. "Back home, you'd never see half this," McBain went on.

"We forget what it really looks like... until it's too late to appreciate it." There was no need for Jacks to say anything. He simply slung his rifle and looked up as if the war had stepped aside for a moment. Archer never moved. His gaze was fixed, waiting for Wetherby's signal.

What came next began as a tremor. Not through the ground, but through the air. A shuddering clank, faint at first, like metal striking stone somewhere far ahead.

Archer straightened.

The second sound came sharper.

Quicker. A grinding crunch, followed by the unmistakable metallic slam of something heavy giving way. Then came the echo, wide and deep, bouncing across the hardpan like thunder bottled in a steel drum. The desert had swallowed everything else, but not this.

Jacks turned sharply. "What the hell was that?"

Another sound followed Shorter, harsher.

The screech of twisted metal.

Then silence.

Archer stepped forwards, his hand unconsciously tightening on his webbing belt. The darkness gave nothing back. No shapes, no lights, no silhouettes. Nothing moved on the ridgeline.

McBain's face had lost its usual calm. "That was the carrier." It wasn't a question.

No one moved.

The moment held, stretched, as if the desert itself was waiting to confirm the truth. Archer swallowed hard, his mind racing. Distance, timing, possibilities. A blown axle? A flipped hull? Wetherby. Rudge. He felt it before he thought it. This was trouble of the highest order.

Jacks shifted beside him, voice low. "That didn't sound good!" Archer instinctively turned to Jacks. "Get the first truck. Let's go! McBain, get your lads back in and follow us up, but take it easy. We've no idea what's up there." The truck, with Jacks now sitting beside the driver, pulled up alongside Archer in moments. He stepped onto the running board and grabbed the edge of the door, bracing himself as Jacks barked at the driver to move. The Bedford bounced and jolted over the uneven ground, each sudden impact sending a shock through Archer's legs and spine. He held firm. Lone rocks knocked the wheels off course, jarring the chassis as he clung tightly to the cold steel.

The driver didn't hang about, urged on by Jacks' sharp commands and clipped encouragements. The engine strained as they climbed the shallow rise, darkness swallowing the faint track ahead. "Stop!" Archer bellowed, catching his first glimpse of what had happened.

Instantly, he leapt from the tailboard, landing hard beside the long bonnet of the lorry, a distance of at least four feet. Jacks was out a moment later, following fast.

Archer turned, suddenly aware that Jacks was still moving at pace. The driver close behind.

"Easy, Jacks! They've gone over!

Look, down there!"

Archer dropped to a crouch and edged towards the lip of the depression. The moonlight cast enough of a glow to make out the shape of the land ahead. There was a sudden fold in the desert, maybe twelve feet deep, steep-sided, and cluttered with rocks and hard scrub.

Not a massive wadi by desert standards, but deep enough.

Hard enough.

He saw it immediately.

The carrier hadn't gone straight in. It had tried to veer off.

Tracks arced at a shallow angle from the main path as though the driver had spotted the drop too late and thrown the tiller hard right. But the ground had offered no grip. Sand over stone, the left track had slipped, catching the edge. The machine had tilted, clawed at the earth for half a second, then rolled. At the base of the cut, it lay on its side in a shattered sprawl, with its open top exposed and hull half-twisted where it had struck the rocks. The steel looked buckled in places, and the corner of the engine cover was torn back like peeled skin.

Gear was scattered across the floor of the wadi.

A spade jammed upright in a crack, a tin helmet lying upside down twenty feet from its owner, a torn haversack spilling its contents into the dust.

A ration box had burst open, biscuits and paper wrappers strewn among twisted webbing, and the shattered remains of a water canteen. The acrid stink of petrol hung in the air, sharp and throat-stinging, leaking from a split fuel tank that still hissed faintly in the cooling night. A coil of signal wire lay tangled in a thorn bush, and someone's torch – cracked and flickering feebly – cast a stuttering beam against the rocks.

The carrier itself was eerily still. Its engine silent. The entire machine resembled less of a vehicle than wreckage left from an old battle. And bodies.

One was slumped against the carrier's side, unmoving, half-pinned beneath the sponson. Another lay further off, awkward and unnatural: a dark shape folded where it had landed. Sergeant Major Rudge's greatcoat was unmistakable, its heavy wool splayed like wings against the stones.

Jacks came up beside him, breathing hard, gaze fixed on the wreckage. "Christ," he muttered. "They were thrown. Must've been going at speed." He paused. "That's Rudge down there, isn't it?"

Archer didn't reply straight away.

His eyes tracked the wreck, its position, the debris field, the distance it had fallen.

"Looks like it," he said finally. "I don't see the others."

He stepped forward, scanning the edge for a safe way down. The walls of the wadi weren't sheer, but they were steep. A jumble of broken stone, sharp ridges, and loose scree that would shift underfoot.

"I'm going down," he said, turning to Jacks. "Give us a hand here."

Jacks moved in without a word, gripping Archer's arm as he swung one leg over the lip. Archer began the descent, his boots scraping for purchase, one hand braced against the rock. A chunk of shale gave way beneath his heel, and he slipped, catching himself on a jagged outcrop. Pain flared through his palm, sharp and wet. He pulled his hand back and saw blood. But not his. He didn't stop.

The rocks were streaked with dark stains, sticky where they'd already cooled in the night air. A torn scrap of khaki cloth fluttered from a jagged branch of a shrub. Bits of kit were embedded in the slope: broken strapping, bent mess tins, a boot with no owner in sight.

Behind him, Jacks followed more cautiously, eyes scanning as he moved. Above, McBain had arrived, and his voice cut the quiet.

"Section, cover them.

Rifles ready. Anything moves, you shout."

Archer reached the base and stepped lightly between twisted metal and bodies. The carrier's hull groaned faintly as it adjusting itself into the sand, its metal cooling under the night air. The stench of fuel was stronger now, undercut by the copper tang of blood and something more; it was that burnt-oil smell of a machine dying too fast. Archer swallowed hard, blinking against the sting in his eyes. Then he started checking for life.

Archer moved slowly, eyes scanning the wreckage with deliberate care. His boots crunched on loose stone. To his right, Rudge's body lay still. His greatcoat was splayed like a shroud, and one arm twisted impossibly beneath him.

Archer stepped over a length of track guard and ducked beneath the sponson. That's when he saw Wetherby. He was partially under the vehicle, not fully pinned, but caught. His shoulders were slumped with his head resting at an unnatural angle against the side plate. His eyes were closed, jaw slack. Blood stained the collar of his great coat, dark and congealing. Archer crouched, reached out instinctively, and pressed two fingers to the side of Wetherby's neck.

Nothing.

He let out a slow breath, staring for a moment longer at the still face. It wasn't the first time Archer had seen a man die, not by a long way. He'd watched men cut down by machine-gun fire, torn apart by mortars, disappear in smoke and flame. Those deaths, as cruel as they were, made a kind of sense. They were the currency of war, paid out in fire and noise, at least with a reason. But this? This was different. No enemy. No glory. Just steel, speed, and a patch of treacherous ground.

Wetherby had been alive five minutes ago, issuing orders with his boots planted firm in the sand. Now, he was sprawled in the dust as broken as any man caught in a barrage. Only this time, there was no one to blame but the desert and the dark. Archer felt the ache creep in behind his ribs, quiet but steady.

The futility of it.

The sheer waste.

McBain appeared beside him, voice low. “Rudge is dead. How’s Wetherby?”

Archer grabbed Wetherby under the arms and began to pull, trying to free him from the wreckage. The body shifted a few inches but stopped fast, pinned at the knees beneath a twisted section of the carrier’s hull. Archer was still straining when he heard boots shifting on the rocks behind him. He paused, realising it was useless. Easing the captain’s body back down with care, his hands lingered for a moment before he turned.

“He’s dead too,” he said. The words came rough, like gravel in his throat. The truth landed hard, cold, and inescapable. Wetherby was gone That left him. Command had found him again whether he wanted it or not.

Out of the darkness, Jacks called, voice tight.

“One breathing over here. Barely. Broken leg for sure. Maybe worse.”

Archer rose quickly and turned. Jacks was kneeling beside a young private, his webbing half torn, face scraped raw. The man’s leg was bent wrong at the shin, and blood soaked through a ripped trouser leg.

His helmet lay several yards away beside a bent crowbar.

“Who is he?” Archer asked.

“He was the driver, I think. Name’s Larkin. He’s out cold.”

A few paces beyond, the fourth man was easy to spot. He lay face-down sprawled across a tangle of gear. His neck was arched back at an impossible angle. A split water tin, drained of its content lay nearby with its handle snapped clean.

Archer gave a short nod. “And him?”

Jacks glanced over, then back to Archer.

His expression said enough.

No need for words.

Archer's thoughts raced.

Three dead.

One wounded.

"Lieutenant McBain," he called, "get one of your sections down here with a stretcher."

He paused.

His mind was already turning through the next decisions. Then, with quiet firmness, "Once they've got Larkin out, have them recover Captain Wetherby, Rudge and the third man. Bury them here." McBain gave a silent nod and turned, picking his way back up the wadi. He stumbled once, catching himself on a slab of rock before disappearing into the dark above.

Jacks had applied a field dressing to young Larkin's bleeding leg and was now walking towards the wreck of the carrier. He leant over a shattered ammunition crate, rummaging through the splinters until he fished out what he needed: two pieces of timber, each about a foot and a half long. Then he returned to Larkin.

With a quick glance at Archer, he said, "Sir, can you give me a hand?" Kneeling again beside the wounded man, Jacks nodded to the opposite side. "Hold these here, Sir. We need to splint this leg."

The young lieutenant placed a hand on each piece of timber, pressing them gently to either side of Larkin's shin. The bone beneath shifted slightly, not much, but enough to make the skin jump. Larkin groaned. It was a low, guttural sound, not fully conscious, but enough to twist his mouth and crease his brow. Jacks didn't flinch. He moved fast, working with practised hands. Tearing a length of cloth from a field dressing, he tied the first strip above the break, then another below. Each knot was firm, deliberate.

"We'll need to keep him flat," Jacks muttered as he worked. "The leg'll hold, just. That's all we can do for now. When he comes round, we'll give him a shot of morphine."

Archer nodded, his hands still steady on the timber even as the soldier groaned again, softer this time. Jacks tied off the final knot and sat back. "That'll do. Not pretty, but it'll get him to the truck in one piece."

The two men held each other's gaze in silence. Neither needed to speak. Both had seen too much already: death, chaos, the slow erosion of certainty. It was written in their faces, in the set of their jaws, the stories behind their eyes. They were soldiers of this war. Not born to it but shaped by it. Men of the moment, doing what needed to be done. Not because they believed in glory, but because they were still standing.

For a moment, that was enough.

A quiet understanding passed between them, not camaraderie.

It wasn't comfort, just recognition.

The silence smothered them while the desert waited.

CHAPTER 5

Dawn was still an hour off, but the desert had already begun to stir, a faint wind brushing over the ridge line, carrying the smell of sweat and sand. Archer stood in the half-light, shoulders squared against the cold, eyes on the distant horizon where the sky was just starting to turn the colour of tarnished steel. As always, there'd been no time to grieve. No pause. Just the facts: Wetherby and Rudge were dead. Larkin was still breathing, barely, and the mission had to continue.

Command had fallen to him now. No ceremony, no confirmation. There'd been no moment to dwell on it. No pause to consider the pressure of it. One second, he'd been a platoon commander, waiting on orders. Then Wetherby was dead, and the company was his. The burden had landed without warning like a kitbag dropped onto his shoulders mid-stride.

It hadn't been fear he'd felt as he'd made his way back to the columns...not exactly. More like a hardening. A quiet tightening of the chest, a narrowing of focus. Just the silence that followed, and the eyes that turned to him. Men were watching. Waiting. And in that moment, he'd known the orders had to come from him now. He'd given them without hesitation, with his voice steady and eyes forwards. But underneath, something else stirred. It wasn't doubt, but awareness. This was his to carry now. Their lives. Their chances. He'd led men before, through fire and retreat. But this felt different. This was a company, 128 men. A whole thread of lives stretched thin across the sand, all looking to him.

There was never any doubt. He accepted the responsibility. They'd laid the trucks up under the cover of a shallow rise. The engines were off with their wheels half-buried with sand and canvas thrown over the cabs to kill any glint of moonlight. A section from McBain's platoon had been left behind at the wadi:

two men to tend to Larkin and four more to see to the dead. Quiet work, necessary. They'd rejoin the company once the burial was complete. Archer hadn't liked leaving them behind, but he hadn't hesitated either. Command didn't leave room for hesitation. The rest had formed up with quiet efficiency, weapons checked, water bottles topped, and their final words had been exchanged in low tones that vanished into the dark. Then they began the march. Three miles of hard, uneven ground. No lights. No talk. Just the crunch of boots, the occasional stumble, and the hiss of breath as the cold bit through wool and sweat-soaked khaki. They were getting close. The final ridge loomed ahead. It would be their jump-off point for the assault.

Behind him, somewhere among the scattered shapes of the platoons, was the Forward Observation Officer and his carrier crew. Lieutenant Innes, Royal Artillery, a wiry Scot with sharp eyes and a sharper tongue. He'd joined them just before the trucks moved out, slipping into the column like a man who knew how to stay unnoticed. Archer had barely exchanged more than a nod with him. But now, with the guns waiting on the call, Innes was the key to everything. Upon reaching the point where the trucks were laid up, Archer had wasted no time introducing himself to the artillery officer.

Innes's carrier was positioned in a shallow fold a few hundred yards back and held the rest of his small team: a driver, a wireless operator, and a signaller. They were Royal Artillery men, sharp-edged and quiet, already setting up the wireless set - a bulky radio powered from the carrier's battery and bristling with cables and valves. The driver handled the machine, the wireless operator worked the big set - a Wireless Set No. 11, and the signaller stood ready to assist by passing messages, rigging aerials, or sprinting with a note if the airwaves went dead.

The engine had been cut to reduce noise, and the aerial was rigged and waiting. Camouflage netting had been thrown over the whole arrangement. Innes hadn't trusted the reliability of his smaller set - the Wireless No. 18 - to function when it mattered. So he'd brought his signaller forwards with him, ready to run the coordinates back to the carrier on foot if the signal failed. Either way, when the time came, Innes would relay the fire order from the ridge, and the carrier crew would transmit it to the battery. From there, the guns would do the rest.

Archer let out a slow breath, watching it drift in the cold air. Around him, his men lay silent in the dust, each one waiting for the light... or the signal.

They had crawled the last thirty yards on their bellies, packs dragged low, rifles hugged close to their chests. No talk. Just the scratch of cloth on sand, the soft chink of webbing, and the occasional grunt as someone caught a knee on stone. The constant low sound of men spitting sand out of their mouths had been the soundtrack to their movements. Archer had led the final crawl himself, placing Innes and his runner beside him, just short of the crest. The rest of the company lay twenty yards behind, spread across the lower slope, keeping low and waiting.

From up in the forward position, Archer had the binoculars already in hand. It was the last fold of ground before the ridge broke, so he could see everything.

The three of them lay behind a shallow rise, the ridge dropping away just ahead. Innes was scanning the darkness with his binoculars raised, searching for shapes or movement or the flat profile of a gun shield. Nothing yet. But it would be there.

It was clear to Archer that the Italians hadn't abandoned the position. As the light crept upwards, the slope ahead began to take shape. He could make out broken lines, the hint of spoil heaps, low shadows where pits had been dug. Archer adjusted the focus on his own glasses and felt his jaw tighten. The position had changed. Since the recce, it had grown.

Wire had been thickened, double-coiled in some places and strung tighter across the slope. The shallow dugouts were now reinforced to be deeper, with sandbags built up into proper firing pits. New spoil heaps suggested expansion. And further back along the ridge, more guns rested in wait. He had seen four before. Now there were at least eight prepared positions. Not all were manned yet, but they were ready.

Behind that position, he caught glimpses of movement. There were groups of three or four men darting between dugouts, some carrying crates or weapons, others simply running. But it wasn't just that. Something in the scale of it made his stomach tighten. With the with the growing light, he could see properly now - the full scale of the Italians' position: the breadth of the trenches, the number of prepared posts, tents staked beyond the ridge line, and the faint outline of what looked like a field kitchen with smoke trailing to the rear. This was more than a few dozen men. This wasn't just an outpost. It was layered, reinforced, supported. It was likely to be a full battalion. Maybe more. Infantry, guns, stores, all dug in and spread across the position like a safety net.

The Italians favoured these kinds of defences: ', strongpoints, fortified boxes, spread out and self-contained. Built to hold, to stall, to bleed an assault dry before it ever reached the main line. They were static and sure. Easy to cut off once you got behind them. But up close, they were something else entirely. Dangerous. Lethal, if you didn't respect them.
And now, Archer and his men were looking at one.

Archer's thoughts started racing. The orders had been clear: hit hard with artillery and take the position. But as he continued to scan the area, it was becoming obvious that what lay in front of them was no mere outpost. It was a formidable obstacle. As the light grew, more Italians came into view, busy with their routines. He spotted two shirtless men with towels slung over their shoulders, clearly heading off to carry out their ablutions. Archer stared at them a moment longer.

Christ, he thought, they've even set up a wash tent. They're not planning on going anywhere soon.

This wasn't just a position – it was built to hold. And Archer's men had been ordered to take it.

Archer's thoughts turned inwards, stepping through the plan once more.

They had now confirmed the position of the Italian guns visually and quietly, and they had received word that Innes' battery of eight 25-pounders was in place, five miles to their rear and ready to fire from 0545 hours. Archer and Innes assumed the timing was linked to the main assault by 7th Armoured. Once Innes had the bearing, he'd call it in. A full battery barrage would hammer the position. As soon as the first shells landed, Archer's company would go up, over and through. Fast and hard.

Archer had asked Innes to keep the fire rolling right up to the moment the men had cleared the perimeter defences. His concern wasn't just the guns. It was the wire, and whatever other nasties the Italians had waiting inside the perimeter. His earlier reconnaissance days had confirmed it wouldn't be easy to breach. He hoped the guns would buy just enough time to get his men through.

Archer shifted slightly in the sand. The grains were cold and damp against his palms, the chill of the night still lingering. Around him, the desert rolled in shallow rises and dips, enough to break the ground but not to hide a man. There was no cover, no comfort, only open space stretching in every direction. A few tufts of brittle scrub clung to the earth here and there, offering no concealment, only the illusion of life.

Archer's eyes remained fixed on the ridge ahead. The horizon was changing. It was subtle at first, then definite. The eastern sky had begun to grey: the pale, bruised light that came before dawn. Overhead, the stars were bleeding out, fading one by one as the darkness slowly loosened its grip. It would be fully light soon. And with it, the barrage.

He continued to review the plan in his mind one more time.

No. 1 Platoon, his, would go in on the left. McBain's No. 2 Platoon on the right. Standard assault formation. Two up, one back. Kingsley's platoon would remain in reserve, ready to plug any gap or, when the moment came, follow through and add weight to the attack. Riley was to remain on the ridge with the HQ Platoon. He had four of the company's Brens, and the rifles of his men trained on the perimeter, tasked with laying down covering fire to suppress the Italian defences during the approach.

The ground ahead was flat, open, and possibly mined. Wire obstacles had been confirmed during the reconnaissance, and Archer hadn't forgotten how deep that barrier ran. His men would move under cover of the barrage. The aim was that it would continue until they were on the perimeter, then cease just as they were going in. He'd told the platoon commanders they'd need to get uncomfortably close before it lifted. Too close for comfort, but necessary.

They had to be inside the wire the moment the guns fell silent.

He'd reminded them that they were likely to be outnumbered - at least two to one. That meant speed and aggression. Hit hard. Keep moving. No time for drawn-out fire fights. It had to be shock and momentum. At 0530, a rumble started.

At first, the sound came low, a distant mutter along the horizon. Archer glanced at Innes who met his look with a nod. Right on time. To the east, the opening barrage of Operation Compass had started. Dozens of guns, maybe more, hammering the Italian strongpoints at Nibeiwa and further south. The real blow was falling. It was a carefully timed symphony of fire and steel, and they were close enough to feel the first bars of it echo through the sand.

In the distance, the sky lit with faint, rhythmic flashes. A dull percussion rolled over the ridge, not loud, but constant. Like the steady drum of thunder moving across dry hills.

Archer drew a slow breath through his nose. "They've started."

Innes didn't reply. He was already adjusting his binoculars, sweeping the ridge below for any sign of movement. He had calculated the coordinates for the Italian position earlier, written the fire order by hand, and passed it to his runner. It had been a contingency in case the No. 18 wireless set failed, which, judging by his grim expression, it already had.

"Go! Keep low!" Innes ordered in a hushed voice.

The runner turned on his belly and crawled away with his rifle slung tight, clutching the folded fire order. His destination was the camouflaged Bren carrier tucked into the fold of ground behind them where the radio operator of Innes' artillery team waited by the Wireless No. 11 with its battery humming quietly, aerial rigged and listening.

Inside the paper, the message was a single line written in Innes' clipped hand: "Target GR 883429. Battery concentration, HE. Commence fire at 0545 hours. Continue until ordered to cease. Observer adjusting."

It was short, precise, and deadly. The coordinates marked the centre of the Italian gun line. If the battery received it in time, and if the guns were ready, the barrage would begin in just under fifteen minutes, and the ridge before them would vanish in fire and smoke. Archer checked his watch again. 0540.

As he replaced the leather cap, his thoughts flicked to Charlotte, just for a second. He wondered what she might be doing at that exact moment. Whatever it was, he hoped it was calm and warm. He was glad it was far removed from the cold sand and rising tension of this ridge. The thought lingered briefly, then faded as he pressed his mind to what was about to come.

He raised his binoculars and scanned the Italian position. Movement. The enemy was beginning to stir, shaken from their beds by the first light, and the distant thunder of the main assault. Officers and NCOs barked orders. Men scrambled into trenches. Others ran to the guns, half-dressed, weapons slung hastily. Well, that's got them going, he thought.

His eye caught one figure, standing awkwardly near the centre of the position. The man looked lost, turning in place like someone trying to remember what came next. Archer lingered on him for a moment before shifting his attention to the barbed wire that snaked across the forward edge of the position. It was layered deep, coils upon coils, double-aproned in places, and staked low and wide. Rusted in parts but it was still sharp; the wire glinted in the pale morning light, almost beautiful if it weren't so deadly. Breaching it would be no easy task. It would slow them, tangle them, expose them. His men would have to find gaps: crawl, cut, climb, probably all under fire.

He adjusted the focus on his binoculars, following the line of obstacles from one flank to the other. The wire was thick in most places, tangled and overlapping. But here and there, he spotted gaps and breaks in the coils where men might slip through if they moved fast and low. Yet none of the gaps looked accidental. Too neat, too deliberate, likely left open on purpose to draw attackers into fixed fields of fire. Archer scanned the ground beyond, narrowing his eyes for signs of scraped earth, disturbed stone, or the flat line of a low sandbagged wall where, most likely, a machine-gun was positioned to cover each gap. He exhaled slowly through his nose. There was no doubt the wire would slow them, but if they were fast, if they struck while the bombardment fell, they had a chance. The air cracked open.

A single roar split the sky above. Then another. All eight guns spoke at once: sharp and violent, hurling their steel-cased high explosives through the desert air with a punctuation of sound that could be felt in the bones. The rounds passed close, low and fast.

Even the ground beneath Archer's body seemed to thump from his feet to his skull as each one tore overhead. His teeth chattered with the pressure of it.

All eight 25-pounders were firing at speed. The crews worked fast, fluid, and automatic. Innes had told him they'd begin with rapid fire. Six to eight rounds per minute before settling into a steady rhythm that would be paced to conserve barrels and breath. Of the drill held, each gun, would land around every fifteen seconds or so. That meant a shell roughly every two seconds was now screaming towards the Italian line. And they would keep coming until Innes told them to stop.

The first eight shells landed almost as one. The Italian position erupted: a string of sudden, violent columns of earth and smoke along the forward slope. Flames burst from dugouts, sandbags were hurled skywards in whirling fragments, and clouds of dust punched into the air. One round hit squarely among the gun pits, and a brilliant flash was followed by a ripple of secondary explosions when stored shells or equipment went up. The next volley struck seconds later, chasing the first like hammer blows on a nail. Earth and debris lifted with each impact, showering the Italians' position in a rising storm of grit and shrapnel. A stretch of the wire sagged as a support post disappeared in the blast. Figures scattered through the smoke running, diving, vanishing.

It was chaotic. Men bolted from cover, some without rifles or helmets, desperate to reach firing positions or deeper shelter. Archer saw one man sprinting toward a gun pit, only to be flung sideways by the next strike, his body twisting in mid-air like a broken rag. The barrage didn't slow. Another round. Then another. Sandbags burst open. Tin helmets flew like kicked stones. Trenches collapsed inwards as the blast wave rolled over them. The gun crews, those still alive, were scrambling, disoriented, and dragging others into cover, or they simply froze where they stood. The desert ridge was vanishing beneath a growing pall of smoke and pulverised earth.

Archer, transfixed by the scene ahead, almost lost himself in the sheer devastation unfolding just a few hundred yards in front. The fire was hitting exactly where it needed to.

Then he snapped back.

The moment was now.

"Let's go!" he shouted.

They rose as one, figures pulling up from the sand in a ragged, urgent ripple. Across the shallow ridge, Archer's company surged into motion. No. 1 Platoon on the left, McBain's No. 2 on the right, and Kingsley's reserve group still crouched low, watching and waiting. Ahead of them, the Italian position was disappearing in smoke and flame, and the wireline lit in brief, stuttering flashes as another shell tore into the forward edge. His men moved fast, bent low, boots pounding the dry earth. Officers and NCOs led the way, flanked by their sections and platoons. Barrels were held tight, swinging left to right, their bayonets catching the pale morning light. Each man scanned the haze for muzzle flashes. The riflemen were spread wide. No shouting. No wasted words. Adrenaline coursed through their veins, sharpening every movement. Every breath.

Behind them, the 25-pounders kept firing. The rhythm relentless. Shells tore overhead in tight intervals, arcs of high explosive landing seconds apart. Each impact hurled up clouds of grit and stone, masking the Italian line and with it, the advancing British infantry. The barrage was a curtain of steel, both shield and sword that cloaked their approach. But Archer knew, the closer they got, the greater the risk. One misfire, one correction too far forwards, and the shells wouldn't fall on the Italians. They would fall on them.

Archer's left flank moved through a stretch of hardened sand, their boots skidding on loose stone as they moved up the far bank without pause. McBain's men crossed open ground to the right, advancing at a crouch, rifles tight against their chests. The smoke thickened with every step, blurring the line between cover and danger. They were nearing the point Archer had feared most: the gaps in the wire. He had seen them through the binoculars earlier, and knew they were too clean, too deliberate. They were places where a man could crawl through, maybe two abreast, fast and low. But he also knew they were perfect places for a trap. He had been sure these spots would be covered by machine-guns, zeroed in, ready to cut down the first section that dared try.

And yet, nothing. No stuttering bursts. No arc of tracer. No sudden flurry of bodies twisting under fire. Just smoke and dust. The steady percussion of shells still hammered the ridge and beyond to create a diversion. The men moved through the gaps untouched. Webb and Evans were the first through on the left, their boots crunching over torn wire and stone. Saunders followed with the rest of his section, rifles raised, eyes wide, scanning ahead. Each man shared Archer's unease about the gaps. McBain's lead section cleared the right-hand break just seconds later, each man emerging from the wire like wraiths, weapons up, waiting for the blow that never came. Still nothing.

The barrage had done its job. The Italian gunners, if they were alive at all, were either buried in cover or too dazed to fight. The wire was behind them now, and the edge of the Italian's position loomed. Archer signalled to his men to get down prone, ready for the next move.

From his position on the ridge, Innes watched through his binoculars, eyes sharp despite the dust and heat rising from the valley below. He had tracked the platoons as they surged forwards: Archer's first, moving fast through toward the smoke, with McBain's not far behind, sweeping in from the right. Then the third platoon had formed up at the edge of the rise, waiting for the order to push in. The wire had been cleared, the gaps used, the men through. He exhaled quietly.

No flare.

No obvious signal.

Just the confirmation in motion with boots beyond the wire, and shoulders ducked beneath smoke. No men fell. It had worked. He turned slightly, signalling down to the carrier, both arms raised and waving, clean and deliberate. The signaller nodded, bent to the radio operator, and within moments, the word was sent. Cease fire.

The guns obeyed with the same discipline they had opened. No grand finale. No drawn-out thunder. Just a final rolling impact across the ridge, then silence.

Archer lay prone and scanned back and forth, checking on his men. He saw that they'd made it through the wire, and one after the other, they were lying low to avoid any debris or shrapnel from the bombardment. He turned to his rear to view the position they had left and saw that Kingsley was already on the move. The shelling lessened before it slowly came to an eventual abrupt halt. Moments passed. Simultaneously, McBain and Archer were up.

"Follow me!" Archer cried.

Each man rose and moved forwards. The first shots were fired by the British as they pushed into the Italian position.

Jacks dropped straight into a trench, both feet landing at once. Two Italian soldiers were curled up at either end, still huddled from the bombardment they had just endured. Without hesitation, he raised his Lee-Enfield and fired into the first who lay to his right. Then he turned and drove his bayonet into the side of the second, the blade slicing through skin and muscle, and splitting bone. The Italian convulsed. His body arched, and a strangled scream tore from his throat. His second cry was sharper and shrill with panic as Jacks yanked the bayonet free, then drove it in again, silencing him. Jacks hauled himself out of the trench and moved forwards.

Webb and Wilson were both on one knee, firing in unison at a position where two Italians had taken cover behind a stack of sandbags. Dust and stone leapt with each shot, and one of the defenders tumbled sideways while the other scrambled to return fire.

Archer led four men into a line of firing pits, each of them engaging without pause. Rifle butts cracked skulls, bayonets punched into soft flesh, and boots stomped down hard. Screaming broke out, high, and desperate. One young voice cried out, clear amid the chaos, *"Mamma!"* It wasn't unusual. Archer pushed it from his mind before it could take hold, wrenching his bayonet free.

The British assault pressed inwards, rolling through the broken Italian defences like a tide over fractured stone. McBain's platoon swept right, clearing trenches and shallow dugouts one by one. Archer, now halfway across the position, was pushing his men left, moving in short, fierce bursts, taking ground in handfuls of yards.

One of his Bren teams was firing from a low rise where an Italian machine-gun had been set up, sending long bursts overhead to keep heads down ahead an advancing section. The trench system, if it could be called that, was shallow and winding, but it was poorly maintained and had taken a severe battering the preceding artillery bombardment. Sandbags were split and tumbled with every step. Earth crumbled underfoot. Most of the Italians were already fleeing deeper into their position, some throwing their rifles aside, others shouting 'surrender' in panicked, garbled phrases.

Matthews and Saunders flanked a low dugout and tossed a grenade inside without a word. The muffled thud came seconds later, followed by a spill of smoke and dust. They didn't pause to check. Matthews was already ahead, checking the corners of a connecting trench with his rifle ready, scanning for movement in the drifting haze.

Archer vaulted a collapsed section of sandbags and dropped into another firing pit, his boots slamming down beside an overturned mortar. A body lay beside it, limbs bent wrong. The face was half-buried in grit. Behind him, Pritchard and Foster moved in with purpose, clearing a sunken weapon pit with sharp commands and short bursts.

Here and there, isolated pockets of resistance flared. A machine-gun raked the open ground before being silenced in a flurry of return fire. A few desperate but determined men held a mortar pit. McBain ordered one of his sections to assault it from his right flank while the rest gave covering fire. They swung around to the right and disappeared into the low pit before reappearing minutes later with three prisoners, hands raised, eyes wide.

The ground was thick with spent casings and churned sand. Smoke curled from shattered dugouts. The smell of cordite, blood, and burnt canvas hung heavy in the air. Still, Archer's men kept moving. They were halfway through the position now, no grand charges, just calculated, relentless clearing, pit by pit, trench by trench.

McBain's voice carried over the noise, shouting orders to tighten his flank. Archer signalled left, calling Wilson to loop towards one of the gun positions. The weapon was long out of action; its shield was cracked, and the barrel was split from a direct hit during the bombardment. But the pit was still occupied. Three Italians lay in wait: one officer, the two rankers. Wilson and his section didn't hesitate. They opened fire at close range, cutting all three down in a snap of sharp, controlled volleys.

Archer paused to catch his breath and take stock. He knelt beside a pile of sandbags and splintered timbers. It was the remains of what had been a small bunker before the bombardment had torn it apart. From there, he spotted Lieutenant Kingsley arriving at the perimeter, his platoon moving in behind him. Archer stood and called out to get his attention.

Kingsley, hearing his name through the noise, turned and moved to meet Archer in the midst of the mayhem.

"They've been knocked about by the artillery. Still dazed," Archer said, gesturing with a straight arm towards the right. "Head over to McBain. Reinforce his push. We've got to keep the momentum. There's clearly a battalion here. Maybe more."

Kingsley's eyes stayed fixed on Archer's. "Alright, Tom. We'll keep it up."

With that, Kingsley turned and signalled for his platoon to follow. As a group, they moved off in the direction Archer had pointed. He turned back and resumed his survey of the action. He saw McBain and his men leaping over obstacles, some firing from the hip, others taking careful aim. A few were clearly driving bayonets into flesh. Moments later, Kingsley's platoon joined them, charging into the thick of the fight and pushing further to the right.

His attention shifted left where he caught sight of familiar figures, Wilson, Matthews, and Pritchard, screaming orders and leaping into trenches, followed by the men of their respective sections. Archer felt a flicker of satisfaction burn in his chest. They were pressing on, hard.

They worked through more than half of the Italian's position. The signs were all there: the Italians were on their last footing. Ahead lay two half-collapsed gun emplacements, one still burning, the other deserted. Webb was covering the left while Wilson and another soldier moved in, rifles raised. Almost at once, the rest of Wilson's section followed, regrouped, and pushed forwards again.

To the far left, Archer spotted Jacks and a private moving in on a low dugout. Both men had just lobbed a grenade into the position, clearly intending to deal with whatever was left inside.

It began with a single figure, his hands raised, rifle discarded, and stumbling out from behind a shattered gun pit. His eyes were wide, and dust caked his face. Then another came, limping from a trench, calling out in broken English and waving a bloodied cloth. Within minutes, more men followed. Groups of three, four, sometimes more, emerged from dugouts with arms up, faces pale, shouting *"Finito! Basta!"* or simply collapsing to their knees in the sand. The Italian position was collapsing around them. The bombardment had shattered their nerves, and Archer's men had smashed through before they could recover. There was no order now. No resistance. Just small, desperate knots of men hoping to survive.

Archer moved through the lines, taking it all in. He spotted McBain ahead, waving a section to hold fire as another group of Italians stumbled forwards with their hands raised.

Webb was covering the mouth of a trench where a dozen men had been holed up. Now, they were clambering out, one by one. Some hurled their weapons aside; others looked too stunned to speak. The battle was slipping into a lull. Gunfire sputtered, then faltered, then stopped altogether as more Italians emerged from foxholes and dugouts with their arms aloft in silent surrender.

Archer stood still, taking in the scene. His soldiers moved cautiously from cover, rifles raised, eyes wary. The Italians they confronted were visibly shaken faces drawn, hands trembling, some weeping, others simply staring in shock. After the brutal bombardment and the swift, vicious assault by his men, Archer was surprised so many were still standing, let alone able to follow the current orders being barked at them.

After a moment, Archer turned and scanned the chaos for a familiar figure before finding him.

"Lockett! Over here!"

Private Raymond "Ray" Lockett appeared through the dust.

His rifle was held loosely at his side, and his eyes were wide and alert, with what looked like the beginnings of a grin. He was the youngest in the platoon, barely more than a lad but quick on his feet and always eager, sometimes too eager, to prove himself.

Lockett's grin widened. "Got one, Sir!"

A little surprised by the declaration, Archer shook his head, then pointed toward the rear.

"Get to Lieutenant Riley. Tell him I want the HQ section and the FOO up here now." Lockett nodded, already turning. "Yes, Sir!"

He was gone in seconds, sprinting between shattered crates and crumpled wire, and past scorched patches of earth where the bombardment had left its mark. Rifles lay discarded in the dust, and the bodies of the fallen, some still twitching, others eerily still, dotted the ground like broken puppets. Clumps of Italians sat or knelt with their hands raised, helmets discarded, and eyes vacant with shock.

Archer watched Lockett go, the young private weaving through the wreckage, his webbing rattling faintly with each step. The fight was over, for now.

CHAPTER 6

Smoke still curled from the last of the dugouts, acrid and low to the ground. Spent cartridges glinted like brass teeth in the sand. Archer moved among the wreckage with the slow, deliberate step of a man measuring consequence. Around him, his men picked their way through the Italian position they'd just taken. Webb and Matthews had their sections working methodically, stepping over discarded rifles and the slumped forms of the fallen. They moved with quiet efficiency, clearing weapons, checking for bodies, making sure the dead stayed dead, and marking the wounded by driving rifles upright into the sand. Lieutenant Kingsley had already located a cluster of Italian stretcher-bearers who'd been corralled earlier. One of them, a lanky corporal with a Red Cross armband, was tending to a groaning Italian soldier under the wary eye of Pritchard. Among the Italians was a medical officer who, along with his Red Cross insignia, wore three stars on his sleeve and shoulder strap, the markings of a Capitano.

Archer appeared at Pritchard's side. The corporal, watching the prisoners with his usual firm expression, turned to him. Both men's demeanour softened slightly, a shared moment of quiet relief at seeing each other safe and whole. Together, they watched as stretcher-bearers, British and Italian alike, carried in the wounded– most of them Italian. The enemy medics had salvaged what they could from the wreckage and were doing their best to make the injured comfortable.

Archer glanced up at the sky which was already brightening with heat before he turned to Pritchard. "We'd best rig something up," he said. "Get them under cover before the sun really gets going." Jacks stood and approached, brushing dust from his pocket as he pulled a battered notebook from the pouch at his side. His sleeve was darkened with sweat and a thin line of blood from a shallow graze on his forearm.

"Initial count, Sir." Archer nodded once. "One dead on our side, Private Morgan. Took it in the chest. Quick," Jacks said, voice flat. "Three wounded, Ellis, Banks, and Hodges. All walking, though Banks'll need stitching. Nothing worse than a cracked bone and a hole through the calf." He flipped the page with a sand-caked thumb. "Italians, one hundred seventy-two prisoners under Wilson's watch. Thirty wounded, half of them stretcher cases. Forty-one dead, mostly taken down in the bombardment."

Archer gave a quiet grunt. The numbers were good, all things considered. Before he could reply, the sound of heavy, deliberate breathing announced McBain's approach. He came flanked by two of his men, marching alongside a grey-haired Italian officer who walked straight backed despite a torn sleeve and dust clinging to his uniform.

McBain gave Archer a nod, his expression unreadable. "He surrendered to me about ten minutes ago," he said. "Colonello De Luca, apparently. Thought you might want a word."

The Italian officer stopped a pace away from Archer and offered a crisp salute. "Colonello De Luca, 73rd Infantry Regiment," he said. His accent was heavy but clear. "I commend you on your victory, Lieutenant, and I thank you for allowing us to tend to the wounded."

Archer studied him for a moment. The man's eyes were bloodshot but steady, his chin lifted. There was dignity there. Defeat, yes, but not collapse.

Colonello De Luca looked every inch the officer: olive-skinned, lean-faced, and grey hair that was almost silver and flecked with black at the roots. Dust streaked his uniform, but his collar was still buttoned, and the laurel-shaped silver crown with two five-pointed stars gleamed faintly on his shoulder board. It was the insignia of a full colonel. He had that easy, inherited poise that was common to well-bred European officers: Mediterranean good looks, straight-backed pride, and a quiet, unfussed composure, even in surrender.

De Luca hesitated briefly, then continued in perfect English. "If I may, I request permission to bury our dead and conduct a service."

"Permission granted," Archer said. "If I may, I would like to join you...for our dead as well. And please thank your medics for the work they are doing." De Luca dipped his head. "Thank you. And of course, Lieutenant."

As De Luca turned and strode off towards the dressing station, McBain gave Archer a look. "Well," he said, dryly, "I've seen sterner defences in a training depot. If this lot are the best Mussolini's got, we might be in Tripoli by February."

Archer didn't smile. He glanced across the scene where stretcher-bearers moved among the wreckage, and Wilson's men were stacking rifles beside a sandbagged parapet. "Maybe," Archer murmured, "but after a barrage like that, most men aren't thinking about fighting. They're just trying to breathe." McBain gave a short grunt. "Suppose so. Still, they had the numbers and equipment too. Just didn't use them."

"We never gave them the chance," Archer said, nodding towards the line of bodies being prepared for burial. "We were quicker, came in hard and fast. Didn't give them time to think. That's how we do it. With speed, efficiency, and violence. That's how you win these things." He paused, his voice lowering. "Well, that's what I've learnt these past few months."

Archer turned to McBain, a flicker of respect in his eyes. "You led that well, Alistair. Kept it tight and maintained the momentum. Could've gone another way if we'd hesitated. Well done." McBain shook his head. "Thank you, Tom."

Archer didn't answer. His eyes swept over the captured trenchwork. The Italian medical officer continued tending to the wounded who were laid out on stretchers propped across trestles. Jacks and a few others were wrestling with a damaged tent, trying to provide some cover. Beyond the perimeter, many of the prisoners, led by De Luca, were digging shallow graves under the watchful eye of a British section from Kingsley's platoon.

Archer had called the Platoon Commanders together at one of the old Italian bunkers. It was a half-collapsed position near the rear of a trench line. Riley had taken it as a makeshift HQ, putting a few of his lads to work, shoring up the walls with sandbags and salvaged timber in an attempt to rig a bit of cover against the sun. Once gathered inside the narrow shelter, McBain, Kingsley, Riley and Lieutenant Innes, the artillery FOO, waited for Archer to start.

Innes was stood slightly apart from the others, a lean figure with dust-caked boots, and a folded map case slung to his side. Like the others, he said nothing, but his eyes flicked across the assembled officers and bunker's walls.

"Gents, first of all, well done," Archer began. "As we're to hold here until further orders, let's start making this place a little more homely. The Italian colonel has requested a burial service which I've agreed to." The officers exchanged brief glances as Archer continued. "Once that's done, get some working parties organised. Kingsley, you take that on. Use wire from the perimeter and form a pen for the prisoners. Riley, they'll need feeding, water, and so on. See what we can salvage from their stores."

He turned to McBain. "Survey the perimeter and set up an all-round defence. You'll likely have to stretch the sections thin. Each platoon is to provide a section for a working party to clear up and improve what we've taken here."

"Lieutenant Innes, signal Brigade. Position secure. One hundred seventy-two prisoners in our custody, thirty wounded, approximately half stretcher cases. Forty-one confirmed Italian dead, mostly from the barrage. One British dead and three wounded. Holding for further instruction."

Archer took a moment as he watched both McBain and Innes set off to deal with their respective task.

The heat hadn't eased. If anything, it pressed heavier now, like the sun was trying to grind them into the sand. It settled on the shoulders, sat in the lungs, turned every breath dry and shallow. The flies were constant, settling wherever they could, eyes, mouths, the corners of wounds, brushed away only to return a moment later. The still air hung thick with the reek of cordite, diesel, and blood, an aroma that was all too familiar to Archer. The sharp, bitter, metallic tang crept into his mouth despite the breeze. Archer stood at the edge of the captured strongpoint, watching his men move with quiet efficiency. The fight was done, but the work had only begun.

Jacks was already organising work details. As ever, his sleeves were rolled high, and his voice was low but firm. Shovels scraped against baked earth. Crates were stacked and sorted; salvaged stretchers were laid in rows along the shade of a collapsed dugout. The wounded had been treated and lay with their dressings pale against sunburnt skin. They seemed to be waiting for what Archer was unsure.

Matthews and Saunders were leading a section down the length of the position, inspecting dugouts and trench bays, calling out for any overlooked weapons. Pritchard crouched beside a bent and broken Italian gun, muttering as he counted crates that he'd got a couple of Italian prisoners to carry and stack. Nearby, Evans sat cross-legged, his face a mask of dust. His Lee Enfield lay across his lap as he tentatively applied a light covering of oil to the bolt he had removed.

The Italians had been put to work without ceremony. Under Wilson's watchful eye, they'd formed ranks and been split into groups – those on the burial duty and those working to fix the defences that had been ruined by the bombardment and assault. These men moved slowly but obeyed orders without protest, driven by exhaustion more than defiance. The burial party had already begun clearing a plot beyond the perimeter wire, hacking into the hard earth with picks and shovels. The dead, British and

Italian alike, had been laid out under canvas sheets. De Luca, stood nearby in silence, his face was unreadable as he oversaw the arrangements for his fallen.

Tents that had survived the bombardment were being re-erected despite their poles being splintered and the canvas being torn, but enough remained to cast some shade. Lieutenant Riley had a few of the prisoners and British soldiers patching together a few lean-tos from salvaged poles, tarpaulin, and the remnants of a mess flysheet. The canvas flapped like damp laundry in the breeze. It was barely enough to block the sun, but it was enough to give comfort to the wounded who were being placed underneath the shelters.

Riley had done a better job with what now served as company HQ. The dugout was shallow, ringed with sandbags and empty crates, its roof built from duckboards and old tent canvas that were lashed with wire and weighted down with rocks.

Archer moved among them without speaking much. Just a nod here, a word there. The men didn't need direction now. They were tired, sun-scoured, and blistered, but they knew what came next. Gear would be checked, rifles cleared of grit, and ammunition redistributed. Water bottles would be topped up from whatever could be salvaged from the Italian stores. Archer realised they had been lucky the Italians had stored their ammunition and food well, so rations were in plentiful supply. It was one less thing for Archer to worry about.

The company's vehicles had been called forwards. Actually, the drivers had been sent back to where they had left them earlier that morning, and the trucks were now laagered in the centre of the position and had been joined by several captured Italian lorries. Every vehicle showed signs of wear. Sand had scoured the paint, and the hulls had been scratched and blistered under the sun.

Inside the dugout, Kingsley was kneeling by an impromptu table made out of Italian ammunition crates, two wide two high.

He was reading his notes in a little, brown mole-skinned notebook. Archer crouched through the opening, "Ah, Tom. Well, we certainly hit 'em hard. I've taken stock and we've captured five Italian trucks, operational, and with minor damage; one light car, it's marked *Comando*. Most of the vehicles were out in the open." He slowed to take a breath and continued. "One field kitchen unit that looks workable although the axle seems to be broken. Six light machine-guns, and stacks of crates marked *Munizioni* and *Razione K."* Not a fortune, but not nothing either.

At that moment, Riley stepped into the dugout carrying, of all things, a battered typewriter and a cracked mirror. Archer and Kingsley glanced up, staring at the young lieutenant with equal parts confusion and curiosity.

Riley caught their look. "What?" he said, his tone nonchalant as if lugging a typewriter and broken mirror was no more unusual than pouring a cup of tea.

Neither officer replied. Archer simply shook his head and returned to the matter at hand. "Right. Speak to the Italian colonel. Have him get his cook to set up the kitchen. I want everyone to have a proper hot meal when the sun goes down."

With that, Archer left the dugout and walked over to where Innes was sitting under a tarpaulin rigged along the side of his carrier, supported by timber poles to form a makeshift lean-to. Monitoring the radio for further instructions, Innes sat on a three-legged folding stool, drinking tea from an enamel mug. Nearby, his wireless operator was perched on a similar stool with the No. 18 set humming quietly on a folding table that looked suspiciously like an old games table. It was the kind Archer remembered playing cards on during school holidays at home. The operator had one hand on the tuning dial, and the other scribbling notes into a hardbacked notebook.

Archer noticed a pair of legs sticking out from beneath the carrier. Another man, who was clearly engaged in a mechanical battle with the undercarriage, twisted and muttered something indistinct.

"Still patchy," Innes said as Archer stepped beside him. "Atmospherics are awful. I've relayed your message and had confirmation it was received, but we've heard nothing further."

Archer nodded. "Do we still have the battery at our disposal?"

"We do. But for how long, I couldn't say." Innes didn't look up; his eyes still fixed on the map in front of him. "Everything's moving fast. Nibeiwa was taken this morning. Sounds like Tummar's being hit now."

As Archer leant closer to the map, a white, enamel mug appeared from his left. The warmth and smell of fresh tea wafted across his face. A grizzled-looking private of the Royal Artillery stood beside him. "Tea, Sir?"

Archer took the mug in both hands, grateful. "Thank you, private," he said quietly before he turned back to study the map.

"I've been listening in all afternoon," Innes murmured, eyes still scanning the grid lines. "It's textbook, really. They're hitting the Italian camps one by one from the flank. Nibeiwa this morning. Tummar West under assault now. From what I can tell, they're just breaking through the Italian line and then smashing each strongpoint before they roll past and on to the next one." Innes was tracing the direction of travel on his map with a small pencil.

Archer took a slow sip of tea. "They're not trying to hold ground, then."

"No, it doesn't appear so," Innes replied, tapping the map with a short pencil.

Archer leant over, tracing the lines and pencilled notes scattered across the grid squares. Arrows swept from Nibeiwa to Tummar West, then curved again towards the coast. He narrowed his gaze, following the progression.

"Looks like they're pushing straight on," he murmured. "Nibeiwa, Tummar... then arcing east, probably towards the coast road. Sidi Barrani, maybe?"

"Do you think?" Innes said, tilting his head as he stared at his markings.

"Cut the road," Archer leant over and with a straight finger pointed on the map. "Trap whatever's left. They're rolling them up in sequence. Not trying to slug it out across the whole line," he continued to gesture across the map. "Just taking each major point in turn and leaving gaps behind."

He'd seen it before, though from the wrong side: fast armour, sudden gaps, lines buckling before men had time to regroup. Only this time, they were the ones doing the rolling up.

Archer straightened, taking another sip of his sweet tea and letting the weight of it settle. "If it works, there won't be much left to fight by the time they reach the coast."

Innes looked up from his chair. "And, what about us here?"

Archer turned and looked out over the position. "We make ourselves comfy and wait to see what's next."

As Archer moved away, he realised the sun had lowered into a molten disc. It was melting into the desert rim and throwing long shadows over the captured position. The heat had eased just enough for movement to feel less like punishment. The wind, such as it was, had turned faint and cool, whispering across sandbags and battered canvas, fluttering an Italian flag someone had tied to tent poles. The scent of cordite still lingered, but now it was joined by cooking smoke, faint herbs, and the sharp smell of disturbed soil.

The burial party had done its work. Shallow trenches had been dug just beyond the perimeter wire: separate rows for British and Italian dead. Each was marked with whatever could be found – scraps of timber, flattened tins, a few crosses fashioned from bayonet scabbards and tent pegs. De Luca had insisted to his men that the digging "...is a duty, and the last act of friendship to the fallen."

Now everyone in the company, along with the Italian prisoners, was gathered in a rough arc around the cleared space. British soldiers stood to one side, still in their sweat-drenched khaki, with faces streaked with dirt, and their rifles at ease. The Italians, in tattered grey-green uniforms, formed their own column opposite. Some were helmeted, others bareheaded, but most had expressions of blank exhaustion. Between them lay the canvas-draped dead: forty-one Italian, one British. Private Morgan's rifle with its bayonet fixed, had been driven into the ground. His tin hat rested on the brass end of the butt, and the chin strap swayed gently in the evening breeze. The same, small ritual had been repeated at many of the graves.

Colonello De Luca stepped forwards, still in full uniform. The creases had softened, and his shoulders carried the weight of the day, but his presence remained composed. In both hands, he held a small, worn book; its red leather was faded and cracked with age. He stood in silence for a moment, letting the situation settle across the ranks, his gaze passing slowly over the faces before him. Then, in soft and formal Italian, he began to speak.

Archer understood only fragments of the colonel's words, but the meaning was clear enough in tone. The words came slowly. Each one was deliberate and shaped with care and weight. Later, De Luca would quietly translate the core of it for him: "We honour the fallen of all nations who gave their lives today. They fought not because they wished to, but because duty called. May they be remembered not as enemies, but as men."

Standing in front of the graves, he read a final passage from the book, still in Italian. The cadence alone carried reverence. Across both ranks, heads bowed. Some whispered prayers under their breath. Others simply stared at the fading line of the horizon as the last light of the day bled out across the sand.

When De Luca finished, he slowly turned and gave a slight nod to a tanned-looking officer who stepped forwards, crossed himself – forehead, chest, shoulders – and opened what Archer recognised at once as the Holy Bible.

The officer began in measured, fluent Italian, his voice rising gently as the words breathed over the graves. Archer bowed his head. He didn't need to understand the language. The rhythm was familiar enough; it was the weight of ritual and reverence.

In that moment, Archer's thoughts drifted to his friend, the padre, Captain James Cartwright. He pictured him back in Colchester, stood before the chapel in his battledress with his cuffs turned back, and the white square of his dog collar pressed neatly under his throat. Archer wondered what he might be saying now. Something about sacrifice, perhaps. Or duty. Or simply the dignity of the fallen, whatever side they'd fought for.

As the Italian's voice came to a soft and smooth ending, Archer lifted his head. De Luca looked to him and gave a slight nod. Archer returned it once, and the colonel stepped back in silence. Archer took a steady breath and stood tall. From memory, he began to speak. It wasn't Keats as he'd first imagined he'd quote, but scripture. The words came clearly, calmly, and were carried by the hush that had settled over the assembled men.

"The Lord is my shepherd; I shall not want. He maketh me to lie down in green pastures: he leadeth me beside the still waters. He restoreth my soul: he leadeth me in the paths of righteousness for his name's sake."

He paused briefly, then continued.

"Yea, though I walk through the valley of the shadow of death, I will fear no evil: for thou art with me; thy rod and thy staff they comfort me. Thou preparest a table before me in the presence of mine enemies: thou anointest my head with oil; my cup runneth over.

Surely goodness and mercy shall follow me all the days of my life: and I will dwell in the house of the Lord for ever."

A moment's stillness followed. Then Archer added, simply, "Amen."

As one, the men, British and Italian alike, echoed, "Amen."

Archer turned to Jacks who called the men to attention. A separate detail, standing to one side, shouldered their rifles. At Jacks' order, they fired a single round into the air. The echo cracked across the desert like a mark of finality. As the riflemen lowered their weapons to slope arms, Jacks gave the order to dismiss. Slowly, the Italian burial party moved forwards, and the filling in of graves began.

The last shovelfuls of earth had barely settled when a faint, persistent growl reached them. It was low at first but grew steadily louder. Heads turned. Archer raised his own slowly, already recognising the familiar churn of a single-cylinder engine. A moment later, a motorcycle burst through the distant shimmering haze, a dust cloud trailing behind like smoke from a fire not extinguished.

The rider cut the engine sharply as he neared the gathered men. He swung a leg off the battered Norton, dust-coated and swaying slightly from the ride. His goggles were crusted white, and the scarf tied across his mouth was stiff with sweat and sand. Above his long leather gloves, Archer saw the chevrons of a corporal. The man straightened, pulled down the scarf and raised his goggles.

"Captain Wetherby?" he called, his voice hoarse. The name was a jolt, a reminder that Archer's commanding officer was dead and that the responsibility now rested with him.

"I'm afraid he was killed last night," Archer replied, stepping forwards. "You'll be handing it to me."

The despatch rider reached into his satchel and pulled out a folded message slip, creased but marked with the clear stamp of 7th Battalion HQ. He handed it over without ceremony.

"Of course, Sir."

Archer took the paper and then paused to study the man. The corporal looked utterly spent. His uniform was caked in fine sand, and his bike showed the strain. The paint was chipped back to bare metal where the desert wind had scoured it clean. "Corporal, where have you come from?" Archer asked, voice level but curious.

"Brigade, Sir."

"And where are they now?"

"East of Bir Tummar. Couple of miles past the old Italian supply post. They're moving fast, Sir."

Archer nodded as he took the folded paper. "Before you go, Corporal, be sure to get something to eat. We've got a cookhouse set up. Get yourself to the front of the line and grab a bite."

The corporal blinked, clearly surprised. He wasn't used to that kind of invitation from an officer. "You'd best get a move on, Corporal," Jacks added, appearing beside them. "It smells bloody good."

The rider gave a quick nod, still not quite sure how to respond, and moved off towards the tents.

Archer unfolded the message, reading the precise instructions in clipped staff officer's language:

To: Captain Wetherby, B Coy 7th Greenmoor Light Infantry

RE: POW Holding Position, Tummar Flank

Time: 1410hrs

You are to maintain control of current position and prisoner strength (172) until arrival of Royal Military Police detachment. ETA: 0200-0400hrs.

Upon successful handover, report to 7th Battalion assembly point at Bir Tummar East. Arrival no later than 0600hrs.

Lieutenant Innes and associated artillery detail are to accompany.

Orders confirmed by Lt Col, Blackstone CO. 7th Battalion GLI

Message ends.

Archer read the message twice, then folded the slip and slid it into his breast pocket. The horizon was already softening with dusk, the wind carrying the last of the day's heat in it.
He turned. "Jacks."

By his side, the sergeant turned and waited with his rifle slung, and his face streaked with dust and dried sweat.

"We're to hold position until the RMPs arrive, sometime between zero-two hundred and zero-four. Once they take over the prisoners, we move. Battalion wants us at Bir Tummar East no later than zero-six hundred."
Jacks gave a sharp nod. "How far's the move?"

"About fifteen miles. Enough to make us sweat if we're slow." Archer responded quickly.
"Understood."

Archer sensing the need for urgency, his voice quiet but firm. "Get the lads squared away. Vehicles checked, water topped up. I think the artillery did its job on the Italian guns, but if not, disable them."
Jacks gave a faint smirk. "Right."

"And scrounge what you can. Food, spares, anything useful. But don't strip the place bare. Leave the prisoners enough food and water to get by. We'll let the MPs sort them out when they arrive."

"Aye. We'll make sure we have enough for a good breakfast."

Archer gave a dry nod, his gaze sweeping the fading horizon. "Don't get too excited. We've still got a night's worth of sand and prisoners between us and that."

Jacks followed his eyes for a moment. Then, without a word, he turned back towards the vehicles parked in the centre that were already slipping into motion, the quiet machinery of preparation beginning again.

The shadows were long now. The last light of the sun caught on the tips of rifles and the edges of helmets. The smell of food had returned, and the scent of tomato and stale coffee drifted from the field stove like a promise.

Archer walked slowly back towards where Innes, the FOO, had set up his carrier, turning the orders over in his mind. The day had already felt full: a battle fought, a position taken, the dead buried. But it wasn't over. Not yet.

He passed Jacks near the aid post that had been hastily constructed earlier to provide shelter to the wounded. He noted Jacks was issuing instructions in his quiet, firm way. A small knot of men dispersed at his word, heading towards the edge of the camp.

Innes was bent over the rear of the carrier, rummaging through a crate of equipment. As Archer approached, the artillery officer straightened suddenly, eyes bright.

"Here it is!" he declared, exhaling with relief, and tossed a tin toward his signaller. The man caught it with both hands, squinting at the label.

"It's a can of peaches, not a Mills bomb, Fraser!" Innes said while chuckling. Fraser gave a sheepish grin and tucked the tin away as Innes turned, catching sight of Archer.

"Lieutenant," he said, brushing dust from his sleeves. "To what do I owe the pleasure?"

Archer stepped up beside him. "Orders are in. We're to hold until the MPs arrive, between zero-two hundred and zero-four, they reckon. Once they've taken the prisoners, we move east. Bir Tummar East. Report in by zero-six."

Innes nodded, already focused. "I'm to accompany?"

"Yes. I want us ready to move by zero-one-thirty. Ideally, we're rolling as soon as the handover's done."

Innes glanced towards the interior of the carrier where Fraser was still inspecting their modest hoard. "Right. We'll be ready." Then, after a pause, he added, "I've just eaten. That little Italian field kitchen, any chance we can keep it? What they conjured up was lovely. Better than anything Fraser here can manage with a tin of hash."

Fraser looked over at the lieutenant with a gaze that said, '*you know what you can do, mate.*'

Innes ignored him, warming to his theme. "They even had coffee. Not terrible. But the food! Bloody hell, it was good."

"I've not made it over yet," Archer said, a faint smile tugging at his mouth. "The thing's immobile now. Axle's gone. Although I did hear Evans is trying to claim the cook as a company mascot."

Innes chuckled. "If we end up requisitioning a Sicilian chef, I won't complain."

Archer turned to go, then paused, tone more serious again. "Zero-one-thirty."

"Understood."

Archer walked off into the gathering dark. Behind him, the camp settled into its quiet rhythm: weapons stacked, rations passed around, and the low murmur of preparation threading through the cooling desert air as the light continued to fade.

CHAPTER 7

The ridge at Ras el Galia, as the maps had started calling it, had been taken with the kind of brutal efficiency officers dream of and men rarely experience. Archer's company had hit the Italian strongpoint under cover of artillery, cleared the trenches, and secured over a hundred and seventy prisoners with only one British fatality. It was, by any measure, a success. But success didn't mean rest.

There was no debrief, no handshake, no moment to stand still. Orders came through while the smoke still hung in the air. They were to hold the position overnight, hand over the prisoners to the Military Police, and rejoin the battalion. By dawn on the 10th, they were moving again, trucks loaded, engines groaning, boots already thick with dust. Operation Compass had shifted gear. What had begun as a limited offensive had become a full-blown collapse of the Italian 10th Army. Its forward strongpoints, Nibeiwa, Tummar East and West, and now Sofafi, had been shattered in a targeted sequence. Thousands of prisoners had been taken. Equipment abandoned. Artillery silenced or captured in place. The rout was underway. British and Commonwealth forces were no longer probing the line, no longer feeling for weaknesses with cautious patrols and limited thrusts. They were racing east along the Libyan coast, driving hard for Bardia and beyond. The pace of their advance had quickened.

The road ahead was littered with the wreckage of retreat, burnt-out lorries, overturned carts, crates of rations left half-buried in sand. Here and there, groups of Italian troops sat cross-legged in the dust with their rifles piled in front of them and hands raised long before a shot was fired.For Archer and the 7th Battalion, the fighting had faded into a blur of movement and debris. They hadn't fired a shot in three days. The men rode in silence, squeezed into the backs of swaying Bedfords, faces streaked with sun and dust. Water came warm when it came at all. Cigarettes were shared without talk. The sun burnt through their khaki by day and sweat dampened on their skin in the bitter desert air by night. Dust got everywhere, into rifles, webbing, the creases of eyes and the lining of lungs. The sharpness of battle had given way to a strange inertia, like following the wake of a storm that still threatened but never touched.

On rejoining the battalion after the attack on the Italian position, Archer had expected questions, perhaps even recognition. Instead, he was greeted with the practical quiet of a unit already moving. His report was taken without ceremony: one man dead, three wounded, position taken, prisoners secured. The figures were noted, and the result was folded into the operational log like any other. It came with a nod from Blackstone.

No speech.

No mention of the man Archer had lost.

No comment on the men he'd brought back alive.

Another officer, Captain Sedgewick had been assigned to take over B Company. Archer had been quietly returned to his previous role: Platoon Commander, No. 1 Platoon. There had been no explanation. Just an orderly with a clipboard, calling out new appointments and truck allocations.

He hadn't shown his disappointment. Not outwardly. He'd saluted, nodded, and found his place without hesitation. But the sting was there. He'd held the company together through a live operation. He'd taken ground, secured prisoners, buried the dead, and sent word forwards. He hadn't expected a medal, but he hadn't expected to be overlooked, either. Still, he was a soldier, and pragmatism came quickly to those who had worn the boots long enough.

Sedgewick wasn't a fool. He was calm, steady, well spoken, and the sort of officer who kept his kit pressed and his tone measured, no matter how thick the dust. He'd come straight from

Brigade liaison, they said, with a record full of clean endorsements and no black marks. He was a staff man who'd asked to return to field command. Educated, articulate, and with a voice that carried across a parade square but never quite filled a trench.

Archer watched Sedgewick closely during that first day, noting the clipped instructions, the tidy posture, the way he unfolded maps like they might tear if handled too roughly. He was no stranger to the forms and the functions of command. But he seemed to lack the smell of it, the stink of cordite and blood, the crackle of shouted orders over bursting rounds, the unfiltered edge of decisions made on the run. He was competent, yes. But as yet, untested.

Still, Archer knew enough to respect the uniform. Sedgewick had been appointed. He wore the pips. And whatever Archer thought of the timing, or the quiet way the decision had landed, it wasn't his call to make. He followed the chain, just like everyone else. Even if the chain sometimes looped back to the wrong hands.

The previous night, he'd said as much to Jacks. They had stood beside the trucks as the landscape quietened around them. Archer had turned towards Jacks and said, "Not our place to question it, I suppose."

"No, Sir," Jacks had replied. Then, after a pause, "But it doesn't mean it was the right call."

Archer hadn't answered. Just lit a fresh cigarette and watched the orange glow fade into the desert dark.

The next few days passed in a steady rhythm, moving forwards, halting, and moving again as the battalion followed the advance along the coast. The Italians were falling back in growing disorder, prisoners taken in numbers, positions abandoned almost as quickly as they were found.

Shortly before first light on the 14th, Archer was called to Company HQ.

A runner found him crouched by one of the lorries, checking the bracket on a spare water can. No words, just a pointed finger back towards the canvas-draped shelter Sedgewick had claimed as his forward post. Archer stood up, dusted his hands off on his trousers, and walked over to the shelter without a word.

The HQ was barely more than a lean-to, a salvaged tent flysheet strung between two Bedfords, crates for a table, a lamp flickering in the corner. Sedgewick stood alone, coat buttoned, hair neat despite the sand. A message slip lay flat beside the map board, anchored with a bayonet. He didn't look up straight away, just motioned Archer forwards.

"Brigade passed this down an hour ago. Colonel Blackstone read it himself. Told me: *'Use Archer.'*"

That last part wasn't offered as flattery. Just fact. A simple transfer of responsibility.

Sedgewick tapped the slip with two fingers.

"Point 208. Minor feature. Suspected movement. Intelligence is vague. You're to investigate and report. If occupied, clear and hold. Support will be limited, artillery on call only."

Archer leaned in slightly, eyes scanning the grid reference, the terrain markings, what little there was. No photograph. No field sketch. Just numbers on paper and a red cross on the edge of the current map sheet.

"Not on our line of advance."

"No. But something's drawn someone's attention. Could be a few Italian stragglers. Could be nothing. But they want eyes on it. And Blackstone wants yours."

Sedgewick stepped back, arms folded, eyes narrowing as he looked at the ridge line beyond the trucks.

Sedgewick tapped the dispatch again. "You'll take your platoon. I'm attaching a Vickers team, Corporal Dalton's crew. You may need something extra; best be prepared." His tone was calm and matter of fact as he continued. "You'll take one of the two-inch mortars as well. Ammunition's limited, but better to have it and not need it."

Archer nodded. "Understood. You mentioned artillery, does that mean we're getting a FOO?"

"Afraid not, Lieutenant. You'll take the No. 18 set. I'm pulling Lance Corporal Lomas to operate it. He's kept it working so far, but it's been temperamental. If it goes dead, no artillery."

Sedgewick ran a hand over the map spread out before him, hesitating for a moment. "If you find something significant, and it's too much for a platoon, get a message back. We'll decide what to do from here."

There was a pause between them, not tension, not exactly, but something that lingered just long enough to be felt. Sedgewick cleared his throat.

"I'm aware you were passed over, Lieutenant. It wasn't a slight. It was a staff decision. Rotation. Timing."

Archer met his gaze, unreadable. "I hadn't given it a thought, Sir."

Sedgewick gave a thin nod, then gestured towards the lorries. "Get your men moving. You're to be off in twenty."

Archer folded his notebook shut and, without another word, stepped out into the grey light of morning and felt the cold already lifting from the sand. By the time he reached the trucks, Jacks was already lacing his boots.

"Orders?" the sergeant asked, standing.

"Point 208. Suspected movement. No detail." Archer replied dryly.

"So, we're guessing again."

Buckling the belt of his webbing Archer turned. "I wouldn't say again. We knew we had competition at the last point. Another thing, Blackstone asked for us."

Jacks exhaled slowly. "You mean he asked for you, Sir. Can't say I approve of your popularity, Lieutenant!"

Just then, Corporal Dalton and Lomas appeared, both weighed down with equipment.

Dalton was solidly built, , and calm under pressure, a man who looked like he'd rather be back behind a Vickers gun than lugging it across the desert. He had a belt of .303 rounds draped over his neck, an ammunition can in one hand, and the small two-inch mortar in the other.

Lomas, by contrast, was younger, wiry, and already sweating beneath the weight of the No. 18 set. He staggered forwards with his personal kit and rifle, his glasses slipping down his nose. Quiet but capable, he'd kept the temperamental radio working longer than most had expected; it was a minor miracle in the desert.

"Jacks, see to Dalton and his chaps. Lomas, you'll travel up front with me in the lead truck. Is that thing working?" Archer nodded towards the large, box-like pack on the young man's back. "It was about fifteen minutes ago, Sir," Lomas replied, turning to scan for the lead lorry.

Archer paused, watching the small group of men heave the Vickers machine-gun towards the truck Jacks had pointed out.

They moved quickly, efficiently, no fuss, no questions. For now, they were his men, and whatever waited at Point 208, it would be him they looked to. He felt the familiar pull of responsibility. It wasn't fear, but a steady pressure, like the first steps into deep water. Better it was him making the call. Better the weight fell on his shoulders than theirs.

Raising his voice, he bellowed, "One Platoon – prepare to move!" The convoy pulled out in a staggered line, engines labouring as they turned west into the low glare of the rising sun. Dust lifted almost immediately, hanging in the air behind them, drifting across the scrub and hard ground in long trailing sheets.

The road, if it could be called that, was little more than a worn track marked by tyres and the passage of earlier units. Here and there, signs of the advance lay scattered: abandoned kit, broken transport, the remnants of a retreat that had not held together.

The men rode in silence for the most part, heads low against the wind and grit, each left to his own thoughts as the trucks carried them further from the battalion and toward whatever waited ahead.

The trucks rumbled to a halt well short of the objective. Archer had ordered the men to debus a thousand yards out. He'd called it early, briefing the platoon that they would go in on foot. It would give him time to assess the ground and decide the best approach.

As the trucks settled, dust hung in the air behind them before it drifted away with the breeze, revealing the vast, open desert. Ahead, there was a low rise of ground and broken stone that gave the faint suggestion of crumbling walls.

Archer climbed down from the cab and raised his binoculars, steadying them with both hands. Around him, the men jumped from the trucks and, began forming an all-round defence with the vehicles in the centre, just as they'd been drilled to. Dalton and the Vickers crew knelt beside their lorry, waiting for Jacks or Archer to place them. The air was warm, and the horizon was already shimmering. Jacks approached as Archer swept his glasses slowly from right to left, then paused, holding steady, studying the ground ahead. No immediate movement or signs of life. It was still.

Archer's focus was on the remains of a small farm, or what had once passed for one. Through the shimmer of heat and dust, Archer could make out two low buildings, sun-bleached and crumbling, their outlines broken and sagging. One had a collapsed roof, the other a jagged window frame gaping like a wound.

The walls looked like stone and dried mud, pale, brittle, and pockmarked by time. There was a rough perimeter wall that was mostly fallen, but it traced a loose rectangle around the place. A few upright posts still clung to rusted strands of fencing wire.

Maybe it had been a goat farm? Archer thought. It had clearly been abandoned long ago and was crumbling to nothing.

Nothing moved.

No figures.

No smoke.

Just silence and stillness, the kind that pressed in. The kind that made your skin itch. “Goat farm?” Jacks muttered beside him, squinting into the distance.

Archer didn’t reply straight away. He kept scanning left to right then back again. Shadows shifted, but nothing gave itself away. He lowered the binoculars and drew a slow breath. The ground between them and the farm was open and flat with a few shrubs scattered across the hardened sand. There was barely a rise to break their approach. On foot, they’d be exposed for far too long. It might be abandoned, but something about the stillness prickled. Too quiet. Too clean.

He turned to Jacks. “Change in plan. Ground’s too open, too long on foot, too many angles we can’t cover.”

Jacks nodded, already reading it. “Vehicles in?”

“Vehicles in,” Archer confirmed. “Fast. We drive right up, drop twenty yards short, then rush in and through. No stopping. I want boots on the ground before there is time to blink.”

Jacks turned away, already shouting for the section commanders. Within minutes, Matthews, Pritchard, and Wilson had gathered behind the nearest Bedford, kneeling in the dust, rifles slung, eyes sharp. Archer crouched in front of them and began sketching rough lines in the sand with the tip of his finger.

“Here’s the farm. Two buildings. Likely abandoned, but I’m not trusting it. Matthews, you push straight through and set up a perimeter on the far side, west side.”

“Pritchard, I want you in from the north. Watch the flanks and any back exit from the structures. Secure and hold.”

Archer continued drawing lines in the line with his finger tracing each man's route to the farm. "Wilson, south side. Sweep round but don't get ahead of us. I want pressure from three sides."

He paused, then looked up. "I'll come straight through the centre with Dalton and the Vickers team, and the rest of the lads. We hit it hard and fast. We clear both buildings. No loitering. If it's empty, good. If it's not, better we're on top of them before they can act." They nodded, no questions. Just the tight focus of men who'd done this before.

"Twenty yards out," Archer repeated. "Engines off. Bail out. Move fast."

The engines coughed into life one by one, the trucks growling low as they rolled forward in a loose single file. Dust billowed behind them in pale ribbons, hanging in the still air as the convoy began its short but deliberate advance. Archer rode in the lead truck, canvas folded down exposing everything to the dust and grit. He knelt behind the cab with Jacks beside him, eyes fixed on the line of crumbling stone ahead of them.

The farm sat quiet, unchanged, still half-swallowed by the heat haze. No flashes. No movement. Just sun, stone, and silence. But Archer's gut said otherwise.

At two hundred yards, he raised his hand and gave the signal. The trucks began to fan out, peeling away from the centre in a smooth, practised manoeuvre.

Pritchard's Bedford turned first, swinging wide to the north, the tyres cutting faint troughs in the sand. Webb sat in the back, checking his rifle again, the butt resting on his knee, face calm and unreadable.

To the south, Wilson's vehicle mirrored the movement, curving away in a low sweep, hugging a shallow line of scrub. The men inside were silent, crouched, poised. Someone murmured a short prayer that was barely audible over the engine's thrum.

The centre held firm with Matthews' truck leading straight on, flanked by Archer's with Dalton's men behind. Matthews stood braced at the tailboard, one hand on the tilt frame, scanning the front of the ruins for movement. His section was alert and steady behind him.

The formation quickly widened into an arrowhead, pushing west, tyres scouring dust into pale clouds that clung low to the ground. Archer glanced left and watched Pritchard's truck bounce through the rough, his men steadying themselves against the tilt struts. To the right, Wilson's section were shadows behind canvas, weapons gripped, eyes locked forwards.

Fifty yards out. Archer leant out over the tilt flap and called back, voice sharp and low. "Debus on twenty! Follow Matthews section, head to the larger building!" Jacks gripped his rifle and was the first to nod.

Forty. The farm began to sharpen against the horizon. Two crumbling structures were visible. Archer saw them take shape - jagged openings and stone walls scattered with rubble and heat shimmer. Still no movement. Too still.

Thirty. Archer could see the window with its the iron hook, the fractured gate half-hanging on its post. Dust swirled in strange patterns around the base of the buildings.

Twenty.

"Now!" Archer shouted.

The trucks slammed to a halt in near unison. Tailboards did not drop. Every man was either over the side or out the back, each landing with a thud. Lomas made an audible groan as the weight of the radio impacted on his back. The men burst out at a run, boots hitting sand, weapons raised, fanning out with trained urgency.

Matthews was moving quickly, leading his section directly towards the ruins. Pritchard's men swept north, wide and fast, angling to skirt the outer wall. Wilson's section broke south at speed, rifles up, eyes sweeping the flanks.

In the centre, Archer landed hard, shouldering his rifle. Dalton and the Vickers team were at his heels. Grit filled his mouth. His heart pounded in rhythm with the drum of running feet. He moved low across the sand. His rifle was tucked tight as their soles whispered over the crusted earth. Beside him, Jacks mirrored the motion, rifle pointed forwards, eyes scanning the crumbling outbuildings ahead.

The farmstead lay ahead, a scatter of stone and silence against the hard ground. At a distance, it was little more than shape and shadow, but as they closed, the detail began to come through.

Walls were half standing. Doors hung loose. There were gaps where the wind slipped through, carrying a low, uneven sound. Archer slowed slightly, eyes moving across it.

A rusted water tank stood above the structures, shifting faintly on its frame, its metal giving a dull, intermittent groan as it moved in the breeze.

No voices.

No movement.

Only the wind.

They moved in closer, boots grinding dry dust underfoot, each step sounding louder than it should. The place felt empty but not settled.

The nearest structure came into full view, a squat, single-room hut, windowless with its door hanging ajar. Archer paused just short, flattening against the wall. He raised two fingers. Jacks nodded, shifting his grip.

A breath. Then Archer swung in.

The door creaked and tore free of its top hinge, twisting on the lower one before it crashed to the floor. Dust rose and hung in the air like smoke. Startled for a moment, Archer swept left. Rifle up. Nothing. Just a collapsed cot, a pair of cracked old pans, and a stack of rotting jute sacks in the far corner.

"Clear," he said quietly.

Jacks stepped in behind. His rifle was still raised as he gave the room another glance. The tension in his body slipped away, and he lowered his rifle. He turned and headed out of the doorway where he saw Lockett and Briggs appear from the other building, raising an arm and calling it clear.

Archer approached from the building and scanned the area. A low stone wall, broken in several places, ran along the far side of the yard. He moved quickly to investigate, noting that one of the gaps offered a clear line of fire to the north, south, and west. He called out to Dalton, signalling for him to set up the Vickers in the break. Dalton gave a curt nod and dropped to one knee, directing the others as they wrestled the gun into position. The Vickers settled, facing the open yard with its flanks angled just enough to cover either side.

The farmstead resumed its still silence as the last echoes of boots and shouted orders faded into the heat. Archer stood near the centre, turning slowly as he took in the situation.

Up close, the place was worse than it had looked. The walls were pitted and flaking, stone and mud crumbling at the edges, brittle to the touch. The roof beams on the ruined building had completely collapsed inwards, leaving a jagged tangle of timbers and tile. The other hut, though still standing, stank faintly of old decay, the kind that soaked into earth and never left.

The waist-high stone enclosure, where Dalton had set up the Vickers, ran along one side. Its shape was roughly rectangular although much of its length had fallen in. The dry wall was scattered with white droppings, baked hard by the sun. Near the corner, a rusted trough lay cracked and empty, and beside it, fencing wire was still caught in splintered wooden posts, grey with age. The gate, if it could still be called that, hung limp from one hinge, its frame twisted and rusted through.

Fragments of the place remained among the rubble: broken tiles, splintered wood, a dented water jar half-buried in the dust. Near the edge of the rubble, something made Archer pause. A small, worn sandal was wedged beneath a fallen stone. Child-sized. He didn't speak. Just stood there a moment longer, eyes narrowing.

Slowly, he turned back toward the centre of the yard where Dalton's men were finishing the Vickers emplacement, and he called Jacks over to review their arcs.

Archer stepped away from the Vickers team. The crunch of gravel underfoot marked each slow step as he paced the edge of the yard. The stillness hadn't shifted. Nothing moved. No sound beyond the wind catching at broken timber. He paused beside a crumbling wall and continued to scan the flat horizon. Nothing but heat shimmer and emptiness. His orders were to investigate and report, clear and hold if occupied. But this place wasn't occupied.

Still, something about it bothered him.

The silence felt wrong. It wasn't the lazy hush of an empty position, but a breath caught in the mouth. It felt like the place had been abandoned in a hurry. He had seen no evidence to that effect, but he had a nagging feeling of being watched.

Archer turned slowly, surveying the terrain yet again. It wasn't a bad position. High enough to offer decent visibility, low enough to avoid standing out against the skyline. It provided cover of sorts: the walls, the outbuildings, the shallow depressions. A company could hold here. Rest. Refuel. Hide, even. He hadn't liked driving straight in, not with so little warning. But the approach had offered no cover with no proper rise to form up behind.

The last ridge had been too far back, and the track had been too open. If there had been an ambush, they'd have walked straight into the killing ground. Now, standing inside it, he realised that same exposure might work in their favour. If they were to face an assault, they would see it coming.

His gaze drifted to the distant track they'd followed in, tyre prints still visible in the sand. No recent movement. No sign of a skirmish or ambush. But no sign of occupation either. No fires. No latrines. No empty tins. No discarded debris. Just heat, dust, and the slow creep of time.

Still, it didn't sit right in his mind.

He glanced back toward the trucks. They were being brought up and parked behind the ruined buildings. The men who were responsible for pulling camouflage netting over the vehicles, were doing their best to break up the familiar silhouette of a lorry.

The rest of the men were digging their trenches. It was a two-man task: each slit trench long, wide, and deep enough for two men to stand shoulder high. Every position had been allocated by Jacks, arranged to allow interlocking fire and ensure each trench could be supported by the Vickers machine-gun which was positioned some twenty yards behind.

Archer stood motionless in the middle of the position and scanned the horizon again with his binoculars. He couldn't rid himself of that itch which told him they were being observed. Yet, nothing he saw told him this was the case. He dropped his glasses into his bag.

"Lomas!" Archer called out.

The wireless operator looked up and started to trot over, the No. 18 set still weighing heavy on his back, his Lee-Enfield swinging in time with his stride.

"Yes, Sir!" His reply came a little strained, breath catching as he reached Archer. "In there," Archer said, pointing towards the more intact hut. "Get the set running. Let's get word back to battalion."

He followed Lomas through the open doorway, both men stepping over the broken door that lay in its new position at an angle across the floor.

"Set up in that corner." Archer's tone was sharp as he nodded towards the far side, below a small opening that offered the only natural daylight in the room.

Lomas gave a brief nod, already shrugging off the pack. Archer watched as he knelt by the wall, laying out the handset and aerial, murmuring to himself as he checked the connections. The soft click and hiss of the set warming up was oddly comforting.

Archer stepped back towards the doorway and called out, his voice carrying through the dead stillness.

"Briggs! Lockett! Get in here. Jacks, too."

A moment later, boots scuffed across the loose stone. Private Raymond "Ray" Lockett appeared first, his wiry frame hunched slightly beneath the weight of his kit, followed by Private Norman "Nobby" Briggs, who was wiping his hands on a ragged bit of cloth. Jacks brought up the rear, eyes already sweeping the room. "This'll do," Archer said, turning to face them. "Set up HQ in here."

Briggs and Lockett gave a short nod at the same time. "Right you are, Sir."

Archer shaded his eyes as he stepped back out into the glare, the heat pressing down with steady weight. Jacks followed, squinting into the light and brushing at the constant clustering of flies. Archer moved up beside him, tugging open his bag to pull out his binoculars for another scan of the horizon.

"Sections are in place," Jacks reported. "We've shifted to all-round defence now the ground's ours." Archer nodded for him to go on.

"Webb's on the north wall. He's got the high corner, watching back along the track we came in on. Wilson's covering the south, tucked in behind that broken well. He's set them low, using what cover there is. Matthews has the west side. Not much out there but scrub and open ground, but he's spaced them wide, and they've got decent sightlines."

Archer took it in, looking intently at each line as it was mentioned.

"And the Vickers?"

"I've left it where you positioned it, Sir.

Covers north, south and west. Good field across the front, and it can swing to support either flank." Jacks extended his arm, sweeping from left to right. "If anything comes from the rear, we can switch to that break." He pointed towards a gap in the eastern wall.

Archer gave a short nod. "Good. You've got them interlocked?", "Within the sections, yes Sir. We may have to shift one or two if one side gets pressed, but we can cover it." Jacks gave a faint grin. "We're well set, Sir."

Archer let his gaze drift to the low rise beyond the yard, fingers tapping the body of his binoculars as the shimmer of heat rose in the distance. "It'll do. If anyone comes for us, we'll see the dust before we see the men."

The conversation was cut short by the arrival of Lockett, moving at pace. "Sir, Lomas has had word from Battalion."

Archer turned at once and headed back to the hut where Lomas had set up the wireless. As he stepped through the doorway, he passed Briggs who had just finished hanging a blanket across the entrance. Archer paused, casting a brief, quizzical look his way.

Briggs, understanding the Lieutenant's curiosity, offered a simple explanation. "Blackout, Sir."

Archer gave the faintest nod, then looked towards the radio set. "Lomas, you've had word from Battalion?"

"Yes, Sir." Lomas handed him a note; his fingers were still smudged with pencil lead.

Archer took it, eyes narrowing slightly as he tried to decipher the messy scrawl. Lomas' handwriting was hurried at best, but after a few seconds of squinting, he made it out.

To: Lt Archer, No. 1 Platoon
From: B Coy, 7th Greenmoor Light Infantry
Time: 1310 hrs
Hold present position.
Rest of company, ETA 0600 hrs.

Establish local defence and await further orders.
Acknowledge receipt.
Message ends.
"Have you acknowledged receipt Lomas?"
"Not yet Sir. Wasn't sure if you wanted to reply."

"Yes. Send the following: message received. Holding position. Defensive perimeter established. Awaiting company arrival. Will report any change." He paused. "That'll do, Lomas."

Lomas nodded, already adjusting the dial and preparing to key the microphone.

Archer turned away, satisfied. It was then he noticed how the small room had been transformed from an abandoned hut into something approaching military order.

What had been bare was now functional. A folding table had been set up in the corner, with the No. 18 set resting on top. Lomas had laid out his notepad and pencils just to the right, ready to log any message that came through. The aerial cable snaked through a jagged hole in the wall, above which a rolled-up piece of canvas hung like a curtain, ready to block out light. Clearly, Briggs had realised they'd be staying the night before Archer had.

He continued to survey the room. Two chairs had been dragged in, one canvas, one wooden, the latter missing part of its back. Lomas sat in it, leaning forwards, tapping out Archer's message in Morse code. In the centre of the hut, four storage cases stood on end, supporting an old sheet of plywood covered by half a blanket to create a makeshift table.

Lockett re-entered, carrying a scorched old biscuit tin filled with sand. The sharp smell of petrol trailed behind him. He set it down by the door. Archer noticed four upturned mess tin handles embedded in the sand; each one was bent into a flattened curve to form a stand.

He watched Lockett adjusting the pieces with quiet focus, like a man tuning an engine. Moments later, Briggs appeared with a pot filled almost to the brim with fresh water.

"All yours, Nobby," Lockett said.

Briggs crouched beside the tin and carefully placed the blackened pot on the improvised stand. Without hesitation, Lockett struck a lighter and touched it to the petrol-soaked sand.

A blue-orange flame flared to life, hugging the base of the pot. Within seconds, small bubbles began to form, rising to the surface. "She'll be ready in no time," Lockett said with quiet pride. "Get the cups ready."

Archer stepped outside, letting the door curtain fall behind him. The afternoon was drawing to a close. The sun was lower, and shadows stretched across the yard. A breeze stirred the warm, dry dust, carrying the faint tang of rust and decay. Men were settling in, murmuring over trenches and water tins.

Behind him, from inside the hut, Archer could hear the faint, soft hiss of the burner, the smell of petrol still lingering. He raised his binoculars once more to scan the horizon. Nothing moved. Just heat shimmer and the gentle lifting of grains of sand in the breeze.

They had done all they could. Trenches were dug, guns were sited, and orders had been acknowledged. Still, he couldn't shake the feeling they weren't alone.

CHAPTER 8

The Italian driver said nothing as the desert unfolded in front of them. Major Karl Neumann sat motionless in the rear seat of his vehicle. His hands were gloved, and his eyes were hidden behind round-lensed sunglasses that had once belonged to a Luftwaffe pilot. The man had been polite and courteous throughout the flight from Grottaglie Airfield and upon arrival, had gifted his glasses to Neumann, stating that he may need them. Neumann had accepted the glasses only in exchange for a small bottle of Schnapps.

The car vibrated faintly beneath him as it crossed from hard-packed road to rutted sand. The landscape blurred between the dust, sky, and low-bleached scrub. Somewhere far to the east, guns had spoken that morning. He had heard them before dawn, steady and deliberate: the British.

He lit a cigarette with care. The match flared briefly and then vanished with the wind. This was not his first war. France had been rapid. Poland brutal. But here, in this vast, indifferent heat, war would be different and likely more dangerous for it. In Poland, you could trust the map. In France, the movement. Here, you trusted neither. Distances lied. Roads faded. Men disappeared not in battle, but in thirst, sand, and misjudgement.

Neumann drew on the cigarette and exhaled slowly. The smoke curled against the roof of the car before slipping out through the open window. His uniform was immaculate despite the dust. Tunic pressed. Breeches sharp. Boots high and black, polished even after the journey. It didn't carry rows of ribbons or gaudy insignia. Just the silver bar of a General Staff officer, and tucked into his tunic buttonhole, the narrow black-and-white ribbon of the Iron Cross which he'd earnt in Poland. It was worn without fanfare but never mistaken.

He was not tall. Not physically imposing. But there was a quiet edge to his stillness, the kind that made junior officers stop speaking when he entered the room. His voice rarely rose. He didn't need to. He was a man who dealt in *effect*, not noise. In that, he had earnt Rommel's trust: not through favour but through results. Files moved faster when Neumann read them. Orders came back sharper when he was involved. His presence was a warning, not theatrical, not cruel, but coldly efficient. He did not waste time or resources. Or men. The driver hit a pothole and muttered an apology.

Neumann didn't respond. He hadn't spoken since they left the divisional rear four hours earlier. Not out of rudeness but because there had been nothing worth saying. The Italians had failed. Again. That much was abundantly clear. British units were advancing at speed, bypassing fixed positions, breaking strongpoints in sequence. Neumann had warned of it days ago. But Rome had dithered. Benghazi had postured. And now the 10th Army was bleeding into the sand. He watched the desert roll by. An ocean without water, no waves, no sound, just depthless heat.

The British were not to be underestimated. Neumann had faced them in France. They were stubborn, orderly, and slow to panic. Not brilliant, perhaps, but never brittle. They had held longer than they should have and bled harder than anyone expected. Yet, they were not insurmountable. Not if you moved faster, struck first, and never gave them time to regroup. That was what this desert offered, space, speed, angles. Here, with no hedgerows, no villages, no forests to hide behind, the war would favour the man who moved first and furthest. That was why he had come. Not to advise. Not even to lead. But to prepare the ground for Rommel and show the Italians how real war was fought.

The car slowed as a perimeter came into view. It was a mess of canvas and lorries, and whitewashed stones marked the edges of what passed for an Italian Regimental Headquarters. Someone had painted a red arrow on a petrol drum, pointing east. Another sign leant drunkenly against a crate: *Comando Avanzato.*

Major Karl Neumann stepped out of the car and brushed sand from his breeches. A pall of diesel fumes and dust hung over the compound. Tents sagged under makeshift poles. Wires snaked across the ground like trip hazards, some leading nowhere. A handful of Italian soldiers stood watch near the entrance. Their rifles were slung low, and their expressions were more curious than alert. He was expected. A German corporal, dressed in desert khaki, appeared from a nearby hut and saluted smartly. "Major Neumann? This way, Sir. Oberstleutnant Westphal is inside."

The command post had once been a stone customs house, flat-roofed, thick-walled, and now half-buried under sandbags and camouflage netting. Inside, the heat was worse than outside. The stale air reeked of sweat, paper, and evaporated petrol. Oberstleutnant Siegfried Westphal stood hunched over a map table, sleeves rolled, collar loose. He was lean and hollow-eyed, the product of long hours and few answers. His hair, once tightly parted, had begun to curl in the humidity. He didn't look up immediately.

"Close the door," he said.

Neumann did.

Westphal straightened, tapping a stick at the map. British unit markers, neatly drawn in blue chalk, were scattered along a north-south axis, pushing hard across the desert floor.

"Nibeiwa fell two days ago. Tummar yesterday. Sofafi is expected to follow tonight or tomorrow morning. Bardia's exposed. The 10th Army is... retreating, though that word doesn't quite capture the scale of it."

Neumann stepped closer; his gaze tracked the pins and notes across the board. "And what's left between here and the coast?"

Westphal sighed. "A few rearguard formations. Italian motorised elements withdrawing in pieces. One or two battalion-strength blocks left to die in place. There's no coordination, poor supply, and no air cover."

He finally looked up. "That's the picture. Berlin is watching this with concern. And Rommel..." He gestured vaguely westward, towards the idea of Germany. "...wants men on the ground."

"That's why I'm here," Neumann replied.

"I need you in the field by nightfall," Westphal said, tapping the eastern edge of the map with a pencil. "The British aren't just attacking. They're cutting. Fast. Simultaneous pushes across multiple axes. If I were them, I wouldn't be marching straight up the Via Balbia. I'd be turning the flank, probing south and east, and boxing in whatever's still standing."

He gestured across the paper where lines marked known Italian withdrawals. "They're methodical, well-supplied, and moving with solid artillery support. What's left of the Maletti Group..."

Westphal caught Neumann's glance and clarified, "A formation of assorted mobile elements. Libyan and Italian infantry, light armour, artillery, all under General Pietro Maletti. Supposed to be flexible. They evaporated in under an hour!"

He shifted the pencil to a wider arc. "Now British armour, 7th Armoured Division, are swinging wide. Skirting strongpoints, punching through gaps, then rolling back in behind. Classic envelopment."

Westphal exhaled slowly.

"They're not holding ground. They're breaking cohesion. Taking strongpoints one by one, isolating, then crushing. And they're fast. Faster than anyone thought possible. Our Italian allies assumed they'd wait for supply. They're not. They're living off captured fuel and pushing again by sunset."

The Oberstleutnant paused, lifting a glass from the edge of the map table and taking a slow sip. Neumann stepped closer and scanned the wide spread of paper and its tangle of markings. He took in the British positions, but more than that, he studied the spaces between them. The gaps. The dead ground. The possibilities.

Westphal's words lingered, but Neumann wasn't thinking in slogans. He was thinking in movements, timings, probabilities. The British weren't advancing to hold. They were advancing to unravel: striking at pressure points and pulling loose the threads before a new line could even be drawn.

He marked two likely arcs in his mind. One towards the coast. The other inland, open, unguarded, and wide enough to conceal a flanking force. If he were them, that's where he'd send it.

Westphal moved to a table and pulled a folded dispatch from a leather wallet. "You'll have use of a truck and six of our own men. Feldwebel Holtz is your senior NCO. They're all good lads." He handed the sheet to Neumann, then added, "And the Italians have been instructed to provide a company of infantry for escort and protection." Neumann raised an eyebrow. "How reliable?"

Westphal exhaled through his nose. "They're from the Catanzaro Division, so technically, very good... but don't expect too much." Neumann scanned the dispatch. He'd worked with worse.

"Who commands them?"

"A Captain Lorenzo Messina. Young. Decorated, and..." Westphal paused while showing a hint of a sarcastic grin. "He is the nephew of General Italo Garibaldi who is currently commanding the Italian 10th Army."

A silence fell between them. The map table, the heat, and the feeling that none of this was quite in control swallowed any sound. Then Westphal added, almost offhand, "You'll be formally reporting through the German Military Mission in Tripoli. But I imagine Rommel will want your assessment directly. Once he arrives."

Neumann folded the orders with care and tucked them into his breast pocket.

"I'll send him something worth reading."

Westphal gave a faint nod. "I expect nothing less."

The sun had climbed higher by the time Neumann stepped out of the customs house and into the chalk glare of early afternoon. The compound buzzed with the idle movement of men with little purpose. Crates were being shifted twice. A lorry engine was tested before being killed again. He adjusted his cap and moved towards the designated marshalling area where a staff truck and two motorcycles stood waiting in a loose crescent.

Six men stood beside them with their rifles slung, and their gear compact and tight. Their uniforms bore the dust of recent travel but little else. No slack webbing. No chatter. Neumann liked that. Feldwebel Holtz, stepped forwards and saluted. "Major."

"Feldwebel. Your men are briefed?"

"Yes, Sir. Reconnaissance and the Italians provide support."

Neumann gave a faint nod. "Good. I expect discipline, speed, and silence. This is not a parade."

Holtz didn't flinch. "Understood, Sir."

They turned as a second vehicle pulled into the yard, a long-bodied Italian truck coated in wind-blown dust. At its front, a young officer in clean khaki sat with his cap tilted just so, and his collar stiff at his neck. He dismounted before the vehicle had fully stopped and marched over with the kind of precision only newly minted captains possessed.

"Major Neumann?" he asked, offering a crisp salute. "Captain Lorenzo Messina, 3rd Company, 2nd Battalion, 141st Infantry Regiment, Catanzaro Division."

Neumann returned the gesture with just enough sharpness to acknowledge protocol. “Captain Messina. I’ve been told you’re to accompany us east.”

Messina nodded. “Yes, Sir. I’ve brought one company though numbers are... depleted. We’re at eighty-six rifles, four Breda light machine-guns, and one mortar team. Transport’s in working order.”

Neumann studied him for a moment. Messina couldn’t have been more than twenty-five. His boots were new. His sidearm holster looked untouched by wear, but his salute had been correct, and he’d arrived on time. “You’ve seen action, Captain?”

Messina hesitated. “Limited. My company held the southern perimeter at Tummar. We were pulled back before the position fell.”

Neumann didn’t respond at once. Then, with a slight turn of his head, “And what’s your relationship to General Garibaldi?”

This time Messina blinked. “My mother is his sister, but I assure you, Major, I earned my commission properly.”

“I see,” Neumann said, voice unreadable. “I ask only because command decisions sometimes reflect politics more than necessity. I prefer clarity when dealing with both.”

The young officer flushed slightly but said nothing. Neumann stepped toward the map case mounted on the bonnet of the lead vehicle. He lifted it free and made his way to the tailgate of the lorry. There, he spread the map across the flat surface, smoothing the creases with one gloved hand.

“Our orders are to assess the entire forward line. I need to see across this entire axis.” He pointed at the map and traced an invisible line with his finger. “North at Sidi Barrani, south at Sofafi, with a detailed assessment around Nibeiwa,” he said, tapping each point in turn.

Messina let out a croak of surprise. “Nibeiwa? That fell on the 9th, two days ago!”

Neumann's voice cooled. "Exactly why we'll be going *around* Nibeiwa, Captain, to see how it fell, and what followed." He continued. "The British have already pushed beyond most of it. We will be moving through what they have left behind."

Messina said nothing further. His face had dropped, the way a boy's might after being chastised in front of the class.

Neumann kept his hand on the map a moment longer before he straightened.

"The route runs approximately one hundred and thirty kilometres. We'll be skirting around Nibeiwa, heading south in stages. Sidi Barrani, then Tummar, then Sofafi."

He paused to let that settle and then nodded to Feldwebel Holtz.

Holtz stepped forwards, his voice matter of fact. "Tracks are mostly hardpack sand but expect some soft ground south of Nibeiwa as we head towards Sofafi. No proper roads. Visibility is good but exposed. We rotate the lead vehicle every twenty kilometres. Dust and engine heat will build fast."

Neumann picked up again. "You'll carry fuel for the full journey. Top up your main tanks, check your cans. No excuses. There'll be three to four days without resupply." He looked across the group.

"Each man is to carry water for seventy-two hours minimum. Rations for three days, preferably four."

Neumann's eyes settled on Captain Messina.

"You're here to provide security, Captain. Nothing more. Keep your men close, and your opinions closer."

He let the silence hold a beat.

"If we need your thoughts. I'll ask for them."

Then he turned to everyone who was gathered and spoke with a solid tone. "We move in 45 minutes!"

The first three days passed in steady movement as they moved around the top of Nibeiwa in a southern arch across the desert. Long hours behind the wheel were only broken by brief halts to check vehicles, take on water, and push on again. The heat pressed down without relief, the air was dry and unchanging, and the horizon offering nothing but distance. By the third day, the wind had changed.

Neumann noticed it by the dust at first. It had become thinner, not rising in the usual loose eddies behind the vehicles, but low along the ground, thin and drawn out, like a tide rolling inland. The smell came with it, burnt fuel, sun-split rubber, drifting from wrecks and cast-off vehicles that lined the edges of the desert track.

In those first three days, they had passed Sidi Barrani and Tummar. Sofafi lay in front of them. The trucks rolled on in silence, their engines subdued, weighed down not by terrain, but by what they had seen, the burnt-out columns, the abandoned guns, the scattered remnants of a force that had ceased to exist.

As they continued to move in an arch around Nibeiwa towards Sofafi, Neumann stood at the side of the road with his goggles around his neck, and his map flapping against his thigh. His hands rested on his hips as he stared across the flat sweep of sand and rock. The horizon was hazy with heat and empty of movement but only in the present. In the last few days, he had witnessed the imprint that had been left on the land. Ruts from armoured vehicles scarred the surface, deeper and fresher than anything Italian. Tracks moved in arcs, not lines. Fast, deliberate. British, he thought. The kind of momentum you only get from confidence.

The advance had been faster than expected. Too fast. The British had already pushed beyond most of what lay ahead of them. What remained was what they had left behind.

Reports had filtered back from Arab informants and scattered Carabinieri posts that whole formations of the 10th Army were falling apart, and command was collapsing under its own inertia. Thousands of their men were surrendering without firing a shot. Trucks had been left in dunes, and machine-guns rusted under canvas. In one abandoned tent in Tummar, Holtz had found a table still set with plates and half-eaten rations. It was as if lunch had simply been interrupted.

Neumann had said nothing, just studied the direction of the tyre marks and moved on.

They had passed through the Tummar camps late on the second day. The British already gone, leaving only the wreckage of what had been. What had once been a fortified line now looked like the edge of a rubbish dump. Blown bunkers, collapsed tents, field kitchens torn open by artillery. Craters and silence. The Italians had not held. They had not even attempted to regroup. It was not a retreat in contact. It was a rout.

That night, at the end of the second day, camped beneath a broken water tower, Neumann had written his first field report by the light of a storm lantern. It was blunt. Italian defensive cohesion was shattered. Divisional command was inconsistent. Brigade-level control absent. Morale had become unrecoverable, and the British pace had increased daily. He had included a final line, short and underlined: *We are not observing a withdrawal. We are witnessing a collapse.*

The fourth day had begun with even more heat. Real heat. It was the kind that settled into the bones and left the sweat clinging in place. Men rode with scarves over their mouths, eyes narrowed against the glare. They skirted wrecked convoys, lorries burnt out and tyres burst. In one case, a Fiat staff car sat alone in the middle of a dry wadi with its doors open, a dog-eared opera programme still wedged in the dashboard. Holtz retrieved it with a grunt and tossed it aside.

It took most of the fourth day to reach Sofafi. Neumann immediately realised what was left of a divisional staff had tried to mount a semblance of control. As Neumann approached the largest tent, a red-tabbed colonel, perhaps once competent, now hollow-eyed, had offered Neumann coffee brewed over a diesel burner and confessed they had lost all wireless contact south of them. A Brigade commander had disappeared entirely. No message. No trace. Just gone. Rumours were that he had been captured with his entire HQ while trying to withdraw eastwards towards the coast road.

Neumann declined the coffee. He did not stay. The fourth day brought no assurance of the Italian position against the British.

At every stop over the previous three days, he had taken notes. Hand-drawn sketches. Vehicle dispersal patterns. Positions of shell craters. Estimated blast direction. Ammunition left behind. Even the way the bodies fell. British tactics were visible in the aftermath: speed, flanking, pressure. It was never frontal unless overwhelming. They did not waste time on dugouts that could be bypassed. They isolated, surrounded, and moved on. The Italians, who were built for static defence, simply folded.

Neumann had stopped looking at the bodies they passed unless he needed to. Most had been stripped of any useful kit by Bedouin scavengers. Some hadn't even been buried. It wasn't through malice, but because no one remained to dig the graves.

What disturbed him most was the lack of battle. Not the aftermath of it, but the emptiness. There were no real signs of prolonged resistance. It was as if the entire front had simply dissolved under pressure. At one point, he had paced the inside of a former artillery position, finding full crates of 75mm shells left behind, still stacked neatly under sheets of tarpaulin. They hadn't fired. Not even moved. Just... left.

By late afternoon on the fourth day, the only contact they had made was indirect. They had spotted a pair of British tanks in the far distance with their hulls low against the sand, and their silhouettes barely visible through the shimmering air. The tanks had turned north-westward and vanished. Neumann hadn't pursued. That wasn't his role. He was not here to fight. He was here to learn.

Messina had asked once, just once, why they hadn't stopped to help a damaged Italian column limping towards the coast. They could see the lorry had a shattered axle, and twenty men clung to its side, eyes hollowed by thirst.

Neumann's answer had been silence.

Messina had said nothing more after that.

As the end of the fourth day approached, they made camp beneath a low ridge as the sun bled red into the desert behind them. Holtz set the watches, briefed the drivers, and checked the fuel reserves without needing to be told. Neumann stood apart and leant against the bonnet of the command lorry, jotting rough lines in his notebook for his latest assessment of the situation he'd witnessed at Sofafi.

His analysis of the situation had led to the conclusion that this had become a chase by the British, or perhaps an avoidance by the Italians.

What Italian resistance remained was fragmented and isolated. The British were pressing forwards with speed and certainty. Neumann was doing everything possible to remain just behind the edge of the British advance, close enough to read it, far enough not to be caught by it.

As his men settled for the fourth night, Neumann knew he would move them on again at dawn. One final leg south. There was nothing marked on the map except a series of hills and shallow wadis. The Italians had not fortified it. The Germans had not named it. The British had not yet reached it. But if Neumann had learnt anything these past days, it was this: that which is not yet significant often soon will be.

Silence settled further into the camp. The horizon was still dark, a deep bruise fading into the belly of the morning. Neumann stood alone beside the lead truck, a cup of gritty black coffee cradled in one hand, the other resting on the bonnet. He wasn't watching anything in particular, just the dark line of sand and scrub that stretched east and south, the same as it had for four days. The night held its chill. No fire was lit, too risky, too visible. The men had curled beneath tarpaulins or in the backs of trucks, wrapped in greatcoats, their breath hanging in the air. The vehicles sat in silence, half-sunk into the sand with their doors closed, and their engines cooling in the dark after a long day's drive.

The column had halted just north of a nameless ridge, some thirty kilometres further south of Sofafi. Nothing marked the spot. No ruin, no track, no settlement. Just empty ground, and the kind of stillness that came before a decision.

As dawn approached, Neumann realised the wind had stilled overnight, and in the soft glow of sunrise, the air felt denser as if the desert were holding its breath.

Neumann sat beside the lead truck, elbows on his knees, a cup of lukewarm coffee between his hands. He hadn't slept. Not properly. He could feel it behind his eyes, the heaviness that didn't come from fatigue alone, but from pressure. Unspoken. Unrelenting. The kind that settled behind the temples and waited for you to make the wrong call.

Holtz approached Neumann from the edge of the column. He didn't ask to sit. He just settled down opposite, stretching one leg out in the dirt, and the other bent beneath him. He wore his jacket open, collar turned up, the brim of his cap low over his eyes.

For a while, neither of them spoke.

Then Holtz reached into his tunic and pulled out a small, battered tin. He opened it, drew out a cigarette, and struck a match. The flare lit the lines of his face. He was older than most, worn but sharp.

"Have you seen enough, Sir?" he asked, exhaling slowly.

Neumann looked across at him but didn't reply.

Holtz tapped ash into the sand. "I have to say, I'm not impressed by the Italians. They seem to turn the moment there's any pressure."

He paused, and then muttered the next part, almost to himself. "Captain Messina...well. If you ask me, he'd crumple at the first sign of trouble."

Neumann stared into the darkness. When he answered, his tone was clipped. "I'm not sure I did ask you, Feldwebel."

He understood the sentiment and had even come to a similar view himself, but he would not tolerate such dissent. Not aloud. Not in front of others. It wasn't the Feldwebel's place to say it and certainly not to a senior officer.

Holtz, a senior non-commissioned officer, realised his lapse. He dropped the cigarette to his side and straightened at once. "Sorry, Sir."

He held his posture, waiting for the next reprimand.

That drew a faint smile from Neumann, tired and rueful. "You're all right, Feldwebel."

He took a sip from his cup, grimaced at the taste, and set it down in the dust. When he spoke again, it was as if to the desert itself. "I thought there'd be more resistance. Even in retreat. Some attempt at order. Discipline. But they didn't fall back. They evaporated. If this continues, the British will clear them out of North Africa altogether."

Holtz nodded slowly. "The British are pushing hard. And in force. Reminds me of Belgium...and France. How we rolled them up."

He hesitated, then glanced sideways.

"Permission to speak freely, Sir?"

Neumann gave a brief nod.

Holtz shifted slightly, eyes on the sand. "Is it true...Rommel is coming here? To take over?"

Neumann didn't answer straight away. He picked up the tin cup again, rolled it once in his fingers and set it back down.

"Well, nothing official yet," he said eventually. "That's part of what we're doing here. We need to make an assessment and report back."

Holtz gave a low whistle. "We moved fast in France...but Rommel, he was a blur. Always forwards. Always out ahead."

Neumann allowed himself the faintest smile. "Yes. He has no patience for slowness. Or excuses."

Holtz looked thoughtful. "Some say, he reads the ground like a map. Sees where the enemy will be before they're even there."

"He does," Neumann said quietly. "But he also expects everyone else to do the same. And if they don't, he moves without them."

That seemed to sit heavily between them. Holtz gave a small grunt of understanding. "Then we'd better not let him down on this then."

Neumann stood, brushing sand from his trousers. His voice, when it came, was low but certain. "No. We'd better not."

He paused, then added, almost to himself, "I served under him. In France. He just understands it like no other man I have met during my service."

He let the sentence hang.

Holtz looked up. "What, Sir?"

Neumann didn't answer at once. His eyes narrowed towards the east. glanced at the horizon. It was still dark, but the edge of dawn was beginning to glow. It wasn't light yet, but there was the hint of it, the change in tone that always came just before the desert stirred.

"I've got what I need," he said finally. "I think it's time to head back," Neumann said, more to himself than to anyone else. He rubbed the side of his face, stubble rasping under his palm.

"Holtz. Get Captain Messina to have his men ready to move out at first light. We're heading straight back to Benghazi."

An hour later, the convoy rolled south-west. The tyres whispered over the hard-packed surface, and engines were muffled by the wind. Neumann sat in the second truck, boots braced, binoculars idle in his lap. His thoughts were already turning west to Benghazi, the report, and Rommel's likely reaction. They had seen enough. The front was in disarray.

Dust kicked gently around the wheels, but the desert still held its silence. A silence that gnawed at the edge of his thoughts. He leant forwards, about to call something to the driver, when he felt the need to pause.

Off to the front, perhaps three hundred metres, there was a scattering of stone buildings. An old farmstead, maybe. Faded walls, sun-bleached wood, a half-collapsed roof. Nothing of value. It was just another relic, another mark on the map left to vanish into the sand.

He raised his binoculars and angled them towards the ruin. One of the buildings was low and rectangular with its roof gone. Another had a doorway yawning wide, like a mouth in the earth. He spotted a few half-standing posts with rusted wire still clinging. Goat enclosure, most likely, he thought. Long abandoned. There was no sign of movement. No smoke. No glint of glass or steel.

Still, something about it stirred a flicker of doubt. He scanned left to right, slow and measured. Nothing. He began to lower the binoculars, then he paused again.

He'd seen a shadow shifting. Not movement. More the suggestion of it. A flicker of contrast behind one of the ruined walls. It was gone in an instant. Could have been a trick of light. Could have been nothing at all. He held his gaze a moment longer, then let the glasses fall into his lap.

Neumann glanced at the wing mirror, catching a glimpse of the vehicles behind. Messina's truck brought up the rear, the last in a column of eight, dust trailing high behind it. In each truck, the infantry sat hunched and silent, looking relaxed. Unbothered.

He reached for his map case and slipped it open. The grid reference matched. Barely a feature worth noting, just a faint square marked in pencil as a possible well. He hadn't given it a second glance when planning the route back. Now, it seemed to pull at him.

Without warning, the wind shifted, carrying a sheet of dust across the bonnet as the convoy rolled on. The farm lay off to Neumann's right now, close enough for its detail to resolve from the broken outline of the ruins. He studied it as they moved onwards and could pick out the cracks in the masonry, the sag of collapsed timbers, and the darker gaps where the structure had given way.

A flicker of movement caught his eye. Brief, uncertain. Gone almost as soon as it appeared. Neumann brought the binoculars up again. Slower this time, he surveyed the ruins with more care. The shapes settled under his gaze, shadows separating from substance, and debris from intent. And then he saw them properly. Lying low against the stone but moving with purpose.

Not rubble.

Not wind.

Men.

The realisation came clean and immediate. Whoever was in those ruins was watching them. Waiting. He leant forwards sharply, his voice cutting across the cab. "Halt! Stop the convoy."

The driver reacted immediately, instinct taking over. His hands moved on the wheel, turning it hard as his foot came off the accelerator. The lorry slewed offline at once. The nose swung as the sudden change in speed and direction pulled it sideways across the dust. Behind them, the rest of the convoy began to react in turn. Brakes squealed. One truck swerved wide to avoid closing too quickly. Another drifted as the line broke apart.

"Get them off!" Neumann snapped, already reaching for the door.

Men in the rear of the lorries were already moving, some dropping from the tailboards before the vehicles had fully stopped, others jumping down from the sides with their rifles clutched awkwardly as their boots hit the ground.

For a fraction of a second, the moment hung, disjointed and uncertain. The convoy was no longer moving as one and had not yet settled into anything else. Then the shot came.

A sharp impact slammed into the windscreen in front of him, and the glass collapsed inwards in a vicious spray. The driver jerked violently sideways, his body twisting as the force of it tore him from the wheel and drove him across the cab. For a moment, he seemed to fold against the door, then the latch gave, and he spilt out, half falling, half thrown, his weight dragging free of the vehicle as blood burst across the frame.

A second burst followed, sharper.

Deliberate.

CHAPTER 9

They lay in silence, folded into the shadows of the crumbling goat farm. Rifles were tucked into shoulders, and eyes were narrowed against the sun's glare. The buildings offered little comfort with their low walls, fractured beams, and splintered stone, but it was more than the open desert would give them. At least, there was a sense of shape here. Angles to fire from. Cover to crouch behind. Lines to defend. It wasn't ideal. The place had half-fallen in on itself, brittle and sun-bleached, the kind of ruin the desert forgets. But for now, it would have to do. The enemy was coming.

Archer moved through the position in a low crouch, his steps hushed on the packed dust. The men were spaced throughout the ruin, tucked into doorways and behind shattered walls. Archer had made sure every man was behind cover. No movement, no profile. Nothing to give them away too early. The Vickers team had removed the machine-gun from its tripod and now lay flat behind a low, crumbling wall. On Archer's order, they would reassemble it in the gap and open fire, but not before.

Further along, Evans and Pritchard crouched behind a collapsed lintel, rifles resting on the stone. Both men peered through a jagged crack in the wall, watching the dust cloud on the horizon thicken and draw closer.

The ground outside the farm was flat and unforgiving, open for too long with nowhere to fall back to. Archer had judged the risk and kept them tight to the ruin. He knew it was better to let the enemy come to them unwittingly. Better to let the walls soak the first bullets. He paused near the rear doorway, eyes scanning the shimmer on the far horizon. A dust plume was rising. Still faint. But getting closer.

The patrol had returned twenty minutes ago, ragged and breathless with sand still clinging to their sleeves. It was Lockett who had first spotted the four returning figures, approaching at a sprint across the flats. Archer had run out to meet them, roughly thirty yards beyond the farm's perimeter, and listened to their report, words tumbling out between gasps. They couldn't be certain the convoy was still heading this way. It was a small column. Six trucks, maybe eight. No armour. No outriders. Just dust trailing behind them like smoke. Heading west. Straight for Point 208.

Archer had brought the men to stand-to and, with Jacks at his side, made sure each man was positioned to deliver maximum fire on anyone approaching. The enemy might be coming from what had been their rear, but it had become their front.

Now, the platoon lay in wait. The farmstead offered cover, but it was tight and uneven, and there was little room to manoeuvre. Jacks had placed the sections well, and each man covered the likely approach. It wasn't elegant, but it would do. They'd have the element of surprise, and in a place like this, the first shots mattered most. There might not be time for second ones.

Archer lowered into the shadow of a half-collapsed wall with the binoculars pressed to his eyes. Heat wavered above the flats, turning the horizon into a shifting line of gold and white. At first, there was nothing except the shimmer. Then a faint, blurred smudge appeared, low against the sun's blaze. He steadied the glasses by bracing his elbows on the roughness of the wall. Shapes began to form. Squat truck cabs, dark smudges of tyres bumping along, their movement jerky. Dust lifted behind them in long, trailing plumes, curling and drifting in the breeze.

Beside Archer, Jacks knelt with one hand resting lightly on the rubble of the wall.

"Still a way off," he murmured. "But they're moving at some pace, Sir."

Taking a breath and not waiting on a response from Archer, he turned to his left and right and pitched his voice a touch louder, knowing that he would not be heard at this distance. "Eyes front! Await the order!"

The Italian trucks rolled on in tight formation. There were eight of them by Archer's count; the gaps between them was barely a vehicle's length. The lead jolted hard over a dip, and its canvas tilt snapped in the wind as it was thrust to one side of the track and then pulled itself back online.

The air carried small, familiar noises from the platoon. Jack could hear a rifle bolt being eased forwards, the muted clink of a canteen cap, and the scrape of a boot against stone. Somewhere down the line, someone coughed, quick, but sharp enough to carry in the stillness.

Jacks' head snapped round. "Quiet over there," he hissed, low but cutting. The culprit ducked lower behind his bit of wall, hands tightening on his rifle. The quiet returned tighter this time as if the whole platoon was holding its breath.

Jacks' sharp hiss carried just enough to pull Archer's attention across the line. He let his eyes travel the position until they found Saunders. The lad was about Archer's age, yet he was always thought of as the youngster. His brow was creased and sweat ran down his cheek. Fear showed in him more than most. It was a physical thing, written plainly on his face. Archer had hoped promotion might steady him, but a stripe was no shield against fear. But Archer knew his man. They all did. However hard Saunders tried to mask it, once the shooting started, the fear would fall away. He would be steady and instinctive, almost as if some sixth sense took hold of his mind and body. Archer had never doubted the man.

Archer pulled himself back to his front and the oncoming trucks. Without warning, the lead truck veered right, and its tyres spit a heavier spray of dust. Archer tracked it, realising it had moved onto a pale scar of an old track that was little more than twin ruts winding towards the farm's exposed flank. "They've picked up speed," he said quietly.

The lieutenant twisted the focus on his binoculars until the grille of the lead truck came sharp. The sunlight flashed on its glass, and Archer saw a figure hunched forwards at the wheel, and another sat beside him with their helmet tilted back.

To the left, Wilson's section adjusted their positions, crawling a yard or two to bring rifles to bear on the new angle. Evans rolled onto his side, rifle pressed into his shoulder, and lips moving in a silent count as the convoy closed the gap. The dust hung low, whipped sideways by the wind. Through the haze, the trucks loomed larger with every jolt over the hard-packed ground, their silhouettes shuddering in and out of focus. Canvas tilts snapped and flapped like torn sails, edges catching the light.

In the open beds, men could be seen now. Shapes that had been barely visible had become figures. Archer watched as he saw the men sway with the motion of the truck, their shoulders rocking side to side, and their knees bending with each rise and drop of the axles. A few clung to the tilt frames with knuckles white as their bodies lifted clear of the benches when the wheels struck hollows. Others sat slouched, faces turned into the wind, one or two raising their arms to shield their eyes.

The rhythm of it carried across the flats; the dull thump of tyres striking ruts, the hollow 'boom' as a chassis bottomed out on hardpacked ground, and engines coughing and grinding as gears strained for power. Then came the sharper note, a metallic shriek of suspension under strain, high and grating, drawn out as if the desert objected to their passing. The sound rose and fell with the bumps, carried thinly on the air until it reached the farmstead, setting teeth on edge.

Archer kept his glasses fixed on the lead truck, willing it to stay true, to carry on into the haze. If it passed wide, the platoon could remain unseen, intact. Fewer shots meant fewer dead men, his or theirs. He shifted along the line of vehicles, counting as best he could. Definitely eight trucks; most with men in the back. A dozen, maybe more in each? Near a hundred rifles against his own twenty-eight. If they turned in, there'd be no avoiding contact. And the odds would be brutal.

Archer exhaled slowly and slipped the binoculars back into his satchel. He no longer needed them. The enemy was straight ahead and clear. He let his eyes travel along his own line. Men lay prone in what little shade the ruins gave with their weapons steady.

"Once they cross that dry gully," Archer said quietly, "if they keep coming, we'll open up at a hundred yards. Pass it down."

Jacks moved off along the wall, crouching low and passing the order in whispers from man to man.

Archer's gaze returned to the lorries. In the back of the lead truck, the two Italians continued to lounge with easy posture. One was gesturing with his hand while the other laughed at some remark lost to the wind. The shimmer was completely gone now. The men's faces were clear, and Archer could make out their relaxed expressions. "They don't know," he murmured.

The convoy dropped into the gully in a rush of dust, then rose out of it still pressing forwards. Somewhere to Archer's right, a rifle bolt slid home with a dry click.

"Two hundred yards," Jacks called, voice carrying just enough.

The farm held its breath with him.

Then something shifted.

Archer frowned, leaning forwards. The convoy had kept its line steadily enough, but now the lead truck jolted and slewed sideways, its brakes squealing faintly through the dust. The vehicle behind it nearly ran up its tailboard before grinding to a halt. Engines rattled, and there was a cough of gears, and then a silence that seemed to fall like a blanket across their world.

One hundred and fifty, maybe two hundred yards out, the Italians were no longer coming on.

Archer narrowed his eyes. He could make out the silhouettes of figures moving against the canvas tilts in the backs of the trucks. Some men clambered to their feet, unsteady with the sudden stop, clutching at the tilt frames for balance. Others were already dropping to the ground, their boots thudding into the dust. Archer watched them hesitate, glance about, and move their hands going to rifle straps.

More shouts carried thin on the breeze, sharp, clipped, urgent. "They've seen something," Archer thought.

Through the haze, he caught a clearer picture. A pair of Italians in the third truck from the front heaved at a weapon. Its barrel glinted as they wrestled it clear. Another group stumbled into a crouch beside a wheel, rifles cradled across their arms. Archer's jaw tightened. It wasn't the chaotic stream of civilians spilling from a bus. These were soldiers, and they were trying to form up. Disjointed, yes. Uncertain even, but enough of them were moving with purpose to make him consider his options on what to do.

Archer could clearly see helmets bobbing, and mouths opening with orders or curses. Arms were chopping the air. With each new movement, dust thickened as men hit the ground, and boots and kit sent small clouds curling upwards. The smell of dust was already on the air, dry and chalky, catching at the back of the throat.

Archer tracked one man who had dropped into a crouch at the front bumper of the lead truck, his rifle angled high. Another darted to the side to scan the ruins, and his posture suddenly stiffened as he hunted for shapes in broken stone.

"They've seen us!" Archer said softly, half to himself. Behind him, the Vickers crew shifted. Others followed. The faint metallic click of bolts being drawn home carried louder than it should in the silence, as each man realised, what Archer new.

The convoy was no longer a column of rolling targets. It was becoming a line of soldiers, uncertain but gathering strength with every man that spilt from a tailboard.

Archer's stomach clenched. The chance of them passing by was gone. Surprise was gone.

"Target! Trucks. One o'clock! Two hundred yards. Platoon, rapid fire!"

His voice cut across the farmstead and out into the desert.

Within a split second, every rifleman was up from cover, and Lee Enfield's were braced towards the Italians. Twenty-eight rifles cracked almost as one: a volley that rolled into a steady rhythm. Shots weren't always perfectly aimed but close enough to matter. Pritchard, with his natural steadiness, dropped the first man his sights touched.

Webb had taken the Bren from Private Atwell, who crouched beside him as number two, fresh magazines ready at hand. The weapon gave its familiar, strangely comforting rattle. It was a harsh counterpoint to the sharper crack of the rifles. Webb had set his sight at two hundred yards and fixed on the second lorry in the column. His first rounds chewed the cab door. The range was good. He worked the gun in short, controlled sweeps, walking his fire up the length of the truck and then across to the figures spilling clear, adjusting each sweep to catch those scrambling for space.

On the right of Archer, Matthews's section added their weight. Saunders was among the first to fire. His shots were quick, and his shoulders jerked with each recoil. Archer saw him pause just long enough to work the bolt smoothly and fire again, jaw clenched, eyes narrowed. The fear that always showed in him before a fight had vanished; he was all instinct. The rifle had become an extension of himself.

Corporal "Tug" Wilson kept low behind a fractured wall, shouting orders over the crack of rifle fire. His section moved with him, only a few weeks of drill binding them together.

Webb was tight to the stone, calm and steady with his Bren balanced across the rubble. His skill with the weapon was second to none. He worked it with a methodical accuracy that seemed never to waste a burst. A few yards back, Arthur "Arty" Beckett shifted rubble for cover with the same quiet strength he used on every march, the engine of the section who never seemed to tire. Frank "Skins" Skinner hunched down beside him, his wiry frame taut as his eyes darted across the land for targets. He had a knack for spotting movement that others missed, and Wilson relied on him to call out danger.

Yorkie Harland knelt in the shade of a doorway, muttering at his rifle as he worked the bolt. His miner's hands were sure and practised. Meanwhile, Young Len Carter hugged the corner; his knuckles were white on his weapon. Keen, too keen sometimes, but Archer's men had taken him under their wing. Atwell, broad as a dockside crane, braced as his Lee Enfield kicked into his shoulder before swinging left to find another target. They hadn't been together long, but under Wilson's stewardship they'd grown into a solid unit, tempered by the challenges of the desert. Now they were set, a rough wall of grit and firepower under Wilson's command.

In the centre, the Vickers crew had assembled their gun, and the tripod legs were spread wide behind the low wall. The gunner traversed left, seeking targets through the chaos of dust and running figures. When he found his mark, the gun opened with its distinctive hammering beat, heavier than the Bren and more deliberate. The machine-gun hammered, its belt laced with tracer, one in five, the red-orange streaks like sparks flung across the desert. For a moment, each hung in the haze before striking home. Glowing dots marked his aim. The fire had a rhythm now, a visible heartbeat, showing Dalton exactly where his line was cutting.

Neumann hit the ground hard, sand grinding between his teeth as he threw himself clear of the cab. Around him, the convoy dissolved into chaos: men spilt from vehicles, shouting in frantic Italian. Some were already firing back in ragged bursts towards the farm. The ambush had struck cleanly, timed to catch them strung out and exposed. Yet, the response was messy, desperate, anything but orderly. But chaos was something Neumann understood.

He spotted Captain Messina crouched behind the rear wheel of his truck, eyes wide, barking orders that no one seemed to hear over the crack of rifles. Neumann moved towards him in a low crouch, stone crunching under his boots.

"Capitano!" His voice cut through the noise like a blade. "Get your machine-guns forward! Now!"

Messina blinked, then nodded sharply. He turned, shouting to his sergeant in rapid Italian. Within moments, two Breda teams were dragging their weapons towards the front of the column, using the trucks as cover.

Neumann scanned the British position. His trained eye picked out muzzle flashes, estimating angles. The Vickers in the gap between the walls. That was the key. Silence that gun and win the fire fight.

"Mortars!" he called to the nearest Italian NCO, a grizzled sergeant with three black chevrons stitched on his sleeve, the cloth dulled by dust and sweat. The man snapped his head round, eyes narrowing as he caught Neumann's signal. Three stripes marked him clearly for what he was, a veteran, used to being obeyed and he wasted no time.

"Target the machine-gun position, there, in the wall!" Neumann's voice loud but authoritative.

The sergeant nodded, blood already streaking from a grazed scalp, and began shouting orders. Bent-double, men ran towards the rear truck, hauling the tube and base plate. Slow by German standards, but steady.

The first Breda opened fire. Its harsh chatter swelled above the rifle shots. Dust leapt from the walls as the second gun joined in, both laying down suppressive fire while the mortar team dropped into position behind the last truck.

Neumann felt a familiar calm settle over him. This was what he did: turn disorder into direction, panic into purpose. At first, the Italians had flinched under the sudden, withering fire, ducking low behind wheels and walls. Some fired blind over cover, others froze as dust and splinters spat around them. It was the instinctive chaos of men caught out in the open. But once the first orders cut through the noise, once NCOs began to bark commands and the mortar tube thumped into place, the panic thinned. Movements became sharper, more deliberate. Riflemen found their sights, machine-gunners shifted forwards with purpose, and the platoons that had seemed on the verge of collapse, began to steady like rope being pulled taut. The Italians weren't cowards; they just needed someone to show them how to fight.

Feldwebel Holtz moved among the scattered Italians with the blunt confidence of a man used to being obeyed. He jabbed a finger towards the British wall. His voice was low but hard, the kind that cut through fear like a blade.

"Dort! All fire there, together!" His German was harsh, but the meaning was plain enough, and he reinforced it by seizing one man's shoulder and turning his rifle into line. Another hesitated, fumbling with his bolt, and Holtz cuffed him lightly on the helmet, barking a single word that needed no translation: "Feuer!" Slowly, the ragged shots began to converge, rifles cracking in rhythm instead of isolated splutters. The Italians drew strength from the certainty in his voice. Panic bled into focus. Under Holtz's direction they were no longer a scattering of frightened men, but a line beginning to act like soldiers under fire.

Neumann surveyed the scene, and felt confidence growing, in himself and in the men around him. Messina was kneeling among a knot of fifteen soldiers, calling out, offering quick words of encouragement. Twenty metres further on, Holtz stalked up and down the line, barking orders and sharp insults in German, none of which needed translating for the Italians crouched before him. Then Neumann's spirits lifted further as, from behind, he heard the first heavy *whomp* of the mortar then a second, and a third, in quick succession just before the explosions crashed home.

Neumann hauled a wounded man by the diagonal leather strap across his chest, scraping furrows in the sand with his boots until they reached the shelter of a truck. The Italian groaned but clung to consciousness, eyes rolling as dust and cordite thickened the air. Chest heaving, Neumann straightened and turned on the mortar team. The first plumes of sand and stone rose up from at least 20 metres behind the British wall.

He ran to the pit without hesitation, seizing the Italian Sergente by the arm, voice crisp and cold. "Adjust! Higher! The range is close. Get on target."

For a moment, the crew hesitated, then, steadied by Neumann's gaze, they began to work. One man wound the elevating screw on the bipod, and the barrel shifted up by slow degrees. Another snatched a bomb from its crate: stubby, finned with a steel nose that was rounded like a blunt cigar. In one motion, he dropped it tail-first into the tube. The primer struck the fixed pin with a flat crack, and an instant later the mortar gave its heavy *whomp*, hurling the round towards the British line.

Feldwebel Holtz appeared at his side, half-hauling another casualty, an Italian corporal with blood soaking his sleeve and dumped him in the shade of the same truck. He gave a curt nod, then followed Neumann's gaze to the low wall where the Vickers still hammered, tracers stitching sparks across the haze.

"There," Neumann ordered, jabbing a gloved finger towards the gap. His voice cut like steel. "Keep the mortars on it until it's gone."

The first bomb landed close. Too close. Archer flinched as the plume of sand and shattered stone spewed up from the desert floor, showering the line with grit. A heartbeat later, the second came. They were walking in tighter, and the flat crack of impact was felt as much as it was heard. The third followed hard after it, and shards of rock whickered through the air. At first, it seemed erratic, clumsy fire, but then the pattern changed. The tubes were ranging in, finding their stride, and Archer could feel the shift in momentum.

At least two mortars, alternating with a dreadful rhythm, lobbed their blunt-nosed bombs in ragged arcs. The desert flared with geysers of earth and dust, each strike closer than the last. What had begun as a nuisance was fast becoming a pounding threat. His men were no longer firing steadily but hunched low, flinching as showers of grit rained down around them.

The Vickers hammered on. Tracers lanced from the gap in the wall. Its rhythm became a steady heartbeat in the chaos but then came the round that found it. A blossom of dust and stone engulfed the position, and when it cleared, the gun was gone. Man and machine were flung in all directions, a twisted tripod tumbling end over end. The heavy gunfire that had anchored their line simply stopped.

Archer swore under his breath, scrambling to Jacks' side. The sergeant's face was streaked with grit. His eyes narrowed, and his jaw was tight. Neither needed to say much; both could see it. The platoon had lost its edge. The mortars were walking in, and to stay put was suicide.

Jacks spat into the dust and leant close. His voice was pitched to cut through the din. "Sir, best get the hell out while we still can. Use the transport before they smash it. No bloody point dying here."

Archer met Jacks' gaze and gave a sharp nod. For a heartbeat, he crouched low. Grit stung his eyes as he weighed up the ground. Point 208 had been meant for reconnaissance, to hold until the rest of the company arrived, nothing more. He was sure this force he had engaged was a coincidence rather than anything strategic. They had struck first and bloodied the enemy. To remain here under mortar fire, against what was clearly superior numbers, and with the Vickers knocked out, was folly.

He ran it through again. No sign nor word from Company HQ or Battalion. Lomas had tried to raise them, but the radio was dead. That meant no artillery support.

The pain in his chest grew sharper. Staying would bleed his platoon white for nothing. It was unlikely they could hold, and pulling out was the only way to keep them alive. Every moment spent here risked the enemy finding their transport, and then there would be no withdrawal at all.

That's it, thought Archer. We need to move! "Jacks, keep the pressure on. I'll get a message out, that we'll be pulling out!"

With that, Archer was up and running to the ruined building where Lomas had set up the No. 18 set.

"Lomas send this, from Archer, 1 Platoon. Contact enemy Point 208. Estimated battalion strength. Supported by mortars. Vickers gun knocked out. Heavy fire. several casualties. Position untenable. Withdrawing to rejoin Battalion. Will report on route.

His thoughts sharpened into a plan. If they were to withdraw, it had to be orderly, section by section, each one covering the next until every man was aboard. Panic now would kill more than mortars ever could.

He pictured the order in his mind, seeing the column reform as they had drilled it. Pritchard's section first, steady and reliable. They would set the pace. Then Jacks with the HQ lads, Lockett and Briggs tight on his heels, keeping the heart of the platoon intact. Wilson's men next. Their lorry was already close enough to cover the gap. Matthews would take the rear, holding until the last and boarding with Archer himself, making sure no one was left behind. Each lorry in turn, no rush, no chaos.

Yes. That was the way. Deliberate. Controlled. Every man knowing his place.

He lifted his head, scanning the smoke and grit, then looked back to Jacks. "We go section by section. Pritchard's first, then you and HQ, then Wilson, Matthews last with me. Get the men ready. Once they're loaded, they move. We will regroup 500 yards that way." Archers outstretched arm giving the direction of travel.

Jacks gave a tight grin, relief mingling with resolve. "Aye, Sir!"

Archer rose into a crouch and made for the Vickers, his boots slipping on loose stone. The air was thick with dust and the tang of cordite. He half-expected to see Dalton cursing over the gun. The belt was twisted, or the tripod shifted, something he could put right but when he reached the gap in the wall, his gut dropped. The weapon was gone, blown clear of its mount. The crew lay scattered around the wreckage. Twisted bodies. Kit flung wide. The Vickers itself was a ruin; its water jacket was torn open, and the metal was scorched and splintered. There was nothing left to salvage.

Tightening his jaw, he ducked back into cover and shouldered his rifle. For a moment, he held it there, steady. The weight of it was familiar in his hands. Then he fired, working the bolt again with a sharper, more deliberate motion than before.

It wasn't the shot itself. It was the feeling that came with it; the same one he had carried out of France and into every fight since. Dalton. The others. Names that never quite left him.

He drove the bolt back and forwards again. Harder this time, forcing the thought down as he settled back onto the sights.

The withdrawal began with Pritchard's section. Archer had signalled them out first. Evans and another man were half-carrying a wounded man whose leg trailed limp with his boots dragging through the sand. Grim faced, Pritchard led them steady; his rifle was in one hand as he urged the others forwards. They lifted the wounded man into the rear of their lorry, and

Pritchard jumped into the cab. Evans banged on the roof to signal all were in. The truck jolted into motion with a roar. Its wheels bit deep as it turned away from the farm. Mortar bombs fell behind them, erratic but close, throwing up fountains of grit as they bounced over the rise and away.

Next came Jacks with the HQ lads, hauling Lockett and Briggs aboard the Bedford. Lomas staggered after them. The bulky No. 18 set dragged at his shoulders as he clambered into the back. Jacks lingered just long enough to give Archer a nod before stamping the starter. The engine coughed, then roared to life before the lorry swung hard on the sand before lurching forwards after Pritchard's vehicle.

Wilson's section followed, scrambling aboard under a stutter of rifle fire from Italians who were pressing forwards with renewed confidence. One man slipped but was seized by Atwell's great hand and shoved bodily into the Bedford as it rattled off. Webb, solid as ever, stayed on one knee, firing controlled bursts from his Bren before finally turning and hauling himself over the tailboard.

Matthews held the rear. Cool as ever, his section fanned into a loose line to cover the withdrawal. Archer caught up at a run. His chest heaved. He snapped a quick count of the men before dropping into cover beside Matthews. Together, they fired a measured ripple of shots out into the haze which bought precious seconds for the last lorry to be loaded.

"Right," Archer called, slapping Matthews on the shoulder. "That's enough! Time to go."

"Dent! Covering fire!" Matthews bellowed, then gave the order many had been waiting for. "Back to the truck!"

He stood in a crouch, waving his arms and rifle as if he could physically push each man towards safety. Archer worked the bolt of his Lee-Enfield with practiced precision, the same precision he had drilled into his men countless times.

Dent dropped his empty magazine with a flick and slid in a fresh one: twenty-eight brass rounds snug in the curved steel box that provided another burst of damage. Longer this time, harsher.

"Dent! Time to go!" Archer shouted, then barked again, "Now! Move!"

They broke cover together, running hard for the truck. Matthews fired a parting shot and saw another mortar round land close. A geyser of stone and dust erupted into the air, no more than ten feet to their right. Archer barely registered it: just one more blast among many. What he did register was the sound Dent's body made as it hit the ground flat beside him.

Archer turned, just enough to confirm what instinct already told him. The Bren gunner was gone. Torn apart by shrapnel. Dent's death had been instant: brutal, final. Archer gave him a heartbeat's glance. No more. Then he forced himself on. The ground around them was already being searched by fire, rounds snapping in and kicking up dust where they lay. Stopping meant sure death.

The final section piled onto the Bedford, boots and rifles clattering against its boards. Archer vaulted onto the tailboard last, twisting round to fire one final shot into the dust before dropping into the bed among the men. The lorry jolted forwards, the suspension groaned as it gathered speed to chase the line of vehicles already pulling away across the desert.

The mortars continued to bark behind them, but the blasts were falling wider now, chasing ghosts in the sand. Archer steadied himself against the side of the truck, the metal hot beneath his palm, and he scanned his men. Faces were grey with dust; their eyes were raw while others were bleeding. They were all too tired even to curse. But they were alive. That was what counted. He risked a glance back across the shrinking distance.

The farmstead was alive with movement now. Italian figures vaulted walls and darted into doorways. Their bayonets glinted as they cleared the buildings one by one. A few of them paused near the gap in the wall where the Vickers had stood. Archer's throat tightened as he caught sight of two men bending over a sprawled form in the dust. Even at this range, he knew it was Dent.

Archer looked away: his jaw clenched. He couldn't afford to hold onto the image. Not now.

The Bedford jolted hard over a rise, throwing grit into the wind. Ahead, the line of lorries stretched out across the desert, engines labouring, tracks smudging the sand with a haze of dust. Point 208 was behind them, abandoned to the enemy.

And for now, that was enough.

CHAPTER 10

The road west was barely a road at all. Just a scar in the desert, rutted by lorries and churned by tracks, marked sporadically by burnt-out vehicles, and the scattered detritus of a retreating army. Archer sat in the lead Bedford, boots planted wide on the floor, fingers drumming against his rifle as the truck rocked and rattled beneath him. Dust seeped in through every gap of the canvas tilt, coating the men in a fine, pale film. No one spoke much. They were used to the silence now.

It had been a week since Point 208. The clash with Neumann's Italians already felt like something from another war, another time. They'd fought hard among the ruins, bloodied the enemy, then pulled back before the farm was swallowed whole. The loss of the Vickers team had been reported, as too was Dent's death. It still irked annoyed Archer and Jacks that they had to leave their bodies behind, but the withdrawal gave no time to collect the dead.

Archer had spent the week chasing the battalion across dust and empty tracks, fuel dump to fuel dump. It had been just him and his platoon: the way he preferred it. Now their nomadic run was ending, folding back into the rhythm of the wider battalion. He sat with his thoughts, pondering the point that the company had never followed, nor had any word come back. The radio hadn't failed. Someone had changed the frequency without telling him. He'd never known that they'd been ordered to withdraw and return. By pure assessment and assumption, he and Jacks had brought the platoon back whole. Archer knew mistakes happened in war, but he couldn't shake the thought that if that order had reached them, the four men he'd lost might still be alive.

As the lorries rumbled on, Archer tried to turn his mind from the grim business of Point 208. He forced himself to conjure Charlotte's image instead, willing her forwards as he closed his eyes, letting her face crowd out the disappointment of the desert for a moment. But the bitterness lingered all the same. New orders had already come down: a rendezvous west of Sidi Barrani, and he had said nothing. Yet the taste of it would not leave his mouth.

They crested a low rise, and Archer stood, steadying himself on the frame, scanning the horizon. The desert stretched out ahead of their convoy, broken only by the jagged shapes of distant trucks, and the dark smudge of smoke curling up into the pale sky. The column slowed. A military policeman stood by the side of the road and waved them on, directing them past a cluster of prisoners seated in the dust. They looked almost bored as they sat with their hands on their heads, being guarded by a bored-looking corporal with a cigarette hanging from his mouth.

Everywhere they passed, the signs were the same. Italian helmets discarded by the roadside. Abandoned guns. They had seen a fuel truck that was still ablaze: a miniature inferno throwing fireballs skywards where they vanished into a thick column of black smoke that climbed high above the horizon like a signal flare from hell. The enemy hadn't stopped fighting so much as they'd stopped caring. There had been no formal surrender, but Archer could feel it in the air: a war unwinding itself.

Jacks shifted beside him, stretching his back. "Don't reckon we'll see another scrap before Christmas," he muttered.

Archer didn't answer. He wasn't so sure.

By late morning, they reached the coordinates given in the orders. It was a shallow basin, encircled with scrub and scattered acacias and trucks that had been drawn up in a rough arc. Tents had been pitched in a hasty command post, and the Union Flag hung limply from a radio aerial. Men moved between lorries and map boards with the slow efficiency of a unit on the march.

The trucks halted. Archer jumped down, his legs stiff from the ride. Jacks followed, nodding toward the cluster of tents. "Reckon that's where they'll be."

Archer dusted off his sleeves and stepped out across the hard-packed sand. A few men from other platoons glanced his way: familiar faces, vaguely surprised. One or two gave him a nod. Another raised a hand in something like a salute. Not textbook sharp, but a salute all the same. Archer didn't return it. No nods, no words. He just kept walking.

When he reached the command tent, he paused at the entrance. A moment to gather himself. Then he pushed through the canvas flap.

Inside, it was cooler. The sun filtered weakly through the flysheet and shadows. A folding table dominated the centre. It was strewn with a map, message slips, and a half-empty enamel mug. Captain Sedgewick stood over it, his arms outstretched either side of the table. His uniform was immaculate despite the dust. To his left, Lieutenant McBain glanced up from a clipboard, his expression unreadable, and his jaw clenched in habitual silence.

Lieutenant Kingsley, 3rd Platoon Commander, leant against a packing crate nearby, one boot resting on its edge. He was tall, narrow-shouldered, with a sharp face and a manner that always seemed halfway between boredom and calculation. Archer noticed a faint trace of dried blood marked his right sleeve. He looked up as Archer entered, gave a short nod, then returned to flicking ash from a cigarette that hadn't been lit in hours.

"Lieutenant Archer," Sedgewick said, his voice neutral. "Back with us at last."

Archer saluted. "Yes, Sir."

"Good to see you back!" McBain exclaimed as he held out his hand to Archer.

"I'll need your report as soon as you're settled," Sedgewick said. His tone was steady although there was a faint edge to it.

"Bit of a mess, all told. Not your fault, I know. Signals were changed without warning, and we moved out. Still, battalion will want it down on paper."

Archer said nothing and released McBain's hand. Praise wasn't expected, but he still couldn't get used to the British Army's matter-of-fact way of doing things. It was one of the things he hated about soldering, the fact that he had to write a report that always seemed cold and never reflected the lives lost. It just never felt right. Each name reduced to a line or two on a page, if they were lucky enough to be written down at all

"We're moving out within the hour. We're still in support of the 11th Hussars. The 4th Armoured Brigade has been tasked with pushing up the western approaches to Bardia. Our role is to dig in here," Sedgewick placed a finger on the map sprawled before them. "It's near Bir el Chleta. We'll carry out patrols, possible probing actions, and security sweeps along the coastal route." Sedgewick's tone was serious as he continued.

"Intelligence suggests the Italians are in a hell of a state, but we still need to be careful. Expect pockets of resistance, stragglers, dug-in crews. Maybe the odd rearguard with a few heavy weapons. It's likely there's no real coordination, but don't assume they'll melt away. Some of them are still fighting."

The tent flapped sharply in a sudden gust of wind. Archer turned as one corner blew loose, and he saw a corporal outside struggling to lash it back down. The canvas snapped and billowed. The sound was harsh in the quiet. He turned back. Inside, the other platoon commanders were still fully focused on Sedgewick's words.

"The Hussars will be out front. We're slotting in behind the armour. We're both on the left flank. We'll move up as usual if they hit anything. Keep your spacing and stay alert. We're not expecting contact, but I don't trust good fortune."

Sedgewick's tone remained serious throughout, pausing only to take a breath before giving a gesture at the map.

"Kingsley, you'll take the lead. This route along the main track, steady pace. Keep your spacing and report anything unusual. No heroics."

"McBain, follow on at interval. Keep your eyes out for soft ground or anything that looks like a wreck. If Kingsley calls a halt, I want your lads ready to move up without confusion."

"Archer, you're at the rear. Stay flexible. If we need to scout off the track or check a flank, I'll swing you out."

He gave a glance back to the map and paused. Finally Sedgewick asked, "Any questions?"

Archer took the opportunity "We're alright for now, but a resupply of rations and ammunition wouldn't go amiss. We've been scrounging along the way."

Sedgewick gave a brief nod. "Speak to Sergeant Major Barker. He's set up just behind the second truck. He'll sort you."

Archer nodded again. "Sir."

Sedgewick looked around the group one last time before looking at his watch "Ok, we move out at eleven hundred. Tom, should give you enough time to restock and grab a bite to eat." He took another glance the men were silent. "Let's go."

The light outside had shifted by the time Archer ducked under the canvas and stepped out into the full glare of the hostile sun, immediately flicking at the flies around his face. The sun had already climbed above the low ridgeline, climbing with a dry, relentless intensity that turned every surface to white and gold. Heat shimmered across the ground, rising in faint, oily waves. The sand slid underfoot where it was powder-fine; most of it had been baked hard as clay, but it always managed to cling to boots, cuffs, and the corners of the mouth.

A faint wind blew in from the west, stirring the edges of old canvas and bringing with it the constant bitter tang of petrol, dust, and something else: the distant trace of scorched metal. The remains of a burnt-out Italian lorry still smouldered in the distance, its twisted frame casting a long, eerie skeletal form.

The trucks had settled, and the men had begun rooting out breakfast and brew kits. Archer scanned his surroundings and noticed Jacks was already crouched over a shallow tin, coaxing a flame from a bundle of petrol-soaked sand. The fuel hissed as it caught, flickering blue and orange beneath the edge of an Arabic-looking metal kettle. It had been dented and blackened from a dozen fires and rested on two pieces of brick that had been scavenged from a crumbled wall. The flame danced wildly in the breeze. Jacks sat beside it, shoulders hunched, hands holding an old, enamelled mug waiting for the contents to be poured.

Dust swirled at ankle height. The whole camp seemed to sway in the heat, and the men shifted lazily between trucks. The hum of an engine sputtering in the distance, and someone coughing from a dry throat carried across the vastness. Time moved slowly here, stretched thin by heat and waiting.

Archer watched Lockett squat next to Jacks. His sleeves were rolled in an attempt at some relief to the stickiness of the heat. He laid his rifle across his knees and straightened as Archer approached.

"Nearly ready, Sir," he said, nodding toward the brew tin. "Got a tin of condensed milk off the Signals lads. Thought it might help." Archer gave a faint smile. "You're an optimist."

Jacks didn't look up. "He's a bloody scrounger. If he keeps this up, he'll out do Evans."

The flame hissed gently as the sand caught. Lockett knelt again, adjusting the kettle with his bayonet. He didn't say much. He rarely did when Archer was around, but his eyes flicked towards the officer every now and then, measuring him. On the sea voyage and before Compass began, there'd been stories that were passed around, stories about what Archer and his men had done in France. How they'd held when others broke. How they'd carried on fighting long after they should have been finished. The details shifted with every telling, but the weight of it remained: Archer had stood fast and brought his men out.

But it wasn't just talk anymore. Lockett had seen him in action now. He'd seen how the officer took command of the company and instinctively knew what to do. Calm under fire. Direct, but never barking. He gave orders like he expected you to follow them, and you did. Not because of rank, but because it made sense.

He'd watched Archer drop to one knee, fire, kill a man, reload without missing a beat, then turn, issue clear orders to one lad to move up, grab another by the sleeve and calmly point him in the right direction. All of it done with that steady, quiet voice. He'd even given a faint smile to the lad, saying it was an easy mistake to make, but he needed to be heading in the other direction instead. All the while, Archer kept the battle going his way.

A gust stirred the edge of the canvas Lockett had strung up along the side of their truck to offer the smallest patch of shade. It wasn't the hottest part of the day, but the heat was rising. Above them, the sun was climbing its predictable path. The flame flickered but held.

Jacks shifted and peered into the kettle. "She'll boil in a minute," he said.

Archer crouched nearby, resting his arms on his knees. He said nothing for a while. He just watched the flicker of flame beneath the kettle. The three men sat in silence, staring at the orange glow dancing around the blackened metal.

It was almost strange, but Archer enjoyed these moments. They were the briefest of pauses where he could sit with a couple of comrades, waiting for something as simple as water to boil. He liked the silence. Sometimes, there was the odd snippet of a man's story: his home life, a memory, or a letter that had been received weeks ago and read now for the tenth time.

Not that they'd seen any post in some time. Still, Archer cherished these moments. For once, his mind felt unladen by the burden of command. Often, a quiet smile would come, brought on by a tale from one of the lads, or by Lockett's dry recounting of someone else's misadventure, half-whispered and half-true.

He'd always made it a point to try and join each section for a brew when he could. He didn't do it out of duty, but so he'd know the men beyond serial numbers and rank. Names, accents, hometowns. A sense of who they were, not just where they stood on parade.

Jacks, ever protective, had tried to steer him away from deepening his connection with the men, warning that the grind of losses would be an unbearable responsibility if he let them in.

Archer's reply had been simple. "Do you think I need to know a man not to feel his death?" The faces still came back in the quiet, whether he wanted them to or not.

The silence lingered, the flames dancing in the brew tin casting a quiet, hypnotic pull as the men stared into them. Each of them were locked in his own thoughts, the quiet giving space for things better left alone.

Lockett glanced around, then broke the stillness. "We heading out soon, Sir?"

"Yes," Archer said. "Eleven hundred hours. Kingsley's leading. We're tail end Charlie."

The kettle began to rattle, steam curling from the spout. Lockett lifted it carefully, gripping the handle with a twisted strip of old towel. He poured the boiling tea into three enamel mugs lined up in the sand.

As the liquid hit, each mug darkened. Lockett had prepared the tea in the kettle; two sugar cubes, knowing both Jacks and Archer preferred it strong rather than sweet. The loose leaves were caught by a small, wooden-handled strainer. Once all three cups were filled, Lockett set the strainer on an old sweet tin and placed it in the sun to dry. "Waste not, want not," he muttered.

Archer turned at the sound, a small grin tugging at the edge of his mouth. This must have been the third time they'd used those tea leaves but that hardly mattered. The act itself was what counted. A brew with the lads. Simple, steady, and quietly brotherly.

Archer finished the last of his tea. Even with only two sugar cubes, it was too sweet for his liking, but this was a communal brew, and all sizes fit all. He stepped out from the shade and stood, brushing the dust from his trousers.

"Lovely cuppa, Lockett."

He turned and walked away, heading towards the rear truck. Lockett watched him go, then looked at Jacks. "He always like that?"

Jacks grinned. "Pretty much. Quiet. Dry. And ten times sharper than anyone gives him credit for."

Lockett nodded slowly. He wasn't one for hero worship. But he'd follow Archer, that much was certain.

As Archer walked past the cab of his truck, he reached in and pulled out his bag and webbing. Slipping the yoke straps over his shoulders, he squinted at the morning sun that was already rising hot and high, and the sky above hazed with dust. Engines were coughing into life up and down the line of vehicles, and the rumble of idling trucks blended with the dry crackle of men shifting kit. The flies were back again, settling wherever they pleased. Archer swatted one from his neck and checked his watch. Eight-thirty.

3rd Platoon were busy getting ready, taking down the tents and various shelters that had been erected.

Archer stepped off heading towards his sections. It had become a habit. One he'd made his own: to walk the sections at least twice a day. He found that doing so during a brew or a meal put the men at ease, made conversation more natural. Less formal. More human. It was another opportunity to get to know who they were, not just what they did.

His gait was measured, and his face softened as he walked. A few of the lads glanced his way, but most kept focused on tightening straps or sipping at lukewarm tea. He preferred it that way. The fewer salutes, the more natural the moment. These men had fought, bled, and buried mates in recent days and now, once again, they were preparing to move forwards into unknown country.

He approached Section 1 first. Wilson was checking the rear canopy of the Bedford, tightening the canvas ties with a half-smoked cigarette balanced in his mouth. He noticed Archer, straightened, and gave a brief nod.

"Morning, Sir. We're good here. No drama," he said, voice low and rough from the cigarette.

Archer nodded, stepping closer. Webb was leant over a crate of the platoon's supply of grenades, sorting them with a kind of reverence. Beckett and Skinner stood just off to the side, murmuring about who had the better brew tin. Harland was oiling the bolt on his rifle with slow, exact movements.

But Archer sensed the silence behind it all, hanging over the men like a shroud. They had lost one of their own, a mate, and for many, this was the first time. His eyes settled on Webb, one of the originals from France. Among the newer men, they'd started calling the veterans *old salts.* Not unkindly: just with a quiet respect.

Webb had finished with the crate of grenades and was removing the spring from a Bren mag and touched it lightly with an oily rag, his movements slow and precise.

Archer dropped to one knee beside him.

"How's everyone doing, Webb?"

"They're doing alright, Sir. Keeping them busy. They'll be fine" Webb's voice was steady. He glanced up just briefly, then returned to his work.

Archer didn't reply at once. He let the silence linger, scanning the faces nearby. Len Carter offered a faint smile. Joe Atwell avoided his gaze entirely. "He was a good lad," Archer said quietly.

Webb turning his head. "He didn't flinch, Sir. Not once." Just then, Private Skinner approached quietly, fiddling with something in his hands. He was a smaller man, quiet and reserved.

"Sir... he asked us to make sure his wedding ring got back to his wife. Can we do that?"

Archer was caught by the moment. Not thrown, but still, it took a breath before he replied. "I'll see to it," he said.

Skinner passed the ring to him. It was a plain gold band, scuffed and scratched from years of wear. Archer turned it once in his fingers, thinking of Charlotte without meaning to. Not all that different, he supposed. Someone waiting. Someone hoping. And somewhere, a woman was about to lose all of that.

He slipped it into his top pocket before tapping Skinner's shoulder and giving him a reassuring nod. Slowly, Archer moved on to Section 2 who were gathered under the shade of a ration tarp. Pritchard sat on a crate, sorting through a box of .303 rounds. Evans leant against the side of the truck, sleeves rolled and expression unreadable. Hale and Donnelly were chatting about home with a dented enamel mug between them. The dregs of a morning cup of tea was still steaming.

Archer paused long enough to hear Hale share something personal from home with the men. "Last I heard, Dotty was thinking of moving her and her mother to her cousins in Cambridge."

Hale was an Eastender. Archer had been well aware of his worries with having a wife and three children back home. Archer had spoken for him at an AWOL hearing. It hadn't been entirely successfully, but Archer had pleaded for a lesser fine. After all, it was hard to blame the man for taking off after a massive air raid in London by the Luftwaffe. The fear of losing his family had outweighed the fear of court martial.

Ernie Foster sat sharpening a trench knife with a worn whetstone, rhythmically, not violently. Alfie Groves sat beside him and watched in silence. They were waiting, keeping their hands busy because idle time let the mind wander too far.

"Pritchard," Archer said.

"Sir," the corporal replied, standing with ease. "We're squared away. Full load of ammo. Water tins topped off."

"Good." Archer lowered his tone. "How are the lads after Palmer?"

Pritchard's reply was calm and direct. "They're steady enough. I told them straight. This sort of thing happens, and they need to get used to it."

Archer had admired Pritchard from the start. The best shot in the old battalion, likely in the entire 7th now. He was a natural stalker, all from a life spent quietly outwitting gamekeepers. It had come in very handy a number of times in France. He usually admired Pritchard's no-nonsense attitude, but just now, Archer wasn't sure blunt truth was what the men needed. Pritchard must have sensed it. "Sir, there's no point sugar-coating it. These are the facts."

Archer held his gaze. "Maybe," Archer said quietly. "Doesn't make it any easier on the ones still finding their feet." Then tapped him lightly on the shoulder and gave a small nod. The corporal meant well, even if his way was different.

Archer walked over to Hale and Donnelly. "Morning, chaps," Archer said as he stepped into the shade. "Hale, I'm guessing you've not heard any more on Dotty?"

Hale gave a short shake of the head. "Not a word, Sir. Not since Alexandria. Mail's gone missing again, I reckon."

Archer nodded, eyes settling briefly on Hale. The man tried to keep his expression flat, but the tension was in the jaw, and in the way his fingers gripped the mug too tightly.

Archer crouched beside him. "I checked this morning. Still no post. Must be hard not hearing from her," Archer said quietly. "We'll ask again at Brigade resupply, but with the ports the way they are, I wouldn't count on it."

Hale gave a small grunt. "Reckon the Jerries are shelling the post boxes same as everything else."

There was a flicker of tired laughter, but Archer didn't smile.

Hale had shared one of Dotty's letters back in October, telling the platoon how relentless the bombing felt, though she wrote with pride about how people were simply getting on with life, hard as it was. He had read her words aloud with the quiet pride only a husband could.

Archer said, "The silence isn't easy. But no news still means there's reason to hope." Hale nodded slowly, the mug steadying in his hands.

"If anything turns up," Archer added, "I'll make sure it gets to you first." He stood and turned to leave but a voice caught him from just behind. "Sir! Quick word?"

Evans stepped out from the shadow of the truck, hands in his pockets, grin already forming. Archer raised an eyebrow but said nothing. Glancing around theatrically, Evans reached under a folded tarp, pulled out a small pack, and produced a dusty bottle. The label was half-peeled, but the amber inside spoke for itself.

"Thought you might fancy something a little stronger than tea. No need for thanks. Found it while we were collecting rations and ammo this morning."

Archer looked at the bottle, then at Evans.

"Scrounged or stolen?"

"Sir," Evans replied with mock disbelief. "Traded, for an Eyetie pistol that was, let's say, liberated." The smile spread wide across his face.

Archer shook his head although a smile crept in at the corners.

"Evans... what are we to do with you? I should have you on a charge for this."

Evans squinted again in disbelief. "What, a soldier's trade? Never stick, Sir."

"If Wetherby ever found out this kind of thing was going on, he'd have it in for us."

Evans tapped his nose. "Wouldn't be so sure of that, Sir. Next time you see him, ask about his new shiny sidearm."

Archer's expression fell into something close to astonishment. "You mean..."

"The less said, the better, Sir, eh?"

The lieutenant let out a quiet chuckle. "Danny, you never cease to amaze."

Archer was already walking away, laughing, and raised a hand in acknowledgement. He moved along to Matthews who was bent over his webbing, a folded piece of paper in one hand and a compass in the other. Saunders leant over his shoulder, frowning.

"That's west, not south-west. We'd be marching into the sun."

Matthews didn't look up. "I'm telling you, this track curves. See the bend here? The marker's off."

"So's your bloody compass."

"Only because someone sat on it in the truck."

Saunders snorted and shook his head, brushing sand from the collar of his shirt. The two had formed a quiet bond since Matthews had joined the platoon. Saunders had once been the youngest of the lot. Raw, nervous before every scrap, but he'd never backed out. In fact, among the old salts, he was spoken of as the bravest man in the section. Maybe the whole platoon. That hadn't gone unnoticed. Archer felt it then: a quiet pride, not in the boy he'd been, but in the man he was becoming. Perhaps that was how others saw him now.

A few feet away, Les Fry and Haz Wilkes were stooped over side by side in the dirt with their knees drawn in, and their backs slightly hunched in an attempt to shield their faces from the intensity of the rising heat. Fry was broad-shouldered, with a thatch of sandy hair matted to his forehead and forearms darkened by sun and oil. Wilkes was slighter, wiry, his sleeves rolled high, as he traced a line in the sand with the tip of a pencil stub.

Between them, the ground had been scratched flat, a makeshift surface for the game. A few bent and re-used playing cards – dog-eared and grease-stained – sat face down in a row.

"Two kings," Wilkes said quietly, laying them down with care.

Fry gave a low grunt and shook his head. "You're either lucky or cheating."

"Can be both," Wilkes replied, not smiling. He glanced up once as he heard the rising intensity of Matthews and Saunders bickering before quickly returning to draw a fresh line. A trickle of sweat ran down the side of his temple, vanishing beneath his collar. A few flies hovered near the rim of a half-finished brew tin beside them. They'd long since stopped worrying about the constant trickle of sweat that never quite dried. But the flies were a never-ending menace.

Neither man spoke much. There was just a quiet rhythm of dealt cards, soft remarks, and the occasional grunt of approval or disappointment. It was a small ritual. One of those invented games that filled dead minutes between orders.

Matthews had ended his minor disagreement with Saunders and was now telling the men to clear up and prepare to move. Billy Joyce lay nearby against his rolled-up trench coat. His helmet was tipped over his face, and the slow rise and fall of his chest was the only sign he was still breathing. One hand rested loosely on the butt of his rifle. Matthews gave his boots a firm nudge to wake him.

Meanwhile, Saunders collected a pair of tin mugs, the metal clinking as he lifted them from the crate. A length of camo netting was being folded nearby, shaking out dust as it went. Someone muttered that the heat was already worse than yesterday. Another swore under his breath, blaming the sun like it might listen.

In an instant, Fry and Wilkes were up from their card game and pulling down the canvas sheet they'd used for shade.

"Lieutenant," Matthews said, spotting Archer. He straightened up and began buttoning his shirt.

"All good here?" Archer asked, still buoyant from his encounter with Evans.

"Just getting squared away. Had a quick brew and a bite to eat, so the lads are steady." He turned away for a second. "Joyce, make sure that crate's strapped down properly this time. Don't want it sliding around again."

Private Joyce looked thoroughly miserable under the corporal's eye. He'd taken the blame for the crate holding the brew kits coming loose and sliding about in the back of the lorry for a good few miles. Joyce had insisted he wasn't at fault, and he wasn't but he'd still caught the brunt of Matthews' wrath all the same.

Saunders handed Archer a cigarette. "How are the others holding up, Sir?"

Archer took it without a word, placed it between his lips, and he leant in as Saunders flicked open a shiny silver lighter. Once the cigarette was lit, Saunders tucked the lighter back into his breast pocket without a word.

"New lighter, Saunders?" Archer asked.

Saunders gave a small smile and turned towards the lorry, saying nothing.

Archer hadn't given it much thought at first, but it was clear now that more than a few of the lads had come away from the Italian positions with a handful of souvenirs: the odd lighter, a belt buckle, even clean clothes. Nothing brazen. Just the quiet, half-approved way soldiers always found a use for what others had left behind. At one point, he'd considered putting a stop to it. But he knew better. A man could be forgiven for pocketing a lighter or a cigarette case especially if it kept his nerves steady or gave him something to trade for tobacco down the line.

He scanned the section. Pike, Murgatroyd, Joyce, all present. All climbing into the back of their lorry.

Turning to Matthews, Archer stated clearly, "You'll be in reserve. Watch the flanks. If anything hits the column hard, I may swing you round." Matthews nodded. "We'll be watching."

By the time he'd returned to the lead truck, the desert was alive with the thrum of engines and shouted orders. The men were aboard, weapons checked, dust already rising from beneath the tyres. Lockett stood beside the vehicle, squinting into the sun. "They're ready, Sir."

Archer said nothing. He turned for one last look at the men he'd just spoken to.

No one had mentioned Dent. Not once. Perhaps they couldn't. Better to keep their heads bent over rifles and grenades. Easier to argue about brew tins and let the silence stand for what they couldn't bring themselves to say. Archer understood it. Grief was a private thing, and in war, it was often swallowed whole and buried beneath the next order, the next march.

But the hole was there all the same. It was an empty void among the living. Archer felt it keenly. His hand brushed his pocket and allowed himself the briefest of moments to think about the plain ring that had been entrusted to him with the quiet story of a dead man, Private Clarke.

With a pang of bitterness, Archer knew it had been different with Dent. Left where he fell. There was no keepsake to send back. No grave Archer could name. Only silence waiting for his family at home. The thought lingered a moment too long. He shut it down before it could take hold.

CHAPTER 11

Dawn broke with a dry breath of wind and the creak of canvas straining on guy ropes. In the soft half-light, the desert looked almost calm, a sea of scrub and dust, faintly silvered, with shadows still clinging to the folds of the shallow basin where the 7th Battalion had dug in.

The rising sun caught the ridgelines first, then crept up to the trucks and trenches, illuminating the grey outlines of rifles, helmets, and the sand-caked backs of men slowly stirring from their sleep. Someone coughed. Another man lit a cigarette, shielding the flame with cupped hands. Petrol fumes still lingered faintly in the air and mingled with the smell of unwashed webbing, scorched canvas. The ever-present dust settled into every fold of clothing and crack of skin, forever leaving its imprint.

It had been months since Point 208. Weeks of movement, chasing Italians, rounding up prisoners, and collecting whatever could be reused. The orders seemed to carry less urgency. Each day seemed to stretch longer than the last, the hours dragging in the heat, broken only by small tasks and the waiting that followed. Waiting for orders. Waiting for movement. Waiting for something to begin again.

By late January, the battalion had been pulled from the armoured columns and reassigned to a coastal sector west of Tobruk. No grand assault. No breakneck pursuit. Just another holding role, watching the horizon for whatever came next. For Archer and his platoon, it was the longest they had gone without firing a shot since arriving in the desert.

The days stretched out now, long and empty if a man let them be. The desert had become an enemy of its own: sand in rifles, thirst in the throat, sudden gales that scoured everything raw, and beneath it all, the dull weight of routine. Too much time to think if you weren't careful. Too much time for faces to return, for names to linger. Archer knew better than to let it take hold. He kept the men busy where he could. The rest, they had to manage in their own way.

Stand-to had been called half an hour earlier. No barked orders, just a quiet word passed along by platoon sergeants, creeping through the sections. Rifles were checked, bayonets fixed, eyes peering westwards. The routine was universal across the British Army. It was a habit older than this war, born of bitter experience. Dawn and dusk were the hours when an enemy was most likely to come. When the half-light gave them cover and the mind still lingered in sleep. So, every man stood ready even if nothing stirred on the horizon. The battalion might have been in a holding role, but Lieutenant Colonel Blackstone insisted they behave as if in the line itself. Reserve or not, his order was clear: be prepared, always.

Archer peered out from his position. Nothing moved. This was no hasty scrape in the sand; the battalion had been in place for weeks, and the position showed it. Trenches had been deepened, dugouts were lined with sandbags and scraps of timber, and the perimeter was enclosed with coils of wire. Even latrines and cook tents had been knocked together, lending the place an air of permanence that sat oddly in the desert. Each fresh delivery of barbed wire had thickened the defences, so low and high strands stretched out from the trench line. Every so often, a used bully beef tin, filled with a few stones, had been hung from the wire to rattle in the dark.

It wasn't much, but it made the men feel a little more settled. So, they kept watch, as they always did, with their eyes fixed on an empty horizon. Archer watched it all without comment, then turned his gaze back to the horizon. Still nothing.

The reason for their location was simple: to set up roadblocks and provide local security along a stretch of the main coastal highway. Built by the Italians and named the Via Balbia, it ran the full length of Libya, hugging the shoreline from Tripoli through Benghazi, Derna, and Tobruk to the Egyptian frontier. The battalion was spread thin across almost ten miles of it, each company taking its turn on checkpoints and patrols. To the British, it was simply known as 'the coast road.'

Archer walked the line slowly. His boots trod on sun-hardened sand that had almost turned to rubble. He passed Section 2 first: Pritchard's lads. Most were squatting or kneeling, rifles across their laps, eyes shaded beneath helmet brims from the approaching sun. Donnelly gave a nod. Foster was already chewing something from a mess tin, expression unreadable. Evans, for once, had little to say. He sat cross-legged, wiping a bayonet he had used to cut up his tinned beef. By his side, there was a neatly dug slit trench with a line of sandbags stacked two high, and a Lee Enfield lay across them.

"Any bother?" Archer asked quietly.

Pritchard shook his head. "No movement. Not even a breeze till ten minutes ago."

Archer nodded and moved on. The early light cast everything in pale gold, and the shadows of trucks and men stretched long and thin across the basin floor. In the distance, the outline of a ruined building rested on a rise, a solid shape against the shimmering horizon.

Late last night, Archer's platoon had returned after a three-day stint manning one of the checkpoints along the coast road. Theirs had been Marble Arch, the fifth of six posts strung out across the battalion's sector. Each post had been christened after a station on the Central Line of the London Underground: a thin slice of home imposed upon the desert. From east to west, they ran in order: Liverpool Street, Bank, Oxford Circus, Tottenham Court Road, Marble Arch and, finally, Shepherd's Bush. Back from their stint at Marble Arch, they had quickly settled into the routine of camp life: watching and waiting.

Archer continued his rounds among the sections. Sedgewick had placed 1st Platoon furthest forwards in the company's sector, with Company HQ set centrally, twenty yards behind 2nd and 3rd Platoon. The company had settled back into position on their return and Archer was satisfied. Most of the men were in good spirits despite the monotonous role they were playing, and rest had not been a problem. On the other hand, rations, the lack of enough fresh water, and the harsh environment remained their greatest trials.

Once again, he moved on, stepping between a pair of slit trenches. Webb and Skinner were working steadily in one of them, deepening the trench where the side had begun to cave. They'd been trying to widen it slightly: not for defence, but for comfort. Their faces were dusted grey, eyes rimmed with grime. Archer paused to check in.

"Morning, lads. How was your night?"

Both men looked up. Webb answered for them both.

"Tight and uncomfortable. Nothing to complain to you about though, Sir." Archer smiled as they resumed digging. He knew the improvements weren't tactical: just a small effort to make life bearable.

At that moment, Jacks appeared. His rifle was slung over one shoulder, and dust and grime clung to his arms and brown legs. His knees were a sandy white from where he'd been recently kneeling. Most of the men had been issued shorts for the desert operations. Even in these early days, the skin on their kneecaps was already becoming coarse and hardened from constant contact with sand and stone.

"Sir, Matthews has returned." Jacks' voice was steady, soldierly, but calm.

Archer felt a flicker of relief. He had sent Matthews out on a patrol. It was one of many. Each company was required to put a section forwards during the day to move through pre-designated areas. Even on returning from Marble Arch, the routine held. Sedgewick had passed the task down, so Matthews went out again. The aim was simple: maintain a presence a thousand yards ahead of their line, watching, searching, and mostly listening out for signs of movement, or a build-up, or worse, a night assault. "Wilson is waiting for your briefing. Then he'll set off."

It was Wilson's turn to be tasked with the morning patrol. Sedgewick had insisted on near-continuous coverage of the forwards ground. Daylight patrols were pushed further out. Often a mile and a half ahead of their line, swinging in a wide arc: north towards the coast, west along the shoreline, then south and back again. Blackstone, and through him Sedgewick, wanted constant assurance that the northern flank was never ignored while their main effort remained on the coast road.

Archer picked up his pace and headed straight for Wilson, "Tug" to his mates. Another old salt who'd been with Archer in France. He was a no-nonsense NCO, steady and reliable when it mattered. Archer never had any worries about when Wilson was involved because it was always done properly.

As he approached, he saw Wilson inspecting each man, checking kit was secured and fastened. Asking each one to jump in turn, Wilson gauged the rattle or the bump of loose gear. It wasn't such a concern during daylight patrols, but essential at night when sound travelled further. This was Wilson's ritual: day or night. He personally made sure every man was good to go.

"Corporal Wilson," Archer called out.

Wilson turned immediately and stood to attention. Archer released him from the sharp posture with a nod.

"At ease, Wilson. You're set? You've liaised with the other companies? Know who's where and where they're likely to be?"

"Yes, Sir," Wilson replied without pause.

Archer looked over the six men under Wilson's charge before taking him gently by the arm and leading him a few paces away. He lowered his voice so it wouldn't carry on the breeze.

"Wilson, this is just a patrol. Go out, have a look around and if there's anything, anything at all, you come straight back. Don't get caught up in anything."

"Yes, Sir. Straight back. I understand."

"Good man." Archer gave his arm a squeeze of encouragement, more for himself than for Wilson.

He hated sending these men out, especially if he wasn't leading them. It always felt like it should be him at the front. Every time. He knew that wasn't possible. There simply weren't enough hours in the day, but the feeling never quite left him.

Archer stood for a good twenty minutes, watching as Wilson led his section through the thin wire lines beyond their trenches and out into the distant desert. The knot in his gut tightened. It was a resignation to the fact that he was now powerless to influence whatever might happen out there. It would stay with him until their return. Eight or ten hours from now.

Archer made his way back to his own position where Lockett was busy improving the trench while at the same time, preparing something that passed for breakfast for them both. Officially, Lockett served as company runner and batman, but the line between the roles was often blurred, and Archer had long since learnt not to question how the private managed to juggle both positions. A few yards away, Briggs crouched beside a battered tin, coaxing a flame from the petrol-soaked sand. The lads had started calling it a Benghazi burner, and it was fast becoming the standard way for a British Tommy to heat food or boil water for a brew. Archer had seen it used on several occasions so far and was always struck by how quickly it brought water to the boil. Most of the men could have a fresh mug of something hot ready in minutes.

Lockett, meanwhile, handled the practical things Archer didn't have time for: brewing tea, sorting kit, making sure his helmet and webbing were where they needed to be. He kept track of Archer's mess tin, dug and maintained their shared trench space, and always had a clean pair of socks tucked away somewhere, just in case. He even managed their cigarette rationing. Jacks had made him personally responsible for ensuring Archer ate at least once a day, and Lockett kept a mental tally of where the rations were. Archer was aware that Lockett was becoming more confident around him. Beyond that, he often served as a quiet conduit between the enlisted men and their officer, a pair of listening ears on both sides.

On top of all that, he ran messages to and from Company HQ without complaint, and regardless of the heat, distance, or hour. Lockett revelled in the responsibility and took immense pride in his role. After all, not every batman got to serve Lieutenant Archer, MC.

Archer had never asked for the arrangement, and he wasn't entirely comfortable with it. But he knew better than to turn it away. Command left little room for routine, changing socks, or chasing down the right fuel tin to boil water. And Lockett, without ever being asked, filled the gaps. Quietly. Capably. Without fuss. Archer had become very fond of him.

Lockett saw Archer approaching, set his entrenching tool aside, and turned his attention to the mess tin on the burner. He had cobbled together a strange concoction for breakfast: crushed hard biscuit, chopped bully beef, a little water, and half an Oxo cube to give it something resembling a meaty taste. He called it biscuit mash.

Stirring it with a spoon, like the best chefs in the world, Lockett took a cautious taste. His expression said it all: reasonable, not great, but food all the same.

From a few yards away, Briggs caught the look and gave a small smile that slipped into a chuckle. Lockett returned the glance, both men recognising the absurdity of it, and with a shrug, he let out a dry laugh of his own. It was the kind of expression that said, 'Well, that's soldiering for you.'

Archer stopped by the slit trench. Seeing the work Lockett had put in, once again, he felt quietly grateful for the man's efforts. "Stirling job, Lockett."

Lockett, knowing Archer's first concern that morning had been the return of Matthews, got straight to it.

"Matthews get back alright, Sir?" he asked, passing over a half-full mess tin with his warm mash inside.

Archer took it, eyeing the mixture, and stirred it with the spoon that was already resting in the tin. Before taking a mouthful, he replied, "Yes, all good. Nothing out there. Wilson's just left."

"Tug'll be fine, sir. One of the best salts we've got."

Archer nodded and took a spoonful of the mash. He chewed slowly. It wasn't his first taste of Lockett's handiwork. In a strange way, he rather enjoyed it. The crunch of the warm biscuit against the softened bully beef, all bound in a thin, meaty gravy that was almost delicious. The Oxo cube had made all the difference. A good, strong flavour that caught the taste buds off guard.

Lockett settled in beside the trench, easing down with a quiet grunt as he balanced his own mess tin on one knee. For a moment, the two men ate in silence, and the soft clink of spoons was the only sound between them.

Archer took another bite, nodding slightly as he chewed. "You know," he said, glancing sideways, "This tastes better than it's got any right to."

Lockett gave a small shrug. "Oxo's the trick, Sir. Bit of salt if you've got it. Everything else is just texture."

They shared a brief smile. Lockett passed over a dented mug of hot, milky tea that was slightly too sweet. Archer took it with a nod of thanks and welcomed the warmth of it.

"You always like this?" Archer asked after a moment. "Taking care of people?"

Lockett thought for a beat. "Not really, Sir. But I like things being right."

Archer didn't reply straight away. He looked out across the position to where men shifted, and the soft murmur of routine starting to build. Then he said, "Well... you've a knack for it."

Before either man could say more, Briggs leant in, mug in hand, the steam curling into the morning air. "Any chance of the recipe, Lockett?" he asked with a grin. "Biscuit mash could make you famous back in blighty."

Lockett rolled his eyes. "You want it, you cook it. Sir's the only one daft enough to eat my experiments without complaint."

Archer gave a faint smile, setting his empty tin aside. "Don't sell yourself short. I am sure when this is all over, I'll miss your breakfasts." They shared the joke, small and fleeting.

Archer finished the last mouthful of mash, chased it down with a swig of dark, sweet tea, then handed his mess tin and mug back to Lockett. He wiped his mouth on his sleeve and let his gaze drift across the position.

Lockett leant closer, lowering his voice slightly. "Sir, now you've finished," Lockett said. "I collected the platoon post this morning. Looks like it was dropped off while we were still at Marble Arch. Came with a bundle of socks, a few fags, and fresh rations. Sergeant Barker asked me to pass it on to Sergeant Jacks, Sir."

Lockett bent down and hauled up a small sandbag, its mouth loosely tied with string. "The post, Sir." He set it on the trench wall beside Archer.

Archer untied it and began sorting through the bundle, his eyes flicking quickly across the envelopes. There were dozens of them, different hands and inks, some smudged with age, others still crisp: the accumulation of weeks of silence finally catching up with them. His thoughts went briefly to Hale and whether there was word from home. He pulled two thick envelopes from the pack, both addressed to Hale one was almost entirely covered in a child's uneven drawings.

"Lockett," he said, handing them over. "Get those to Hale. He'll want them straight off." Lockett nodded and moved away.

Archer continued to sift through the bundle. Clarke. Palmer. Dent. He set them quietly to one side. They would never be opened here. For a moment, his hand lingered on the top envelope, remembering the men who would never read them.

Archer found one addressed to Lockett and another to Briggs and as Lockett returned, Archer passed the envelopes over without comment. Both men took them silently, the weight of paper heavier than any ration tin. "Go and fetch Jacks," Archer said, still sifting.

Briggs nodded and moved off. Archer continued, stacking the letters into a neat pile ready for the sergeant. By the time Jacks arrived, Archer had them squared away with those that wouldn't be read set aside, and the letters for the living piled up, ready to be called. It was the cleanest way. The men would get their letters, but not the sting of hearing names that would never answer.

"Jacks, once you have distributed the post, get over to company HQ. There appears to have been a supply of socks and stuff. Make sure we get our fair share."

Although giving an order to Jacks, Archer was clearly distracted by the six letters he still held in his hand. Each was marked in the same plain way: rank, serial number, name, battalion and yet somehow the system had carried them across oceans, ports, convoys, and endless desert tracks, all to land in his hand in a slit trench in the middle of nowhere. The thought struck him harder than he expected. That voices from home could travel so far, through so much, and still reach him here, that was impact enough, before he even broke a seal.

He chose the top envelope. The hand was unmistakable, and he unfolded it carefully.

1st December 1940 St. Luke's Chapel, Colchester Garrison

Dear Tom,

I write this in the hope that it might reach you in time for Christmas. With it comes a warm wish for a Merry Christmas, and a gentle reminder that many of us here are thinking of you. I can only assume the mail is patchy as always, so this may be a little wishful. Still, it is that time of year.

I hope you are finding your feet out there or at least managing to keep them free of blisters and out of the worst of the sun. The word coming back is sparse, but I trust you and your chaps are settling in with the 7th Battalion. Pembroke was saying they have always been the lesser battalion, and that now you are with them, they might soon be up to scratch. He misses you, I can tell. And not just because he has lost his best batsman.

Things here are quiet, cold, and familiar. Mallory sends his regards. I saw him at this morning's service. He is now officially the Regimental Sergeant Major of the 9th. You should see him striding about like a man with a spine made of steel. He was clearly born to it. He misses Jacks, of course, though he would never say it aloud.

Pembroke is well. His inevitable good nature keeps shining through, even though he is busily reorganising D Company. He insists on referring to it as 'D Coy,' though I think he may be the only man left from France still serving in it.

Tom, speaking of France, I am not, nor ever will be, able to thank you properly for what you did for me and all the others to get us home. I am not even sure I ever did thank you. Everything moved so quickly. That they have thrust you back into the war, so soon after that disaster is, to me, incomprehensible. But that is the Army, I suppose.

Ellis has now been formally confirmed as Commanding Officer. Whether they will promote him to full Colonel remains to be seen, but for now, he wears the rank of Major, though none of us refer to him as such. In my limited military knowledge, I would say he has more than earnt the step up, but I have no doubt that rank will never get in the way of his work. He is in full stride, throwing himself into the rebuilding of the 9th with the same vigour, strength, and professionalism we saw in France.

Every few days, a new group of men arrives. Each of them raw and fresh from basic training, all wide eyes and stiff salutes. Ellis and Mallory waste no time in sorting them out and setting them straight in the 9th Battalion's ways. The heart of the old unit beats on, though quieter now. Mallory's been drilling them hard, which, in truth, they need. Pembroke, for his part, has taken a few of the junior officers under his wing. All in all, the battalion is coming along in good order.

I recently met another face you may recall, a Corporal Turner. He said you would know him as 'Sparks.' He was wounded at some bridge, he said, but was extremely pleased to hear that you and a 'Scouse' Evans had made it back. I assume that is Lance Corporal Evans. Apparently, they were great pals.

Now, something that may surprise you, I had lunch with Charlotte last week. Pembroke and I were in London for a day or two on battalion business, or at least that is what he told me. Why he needed a padre for administrative errands, I am still unsure. Perhaps he thought having me along would make it easier to disappear unnoticed for a while. In any case, he arranged for us to meet Charlotte and a friend of hers, a bright young woman named Virginia, at a little café just off the Strand.

Both ladies were in their Wren uniforms, and both looked quite impeccable. Charlotte, as you might expect, was full of gossip, all of it about you. From the moment we sat down, the conversation was peppered with names: Jacks, Pritchard, Webb, even Saunders. She told us how she hangs on every word you write and how your last letter, which arrived slightly crumpled, has already been read and reread several times.

What struck me most, though, was the way she spoke of you. Not just with affection, though there was plenty of that, but with pride. Quiet, unwavering pride. She said, and I quote, "Tom reveres you, Padre. He spoke of you more than you might imagine." I must confess that gave me pause. One seldom hears such things said with such conviction. It reminded me why I do this.

We sat there a good while, the four of us, talking of everything and nothing. Charlotte has a laugh that catches you off guard, and Virginia, well, I suspect James invited her for his own reasons, which became clearer as the lunch wore on. I may have been something of a chaperone, though I did not realise it until afterwards. Still, it was a lovely afternoon. After lunch, we walked through Victoria Embankment Gardens just as the light was starting to fade. The leaves had mostly turned, and there was that crispness in the air you only get before Christmas. Charlotte spoke fondly of you as we walked.

We ended the day at the theatre. Pembroke had managed to get tickets for The Man Who Came to Dinner at the Savoy Theatre. I had not expected to enjoy it as much as I did. Virginia was in fits of laughter at one point, and even Charlotte had tears of joy. I caught her glancing at the empty seat beside her more than once, and I could not help but think she was imagining you there. Finally, the wonderful day came to an end, and Charlotte made me promise to call her when I was next in London. I say this plainly: she is certainly a wonderful young lady Tom. She cares for you deeply, and I believe that knowledge alone would lift any man's heart in your position.

I must bring this to a close as its almost three, and I am having tea with Major Ellis and his wife at four. I still have a few things to complete before I leave.

If this letter finds you before Christmas Day, I hope it brings a little warmth. If not from the words, then from the thought behind them. Look after yourself. We will raise a glass to you here.

God keep you safe. And may this note, however delayed, remind you that you are missed, remembered, and prayed for.
Yours ever,
James Cartwright Padre,
9th Battalion Greenmoor Light Infantry

Archer read Cartwright's words slowly, line by line, as if he could hear the padre's voice beside him: calm and measured, with that quiet certainty that never seemed to falter. By the end, the letter felt like a firm, steady hand on his shoulder, and it was oddly comforting after so many weeks of dust, routine, and silence.

Archer sat still, staring at the page long after he had finished. His throat felt tight with something he couldn't quite name. It had been a long time since anyone had spoken to him like that. Not as an officer, not with orders or reports, but simply as Tom, a man who was remembered, missed, and prayed for.

He folded the padre's letter carefully, almost reverently, but the others he lingered over. Four from Charlotte, her hurried, slanting hand instantly familiar. Each envelope felt different in his fingers, each carrying a little of her with it. One letter was filled with London chatter, trains, queues, the sound of sirens at night and for a moment, Archer could almost hear her voice spilling the words in a rush as though she were sitting opposite him. Another was steadier: written late in the evening with a tighter script, more thoughtful. There were lines of affection that caught at him. Simple phrases that mattered more than any grand declarations and were deep reminders that she cared, that she waited, that she believed he would come back.

He didn't read them all at once. To devour them in one sitting felt almost wrong. Instead, he tucked three back into his pocket, keeping one open in his hand a little longer and letting the words settle. Out here, where the desert stripped everything down to sand, steel, and silence, Charlotte's letters were colour, warmth, and memory. They reminded him that he was more than a uniform, more than a name on a roster. They reminded him he was hers.

In that moment, he made himself a promise: he would marry her at the first chance he got. Slinging his satchel over one shoulder, Archer rose and went to find a quiet spot, somewhere apart from everything else, where he could write to Charlotte about this very morning and about how her words, and the padre's, had reached him here.

CHAPTER 12

The convoy rolled eastwards through the night, engines grinding low and headlights masked to narrow slits. What little light they gave was swallowed almost at once by the desert's vast emptiness. Only the stars marked the way: pale and cold against the black sweep of sky. The men rode in silence, packed into the back of the Bedfords, each lost in their own thoughts. Dust hung behind them in long ghostly trails. Some tried to sleep with their heads lolling against wooden slats or with packs used as makeshift pillows, but the jolting suspension offered no mercy. Every rut in the track sent helmets knocking together, and a chorus of muffled curses. One man shifted his boots to stretch out, only to earn a sharp kick from his neighbour.

"Bloody hell, watch it," came the hissed complaint, answered by a muttered expletive that died away as the lorry rocked on.

Occasionally, a flare of orange lit a hollow-eyed, dust-caked face as the tip of a cigarette glowed fiercely before it was hidden again by a cupped hand. The smoke mingled with the fumes of petrol and hot oil. It was thick in the men's nostrils, leaving a bitter taste on the tongue. Someone stifled a cough, another muttered for quiet. The sound of the convoy dominated everything. Its low, ceaseless rumble seemed to carry them deeper into the darkness.

The Bren carrier rattled westwards through the night. Its tracks clattering over the hard ground, engine note droning low and steady. The blackout hood masked the headlamp to a slit, so its pale glimmer barely marked the path ahead. Beyond it, the desert was nothing but darkness, and its vast emptiness stretched onwards to the horizon. Only the stars offered light: cold and sharp against the black dome of sky. Behind them, the battalion column was spread out, forming a chain of lorries and carriers snaking along the coast road. The engines rose and fell in ragged chorus, echoing off the dunes and the unseen sea beyond.

Archer felt it keenly. Every man, every rifle, and every crate of ammunition depended on the line his carrier traced through the dark. One missed turning, one broken-down vehicle left blocking the road, and the whole battalion would be stalled and exposed, pinned in the open with nowhere to go.

Inside the carrier, the HQ section rode close, shoulders brushing in the cramped steel box. Archer sat forwards with the map board balanced across his knees, a canvas front that was strapped over a rough seat flapped in the draught. Beside him, Jacks shifted uncomfortably. His greatcoat collar was pulled tight, and his eyes were fixed on the road ahead. Lockett was couched against the side plate. His helmet was tipped low, and he was half-dozing until each jolt of the track shook him awake. Briggs had the wheel, and his hands held firm on the controls. The faint glow from the headlights through the metal slit allowed the minimum of light to brush his face. The flying goggles he wore caught the light, but the lenses were already hazed with dust. Evans had scrounged them from some RAF source weeks before and now every man in the carrier had a pair, along with neckerchiefs pulled high across their mouths. They looked like bandits in battledress, eyes peering through scratched glass which were dulled against the grit. Even so, Briggs squinted hard, shoulders hunched over the wheel, fighting to pick out the pale strip of road through the gloom. Each bump sent his goggles slipping, each swirl of dust reduced the world to a blur of shadows and engine noise. His jaw was set hard, and every line of his face was fixed in total concentration as he fought the wheel and the desert alike.

Jacks adjusted the strap of his goggles, tilting his head to catch the faint starlight through the scratched lenses.

"I'll give Evans this," he said, voice muffled behind his neckerchief. "He's got a bloody talent. RAF, was it? Must've talked some poor 'erk out of half their stores."

Lockett gave a short laugh, and the sound was instantly carried away by the engine's thrum.

"Wouldn't surprise me if he came back one day with a Spitfire on tow."

Archer said nothing but allowed himself the ghost of a smile. Evans's scrounging often skirted the line, but there was no denying his finds kept the men going, the little extras taking the edge off a life that offered very little comfort. In the choking dark, with sand drifting like smoke, the goggles were worth their weight in gold.

The desert night had a chill that crept through their battledress and greatcoats, but it wasn't the cold that unsettled Archer. It was the haste with which they were on the move: the way the order had come down with barely an hour's warning. A scribbled map, a set of grid references, and the insistence from Brigade that they were to reinforce the line at Mersa Brega "with immediate effect." No more detail than that.

A bump jarred the carrier, knocking Jacks' elbow into Archer's ribs. "Sorry, sir," he muttered.

Archer shook his head. "Not your fault. Bloody road."

From the rear, Lockett stirred and grumbled, rubbing his shin where he had caught it against the metal frame. "Christ almighty. Could you give us warning before you find another crater?"

Briggs kept his eyes ahead, unruffled. "Road's nothing but craters, mate. Be thankful you're not driving."

That drew a low chuckle. For a few moments, they sat in silence again. Only the rattle of loose kit and the steady roar of the engine disturbed the night. Archer glanced down at his map with his covered torch. Its faint red pencil lines blurred with each jolt. He knew he was on the right road but needed to estimate how much further they had to go.

His unease at their current situation reminded him of France. Once again, they had been called upon in haste, ordered forwards with little warning. Blackthorne had been brief to the point of bluntness.

"The balloon's gone up. Jerry's not wasted any time, and he's on the move east. We're to meet him at Mersa Brega, and we move now."

As Archer, bouncing uncontrollably in the carrier, bemused by Blackthorne's earlier orders: meet them at Mersa Brega? Meet what? He raised his head from the map, and Jacks turned to him.

"Feels like we're being thrown into the dark, Sir," he muttered.

Archer glanced at him. "You're not wrong. Orders were thin enough to fit on the back of a ration slip."

Jacks exhaled slowly, returning his eyes on the road ahead. "I thought it was a bit too good to last, sir. Thumping the Eyeties the way we did... Jerry was bound to show up sooner or later."

The carrier jolted and the men cursed. They drove on. The night seemed endless, punctuated only by the occasional flare of an exhaust or the stutter of a misfiring engine quickly coaxed back to life. Somewhere far off towards the coast, the sky lightened with several flashes that lasted a few minutes. Both Archer and Jacks immediately knew what it was: artillery. Both men stared at each other. Was it theirs or the Germans?

By the time the column halted, the eastern horizon had begun to pale. A thin wash of blue hinted at the first promise of dawn. The men clambered stiffly down from the lorries, stretching and rubbing at their eyes that were raw with fatigue. Ahead lay Mersa Brega: a small, old, historical looking fishing village. Jacks was already among the NCOs, snapping at them to shake the men awake.

"We're forwards now. So get a grip and be ready to move!" he barked, his voice carrying across the chill morning air.

He singled out Corporal Matthews, jabbing a finger towards the track.

"Matthews, get the drivers to pull the wagons over into that clearing. The whole bloody battalion will be on top of us any minute!"

As the platoon's Bedfords began to grind into place under Matthews's direction, Archer paused a moment to watch. The first of the battalion's vehicles were rolling in behind them. The rumble and rattle of that mixed bag of machinery seeming to shake through his boots into his very bones. Almost out of nowhere, a squat, little car nosed its way past the column, bouncing lightly over the ruts.

It was one of the new light utilities the men had started calling *Tillys*. A Morris, by the look of it was civilian in origin but had been stripped down and rebuilt for war. Its boxy body sat low over narrow tyres, with a short and stubby bonnet, and mudguards cut square. The khaki paint was already dulled by desert dust. Its glass screens were half-masked with anti-glare slits, and the whole machine looked both flimsy and stubborn at once, like something improvised and pressed into service because nothing better could be found.

Behind the wheel, a young driver hunched forwards, cap pulled low, knuckles tight on the rim as he wrestled the little car through the sand.

In the rear seat, half hidden by the tilt, Archer caught sight of Colonel Blackstone. His cap badge glinted as he leant forwards, pointing across the bonnet towards some rise on the horizon. Beside the driver Major Markham sat with a map open on his knees, stabbing his finger at features as he muttered directions. The little Morris utility looked absurdly overloaded, and its springs groaned under the weight of too many officers in one place.

When the car jolted to a halt, the side doors burst open almost at once. Captain Sedgewick unfolded himself stiffly from the rear, followed by Mallinson of A Company, Fletcher of B, and Denholm of D. Each man blinked in the sunlight and brushed dust from his shirt, trying to regain dignity after being wedged shoulder to shoulder.

For a moment, Archer thought it comical: a company's worth of brass hats crammed into a vehicle barely fit for two men and a dog. The soldiers nearby grinned, trying not to laugh outright.

Blackstone was the last to emerge. He was composed despite the cramped ride. The cap badge caught the sun as he gave the briefest glance around. He stepped back towards the car, , said something sharp to the driver, and in another moment, the little vehicle had bounced away in a cloud of dust, carrying him off to meet with 2nd Division.

The moment the little Morris sped off, the assembled company commanders exchanged quick glances, muttered farewells, and peeled away to find their respective companies. That left Sedgewick alone, smoothing his uniform and squinting into the sun. Having made the best of a graceless arrival, he now strode towards Archer.

"Get the chaps. We'll have an orders group." He paused, eyeing the ground, then jabbed a finger towards a parked lorry. "Over there."

Archer turned at once, moving back through the jumble of parked and parking lorries in search of the other platoon commanders. He found McBain and Kingsley together, sharing a cigarette against a tailboard.

"Either of you seen Riley?"

Both shook their heads.

"Sedgewick wants us. Make it lively." Archer turned and pointed to where the captain had called them to gather. He pressed on, eventually spotting Riley in the back of a truck, half-buried in kit, rummaging through an old case and cursing under his breath about something he was sure he'd packed and why the bloody hell he couldn't find it. "Riley!" Archer snapped, his tone sharp. "O Group, now. Come on."

Once assembled, Sedgewick acknowledged them, "Gents." He unfolded a hastily hand drawn map and placed it onto the lowered tailgate. His peaked cap was pulled low, but his eyes still stung from the glare.

We're now under 4th Infantry Brigade, attached to 2nd Division." He paused to let that sink in, then continued. "From what I've managed to cobble together from brigade and battalion, Jerry's made a strong push straight down the coast road, heading east and directly at us. Strength is estimated at maybe two German divisions with at least two Italian divisions in support."

Sedgewick was clear, and very matter of fact in his delivery, pausing at the end of each statement before moving on.

"Blackstone is going ahead to link up with 2nd Division. He wants a better picture of the situation, as the information we have is not overly reliable. That said, we do know C Company is to move into a prepared position twenty minutes west of here – an old Italian blockhouse with a few ruined concrete buildings. The place has been wired and partially dug in by the Sappers. Strong enough to hold a flank, though not perfect. We move out as soon as I've finished here."

Sedgewick glanced around the small group. "Any questions?"

Archer cleared the dust from his throat. "What about support, Sir? Ammunition, rations, water? Do we have artillery cover?"

Sedgewick gave a short nod, his voice clipped. "Ammunition and rations will be what we've brought with us. Same for the water. So make it last. Beyond that, gentlemen, it's down to us. We hold until told otherwise."

He let the silence linger.

Archer broke it. "And support, Sir?"

Sedgewick's gaze flicked to him, then away. "Can't say at this stage. I'll need to find out."

Archer pressed once more. "And how do we talk to whatever support we get?"

For the first time, Sedgewick's composure faltered. His jaw tightened. "What I've told you is all I know, Lieutenant. That's that."

Archer knew pressing further would win him nothing but the wrath of a senior officer. He let the words hang in the warm air, heavier than the dust. His thoughts turned to France, another position, another stand. When were they going to learn?

The orders were given quickly after that. Men moved without fuss, kit checked and stowed with the quiet efficiency of those who knew the rhythm of it. Engines coughed into life one by one, the convoy forming in a loose column as the last of the stragglers climbed aboard. They rolled out within minutes.

The desert swallowed them almost at once. Dust billowed up behind the trucks, hanging in the still air, turning the world into a shifting haze of brown and gold. The sun climbed higher, hard and unforgiving, pressing down on metal and men alike. There was little to see beyond the track ahead, just low scrub, broken ground, and the occasional scatter of rock that hinted at something older buried beneath the sand.

No one spoke.

It was a short run, no more than twenty minutes, but it felt longer: the heat, the noise, the constant jolt of the vehicles stretching time into something heavier. Then the lead Bedford slowed. Low, angular shapes began to form through the dust, unnatural against the land. Concrete. Broken walls. Wire.

Archer's carrier pulled in behind the lead Bedford, dust rolling past the so-called blockhouse that had been promised to them as a prepared position.

Up close, it looked less like a fortress and more like an abandoned outpost. The main building was a squat concrete box, sun-bleached and cracked with loopholes that were little more than narrow slits and would give scant view of the approaches.

The roof sagged under its own weight. Its corners were scarred where weather and neglect had done more damage than shellfire ever had.

Scattered around it were the remains of an Italian garrison post: a pair of low huts with rusting tin roofs, half-collapsed lean-tos that might once have housed stores or a field kitchen, and a battered water tank perched awkwardly on a crumbling stand. The Sappers had cut a few trenches and rifle pits around the perimeter, but they were shallow, and their walls already slumping. Barbed wire was practically non-existent, just a few coils had been strung between leaning pickets that would never stop a tank and barely slow an infantryman.

It was a place built for show, Archer thought. Not for war. A colonial police post dressed up as a defensive line. Now, it was meant to serve as the far southern flank of the British line at Mersa Brega The last position before the desert simply opened out.

There was no high ground here. Only the faintest of rises lifted the blockhouse above the salt pans to give a modest view towards the coastal road. From a distance, it looked commanding; up close, it was little more than a bump in the sand.

Geographically, it was clear enough. The blockhouse sat on the southern shoulder of the Mersa Brega line and was an anchor point in name if not in strength. To the north, the Via Balbia threaded past the marshes and was the obvious axis of advance for armour. To the south, the desert stretched out in a flat, shimmering sheet and was treacherous ground where wheels would bog and tracks would churn themselves in circles. No army in its right senses would try to push a column through that, though patrols might skirt the edges.

Here, on this flank, Archer guessed they were meant to hold anything trying to swing around Mersa Brega. They were the end of the line. A battalion might look solid enough on a map but in reality, it was spread over a mile, with C company covering barely four hundred yards. They were thin. At least in France, they had been concentrated and able to pack a solid punch that could hold. Scanning the horizon, Archer thought they would offer nothing more than a tripwire. Enough to make the Germans slip, but not to stop them. He kept studying the ground and noted the broken line of scrub, and the faint undulations in the sand. No ridges. No wadis deep enough to hide in wait. Just open ground.

For them to offer any real resistance would take more than half-dug trenches and broken wire. The blockhouse might give cover against rifle fire, perhaps even some shelter from tanks and artillery, but not for long. His mind flicked back to France, to the bombardments that had pounded them without pause, the bone-shattering percussion a man felt with every explosion.

He straightened, voice cutting through the stillness. "Jacks, this is a shithole, but it's our shithole. Follow me, let's get the men to work!"

Archer moved off at once, Jacks falling in beside him. The blockhouse stood to their right: squat and pitted, its shadow short in the midday sun. Archer paced a slow circuit. His boots crunched over the brittle crust of sand, and his eyes narrowed as he traced the lines of fire each section could cover.

He raised his voice. "Section commanders, on me."

Wilson, Pritchard and Matthews closed in, crouching as Archer took a knee. Brushing a patch of sand flat with his hand, Archer cleared away the loose grit. He drew a quick line with his finger. "That's the sea to the north." Another line, lower down. "Salt bog to the south. They're not coming through that."

He marked a rough line between the two. "That leaves this. Our frontage. Sixty, seventy yards at most."

His finger tapped the centre. "We're here. Southern end of the battalion line – and the end of the company. Nothing beyond us."

"This is the line, runs for eight to ten miles.

“The company is on the extreme left of the battalion, and we are the extreme left of the company.”

Archer rose up, turning to their front. “Our front stretches from here to that low rise and scrub, about sixty to seventy yards to the south.” Archer’s outstretched arm pointed the line.

The corporals now stood alongside him and kept their gazes on Archer, hanging on every word. Each man knew Archer’s decisions were for their best interest.

“The other two sections keep the same line up to the blockhouse, that’s where Company HQ will be. A and B companies are over to our right, pushing north towards the coast road. It’s a thin line. The battalion’s stretched almost a mile to our north. No real depth.”

For the first time, the corporals glanced at one another. The seriousness of the situation landed between them.

“I don’t know if we have artillery support, or, in fact, any support at all. We’ve to rely on ourselves, dig in and hold.”

Wilson broke the pause. “So, business as usual then, Sir.”

All four men gave a wry smile and let out a short chuckle.

“Yes, Corporal.” Archer smiled, then his expression straightened, and he went back to the business of soldiering.

“Section One here. Wilson, your arc will sweep across the open ground. Not much cover, but you’ll at least have a field of fire.” The corporals followed the line of his arm, eyes moving over the ground, already judging angles, cover, and how their lads would fit into position.

They moved on, circling south. The earth was softer here, and sand drifted into the half-dug pits the Sappers had abandoned. Archer crouched, scooped a handful and let it spill through his fingers.

“It’s not ideal. Pritchard, you hold this section. Get them digging in and improve those slits.” Jacks gave a grunt. “Not much of a start.”

Pritchard, in his usual no-nonsense way, said, "I'll get them straight on it, Sir."
Archer nodded and tapped the corporal's shoulder. "Good."

As Archer moved south along the half-built trenches, the line bent slightly; a scatter of scrub and clusters of white stone marked the ground. He paused, judging the slopes and angles.

He fixed Matthews with a look. "Matthews, you're the anchor. This is the end of the line. Improve those trenches. This is where they'll hit hardest. Bring your section a little closer together; you'll need maximum fire here."

He had placed Matthews deliberately. All his NCOs were reliable, but Matthews had a knack for getting the best out of an impossible position.

Archer took a further moment to take in the surroundings again. The wire that stretched along their line sagged miserably; a mix of rusted strands and newer loops drooped between leaning posts, some old, some freshly emplaced and already showing salt. He turned his head, angling his gaze down the line, and saw the small earthworks the Sappers had managed to start. There were shallow scrapes, a few trench sides roughly shored up and half-built with loose stones, and a ragged bank here and there where a man could kneel and fire. He witnessed his NCOs putting the men to work, improving their positions. Close to Matthews' end, a shallow pit had been hollowed for a small mortar, probably a two inch. Nothing more than a lip in the sand and a scattering of sandbags: unfinished and exposed.

"Jacks, let's put HQ in there." Archer pointed towards the mortar pit. "Get the lads to work on it. We can offer support to both Matthews and Pritchard from here."

He just instinctively knew this was going to be the point where he would need maximum effort. It would be cramped between the four of them, but it would have to do.

Jacks spat, a thin sound, globule into the sand. "Bit tight, but I'll get 'em on it, Sir."

Archer took a long look at the position. Decisively, he turned back along the line, already picking out where the wire needed lifting and where the scrapes needed deepening.

A voice carried over the wind. "Sir!"

Lockett came up at a half-run, breath short but controlled.

"Captain Sedgewick wants you. Now, Sir."

Archer paused only a moment, glancing once more at the half-finished position, then turned back to Jacks.

"Keep them at it. I won't be long."

Jacks nodded. "Right, Sir."

Archer turned and followed Lockett back along the line.

The blockhouse smelt of dust and old timber, and its walls were thick with whitewashed plaster that flaked in the heat. Shafts of light speared down from gaps in the corrugated roof, turning the air into shifting bands of glare and shadow. At the centre, there were two trestle tables, nothing on them but some man's webbing.

All the officers of the platoon stood in a loose arc, their boots scratching on the concrete floor as they shuffled into position. They kept their voices low as the heavy door clanged shut behind them. The space was cooler than the sun outside but no less stifling. The air was close with sweat and the faint reek of oil that seemed to cling to everything these days. Cigarette smoke hung in slow layers beneath the rafters, blue grey against the shafts of light that cut through gaps in the roof. It mingled with the dust and heat, giving the whole room the sour, cloying weight of a barracks canteen left too long without air.

The impromptu conference began at once, each officer seeking clarity on their position. Archer glanced around the room and crossed to where Kingsley, McBain, and Riley stood.

Sedgewick appeared in front of the group. He paused, drawing a breath. "All right, listen up," he said, voice quick and businesslike. "There are no radios at company level. Battalion has the only set available, by that I mean working! We'll operate on runners."

Riley blinked. "Runners, Sir? Over this distance?"

"Runners, yes." Sedgewick's jaw was set. "It's all we have."

Archer took a second and answered for all. "Understood, Sir." Sedgewick gave a short nod and placed both hands on his sides as he looked forwards. "Major Markham is concentrating the mortars. He's pooling every two-inch and any spare medium tube he can find. He'll place them centrally between the companies and it will be his call on when and where to use them."

Archer frowned. "Pooling mortars makes sense. We'll need the punch in depth. Are the runners to go through you, Sir?"

"No, they go straight to Major Markham. CSM Barker takes the Boys rifles," Sedgewick said. "They're to be mustered as one mobile anti-tank group under his charge. He will move them to threatened sectors." He paused for a small breath. "Riley, collect the mortars and the Boys and get them to company HQ as soon as we finished here."

Archer had let out a short laugh, though not entirely amused. The Boys were useful enough against light armour and armoured cars at close range. Against a real Panzer, they might as well be peashooters. He'd have traded the lot for a brace of 2-pounders.

He kept the thought to himself. No sense adding to the apprehension among the others .

Sedgewick noticed Archers laugh but did not flinch.

"Markham's trying to scrounge a 2-pounder or two. He reckons our end of the line is where they'll come, punch through, then swing round to cut the coast road, scooping us up in the process."

"Well, that's what they did in France, Sir. At least we've the sea on our northern flank." Archer's tone made plain his agreement with Markham's view.

"I wouldn't be so sure, Archer. We're thin. 2nd Armoured is a shadow of itself. Most of its armour and guns are out of action.

We're an understrength infantry brigade, scratched together with whatever we carry, expected to hold against at least one German division and two Italian besides." Sedgewick fell quiet. There was nothing more to add.

For a moment, the five of them stood where they were, the wind pushing dust through the open doorway as the room began to empty and the silence settled in. Kingsley shifted first, adjusting the strap of his helmet. "Right then."

McBain gave a small grunt. "Aye."

Riley glanced between them, then gave a thin half-smile. "Could be worse."

No one asked how.

Archer lingered a moment longer. Sedgewick was already elsewhere; his head was bent over a scrap of paper a runner had just handed him.

Archer watched him for a second, then said quietly, "Good luck, Sir." Sedgewick didn't look up. "You too."

Archer turned and followed the others out. The four had all stopped outside, and Archer looked at the group.

"Well then," he said quietly then jerked his head towards the line. "Back to it."

They broke apart without another word.

Archer turned and made his way back along the position. The ground was already beginning to feel different underfoot.

Behind him, the low murmur of voices picked up again, orders passing, tools scraping, men digging in.

Ahead, the line waited.

CHAPTER 13

Barely a fortnight after setting foot in Africa, and Rommel was already on the move. Berlin had urged caution, told him to dig in and wait until his division had arrived in full. He ignored the advice. He had seen enough in France to know hesitation was death, and in this desert, with the Italians reeling and the British stretched, speed was everything.

He believed the British were vulnerable, overextended by their own success. Operation Compass had driven them deep into Libya on captured fuel and supplies. Their columns were thin, and their lines of communication grew longer with each passing day. To Rommel, that spelt opportunity. The Italians had sat passively in their fortresses and been smashed apart one by one. The desert, he knew, punished the static and rewarded those who moved first, struck hardest, and those who never allowed the enemy to settle.

Berlin wanted a shield for Tripoli. Rommel intended to build a sword. With only a regiment of panzers, a battalion of motorised infantry, and a handful of 88s, he would not wait for perfect strength. The 88-millimetre gun had been designed to sweep the skies, but Rommel's officers had learnt in France how its flat trajectory and power made it lethal against tanks and bunkers alike. It was a weapon that unnerved the enemy and stiffened his own ranks, a force multiplier in the open desert where there was little to hide behind. It was something Rommel would grasp at once and use with ruthless efficiency to build his own legend. He was now throwing forwards whatever he had, knowing that boldness could mask weakness. A quick blow at the British flank might steady the Italians and buy time for the rest of the elite Deutsches Afrika Korps to land.

The Italian 10th Army was in ruins. Shattered in weeks by Operation Compass, it had left behind a coastline littered with wrecked lorries, abandoned guns, and prisoners who seemed almost grateful to surrender. What remained of Mussolini's divisions, now clung to the Libyan frontier like driftwood in a tide. Rommel had been sent to stiffen that line and to buy time for reinforcements still unloading at Tripoli. Instead, he chose to seize the initiative, pushing forwards with Kampfgruppen, their ad hoc combat groups built from whatever had already arrived. Not enough for a grand offensive, but more than enough to strike, to probe, to harass, to force the British to react to him.

At the tip of that effort rode Oberst Karl Neumann. Promoted from staff to field command, he now led a forwards Kampfgruppe of panzers and motorised infantry: a mixed blade designed to cut where the enemy was thin. Only weeks before, he had briefed Rommel on the state of the front, reporting that the Italians had faltered but the British were dangerously overextended with their lines stretched across too much ground. It was an assessment Rommel had seized upon, and one that helped convince him to strike without waiting. For weeks, Neumann had watched the Italians bypassed and crushed, their fortresses crumbling in succession. Now, at Mersa Brega, he intended to prove his point and show them how a modern army fought.

Engines droned across the flats, trucks and armoured cars kicking up long veils of dust that blurred the horizon. The column rattled past salt pans rimmed with brittle scrub, and the air was sharp with fuel and grit. Neumann sat stiffly in the lead car with the map board across his knees vibrating with each jolt. He had seen this country for weeks now: broken fortresses, abandoned guns, and Italians trudging back with blank eyes and empty canteens. Each mile convinced him further that his assessment had been right: the British had struck hard, but their strength was paper-thin, stretched along a line too long for their numbers.

Ahead, the salt pans gave way to shallow dunes, and their pale ridges ran down towards the coastal road. It was here, Neumann recalled, that he and Rommel had agreed the British would most likely try to stand: a line more than thirteen kilometres long, anchored on the sea and the marshes where they could mass armour, artillery, and infantry in depth to create a defensive block.

Leading the column were three Sd.Kfz. 222s squat armoured cars. Each of their open turrets was equipped with a 20mm cannon and a machine-gun. Their crews scanned the horizon as dust streamed off their tyres. Neumann sat in the third vehicle, a folded map in one hand, binoculars slung around his neck, and a torn cloth tied across his face against the dust and grit that still seeped into everything. Feldwebel Holtz, his driver since November, was sat at the wheel, ever-present at Neumann's side.

For days, they had passed the signs of a retreating army: gutted Italian blockhouses, overturned lorries, stranded guns and equipment scattered across the desert floor. Neumann knew all too well the Italians' failings, and how they had faltered by clinging to static strongpoints, blind to the modern war of movement and machines that he and Rommel had exploited in France. By contrast, the British advance had been rapid, but to Neumann's eye it was also reckless. He repeatedly told himself: their columns are thin, their supply lines are long, and their positions are stretched across too much ground. His own report had argued as much, and Rommel's orders were clear, strike forwards, probe, and discover just how deep the enemy's strength really ran.

He lifted the map and studied it for a moment before reaching for the FuG 5 radio set. - It was a compact transceiver that had a range of four to five kilometres, enough to keep Neumann in touch with his lead cars and the rest of the column as they moved.

Neumann pressed the handset close, his voice firm and clipped. "Kolonne Halt, Halt!" The reply crackled back at once, and the column slowed, dust rolling past in long curtains as engines throttled down. Holtz eased their car off the road, and within moments, two armoured cars emerged from the haze, scouts returning from their sweep ahead. Their commander, a young Leutnant, swung down quickly with his dust mask still around his neck.

"Herr Oberst, the position ahead looks lightly held," the young Leutnant reported, voice sharp. "It's a prepared line, but the wire is thin and patchy. The British are still digging in. I saw only a few guns. An old Italian fort sits astride the road."

He paused. Neumann listened without interruption, raising his binoculars to the horizon. The junior officer pressed on. "Some vehicles are moving within their positions, but no sign of armour."

Neumann swept the horizon, his gaze drawn into the featureless expanse. Salt pans glared white, and dunes folded pale towards the coastal road. He lowered the glass and turned to the dust-covered Leutnant.

"What about the ground to the south?"

"Marshy, Sir. We almost bogged down ourselves. I would assess it as impassable for armour."

Although the binoculars hung around his neck, Neumann still held them tight against his chest as if their weight alone gave him steadiness. He let the silence stretch a moment longer, then gave a sharp nod.

"Sehr gut, Leutnant." Turning to Holtz, he ordered, "Assemble the commanders."

Holtz was already signalling. Within minutes, the dust-streaked officers of the Kampfgruppe gathered round the bonnet of Neumann's staff car. He unfolded his map, pressed at the stubborn folds, then pinned it flat on the ground with a water bottle, his binocular case, and an old brass-cased compass. The Leutnant, who had led the reconnaissance, stood by and waited for questions.

Neumann swept his hand across the paper.

"The British appear to be digging in here. Their line runs from the salt marsh in the south to the coast in the north. It is good ground. Flanks are protected by sea on one side, marsh on the other. Reconnaissance reports say our armour will not pass the marsh without bogging down."

The officers listened intently, taking in every word.

"We assess the line to be thin but that remains only an assessment. Here," he tapped the symbol for the old Italian fort beside the road. "I expect strong resistance. They will use it to deny us a direct push along the road." Neumann took a breath, eyes still on the map.

"We will not assault the fort directly," Neumann said and with split fingers, he tapped two patches on the map. "First the guns. Two short, crushing concentrations, one north of the road and one to the south. While the British are fixed by the barrage, Hauptmann Keller, your armoured company will split in two and drive in on both flanks."

Keller stared at Neumann. He was a capable officer in his early thirties, fair-haired in the Nordic mould. Sand clung to his features, tracing the rims of his goggles. He had cut his teeth in armoured warfare. First in Poland and then in France, where his platoon was among the first to reach the sea at Abbeville under Guderian's command as part of Panzer Group Kleist.

"Oberstleutnant Lang, your infantry will be split likewise," Neumann continued. "They will follow the armour, dismount and engage the enemy in their defences."

Oberstleutnant Heinrich Lang stood a little apart, pencil and small leather map case in hand. He was in his early forties, a career professional from the Reichswehr. His dark hair was greying at the temples, and a thin scar marked the left side of his jaw. Although he held the same rank as Neumann, Rommel had appointed Neumann as Kampfgruppeführer, making Neumann the senior officer.

Pointing to a small mark on the map, Neumann focused on a track from the town which forked into the main coast road. "Both forces will push through and converge here. At this junction, we form up. Krüger, you will direct your artillery on the fort area. Once the barrage lifts, we will assault it from the rear as one."

Oberleutnant Hans Krüger was in his early thirties, and he stood with a small leather notebook open on his knee. He kept the firing tables tucked beneath the book, pencil poised. Methodical by habit, he took quiet pride in the precision of his guns.

"Herr Major," Krüger said, tapping the page. "My 105 battery will fire upon the northern point and the 88s will concentrate on the south." The efficient officer glanced at his senior officer with a dry menacing smile. "Four-minute concentration. I'll keep their heads down."

He closed the notebook with a neat, practised motion. His speech was slow but certain; the men around the map felt the steadiness of it. Neumann nodded once. "Good, Krüger." He looked at his officers. "We strike immediately. Let's not give the British any more time to prepare. Forwards, men!"

With that the small group of officers turned and ran for their vehicles. In no time at all, the German convoy's engines were roaring, and the column was preparing to move. The gunners uncoupled the pieces, swung them into position and emplaced them, ready for what they were about to unleash.

Meanwhile, Archer stood in the mouth of his slit trench, fingers worrying a loose strap on his webbing. Around him, the platoon moved with the practiced economy of men who had been given little else to do but prepare. Sergeant Jacks walked among the men, pointing out weaknesses or generally offering motivation. Lockett was packing away the brew kit that he had used to brew up to provide many of the men with a cup of tea, knowing that this would steady their minds, in between digging.

Wilson was knelt beside Webb who was standing up in his slit trench wiping over the Bren. The two men chatted back and forth. The late morning air was hard and flat; even the heat seemed to be waiting.

A low rumble came from Archer's right. It was soft at first and then grew until every man turned in its direction. The approaching column slowed, and a battered 15-cwt truck drew up, men clinging to its tailboard.

Sedgewick was there in a moment, wiping dust from his face. "Major," he said, more a statement than a question. Markham climbed down from the truck, his shirt dark with sweat, and the two officers exchanged a look that needed no ceremony.

"Three 2-pounders," Markham said, nodding towards the three Morris C8 "Quads" that had been drawn up on the hardpan. Flat-nosed, flat-bonneted and squat, each Quad had an open-topped cab with two gunners at the front and three more in the rear with ammunition and kit for the gun. A spare wheel was lashed to the sloped top and their 3.5-litre engines ticked and growled as they idled.

Archer jogged over, breathless with the short run in the heat, acknowledging Sedgewick and then turning to Markham. "They will come in handy, Sir!"

"I managed to convince the General that leaving his southern flank totally exposed to armour was not a very good idea." His grin was quick, gone as soon as it arrived, but the meaning stayed.

Markham barely took a breath. "Captain, I'm going to place the three guns through your frontage, preferably on that rise." He pointed to where Archer's men were improving their positions. "From there, they'll cover the whole battalion front. At about 500 yards, they should provide a serious deterrent to anything coming up the southern approaches."

"Yes, Sir. Archer, get them up there and dug in as quick as you can!" Sedgewick answered at once.

Archer sprinted to the nearest Morris, shouting for the other two to follow. He clambered into the forwards cab, told the gunner in the passenger seat to shift over and pointed the driver towards his platoon. As the vehicles drew up alongside the line, he called them to a halt.

"Jacks!" he barked, and the sergeant ran over. Archer began directing each gun into position. He placed the first between his platoon and the third platoon on his right before he motioned the second into the centre of his frontage. He then pushed the third out to the far right. The guns were roughly thirty yards apart.

"Jacks, get each section to a gun and help dig them in," Archer ordered. He repeated the command, sharper, "Dig in. These are likely to be our lifeline. The whole battalion will rely on them. Keep them covered."

The sections fell to work with the practised hands of men who had done jobs like this many times before. Shovels bit the baked earth in a neat, steady rhythm, and the ring of metal on stone became a small, regular tune Several men carried filled sandbags, placing them along the top edge of the cut that the spades had made. The sergeant from the 2-pounder anti-tank gun moved among them, calling out measured corrections in a short and precise voice, yet it was threaded with gratitude for the help they were giving. Before long, they had cut a three-foot pit with a single layer of sandbags along its rim; the floor was levelled so the gun could be rolled up into position.

The gunners rolled the piece up to the start of the pit. Four men hauled on the trail, and as they got to the edge, they swung the gun 180 degrees and eased the weapon into the pit until the muzzle of the gun cleared the sandbagged escarpment by six inches. Then the men set to work, getting the gun ready to fire.

They splayed the split trails and engaged the leg locking mechanism, levering the hinged, retractable legs until the two trail-ends lay at the correct angle to take the recoil. A pair of men knocked wooden wedges under the blocks and drove them home while another checked the lunette and the towing-eye to make sure everything was secure for when the quad came back. The road wheels were pulled free and stacked to one side, and the tyre and rim were placed out of the way. By removing the wheels, the carriage would sit lower in the pit and reduce the gun's silhouette. This would allow the trails and spades to bite into the ground, so the recoil would be taken by the earth rather than by the axle.

Finally, they pegged down rope stays and clipped a length of loose netting to the rim to stop the wind from filling the pit with grit. A loader crouched by the breech with spanners at hand while the sergeant ran a practiced eye over the work and called out the last measured adjustments. Finally, the gun sat low and steady, and the crew were set to mount the breach and make ready to fire.

One of the section men, Lance Corporal Saunders, stood with his shovel hooked over his shoulder and watched, a small smile tugging at the corner of his mouth. There was something about the way the gun crew moved together, each action answering the last, that caught him. The quiet economy of movement, the way a heavy thing became manageable when every man knew his place was like a symphony. For a moment, Saunders forgot the grit in his throat and the heat on his neck, totally absorbed in the practical poetry of it.

A short, harsh voice cut through his reverie. "Right, back to your posts, men," Corporal Wilson barked, stepping forwards with the authority that kept the section level. He pushed his shovel into the sand, and he pointed towards the line with eyes that wouldn't be argued with. Hands tightened on tools, shoulders rolled, and the men swung back into their allotted gaps, their muscles switching from the slow, careful work at the gun to the sharper readiness of a fighting line.

Saunders stole one last look over his shoulder, admiration still warming his face, and then he fell in step with the others. The pit and its crew became part of the background. Another piece of preparation was completed, so the men returned to the watchful business of holding what they had.

The men of the 7th were busy with small, human tasks. Lieutenant Tom Archer moved slowly down the line, checking on his men and their kit. Little things to make a difference, straightening a sandbag, congratulating one or two on work done in their slit trenches, offering a quiet word here and there. He knew only too well the nervousness that came with waiting... how the mind liked to invite horrors when a man was left idle. Corporal Matthews, a former Sapper with the Royal Engineers, had his section dug into regulation: men buried to shoulder height so that only shoulders, heads and rifles were exposed. Matthews met Archer's eyes.

His voice low and almost private, Archer said, "Major Markham's done us a favour getting the 2-pounders up here. I feel we have a fighting chance now."

Matthews met his eye, expression set. "We always have a fighting chance, Sir. The real problem is, so does Jerry."

Archer gave a small chuckle. Then his demeanour grew stiff and serious. "This is going to be a real test. We're so thin; I don't know how we'll hold if they come on like they did in France."

"We survived France, Sir," Matthews said, trying to sound reassuring.

Archer let the words hang for a moment and then softly added, "That's all we did, Pete."

A distant boom cracked the air like a thrown stone. For a second, the men looked at one another as if someone else might explain it away. Then a high, whistling scream split the sky.

A shell coming in.

A shout rose from the line. "Take cover!"

Matthews dropped, head tucked to his chest, hands scrabbling for the rim of his steel helmet. Archer did not wait. He sprinted the yards to his cut in the earth and dived in both feet together, landing beside Lockett. His momentum pushed him into the poor unsuspecting Lockett and squashed him against the side of the slit.

"Jesus Christ!" The yell came from the contorted body.

"Sorry Lockett. Keep your head down!"

The distant booms were merging into one sound. The air was split again and again. Archer felt it more than heard it: multiple clean shocks that travelled down his spine. He stayed low for a heartbeat and then forced himself up to peer over the lip of the trench. Roughly fifty yards to the north, the ground broke open in grey and yellow pillars; each shell landed with a dry, savage clap that sent a column of sand and grit skywards and left a shallow, ragged crater when it settled.

The smell of cordite travelled on the breeze with the second impact: metallic and sharp. Archer watched men flinch where they knelt beyond the line of pits, heads ducking and shoulders hunching under the invisible push of air. A private spat and wiped his mouth, coughing at the grit. Someone swore; someone else made the sign they did in the open when there was nothing else to do.

Archer's voice cut the small, stunned silence. "Keep down. Keep your heads!" he ordered, low but hard. He did not look away from the blasts. Each impact told him how the barrage was ranging, how close it might come and for all his experience, a cold, clean worry ran through him as the shells continued to come in measured beats.

He watched them creep in, each detonation a footstep closer. The first group had fallen wide. The next bracketed left and right as if the guns were measuring, and then the pattern narrowed.

A flash.

A lift of dust.

A throat of gravel, and the explosions began to march. No longer random but deliberate. One after another, edging along the line, closer and closer like a man picking his way across a field.

The light from each burst seared for a second. Then it left a ragged afterimage of flying grit and jagged stone. Where the rounds landed, the air tasted of burnt metal and a dry, iron tang. Small pebbles spat across the surface and pinged off stone; a chip of stone nicked a man who foolishly raised his head, Archer watched as the body fell back into its ready-made grave. Men who had been steady a breath earlier, now flinched, their shoulders hunching and fingers tightening on rifle butts as the impacts tightened their ring.

Archer felt the distance shrink in a way that had nothing to do with numbers. Fifty yards became thirty, then twenty, in the hard arithmetic of blast and flash. The ground between them was being rewritten in a series of shallow bowls; each new crater brought the concussion nearer, the push of air like a hand on his chest. He kept his head low and only his steel helmet and eyes showed above the trench. One eye followed the blasts, the other watched his men and, most importantly, the 2-pounders. If they took a hit, the day would be very different. Only when the shells were yards away did he drop to the bottom of his pit. He felt Lockett press against him; both men had tucked their chins, drawn up their knees and braced for the impact.

The barrage, smaller than any Archer had seen, passed over him and his trench, each impact rattling the earth. His thoughts were split between the blunt business of surviving this small hell, and a grudging note of how quickly the German gunners had found their range and worked the line. As the last shells fell, there came the usual, stunned silence, and then the cry of help, the bark of orders, and the raw screams of the wounded.

Archer was up at once, letting the dust fall from his sleeves. "Stand to! Stand to!" he roared.

He vaulted the trench lip. Sand hissed from his boots as he ran for the gun furthest to the north. From where he was, he couldn't tell if the pieces were knocked out; all he saw were figures moving frantically about their positions. As he ran, he barked the orders that would matter first. "Jacks, check the southern 2-pounder! Pritchard, check the centre gun!"

CHAPTER 14

The bombardment had stopped as suddenly as it had begun, leaving only the echo of it hanging in the air. The silence that followed was strange: too heavy, too still, and only broken by the slow patter of falling sand. Archer ran hard across the trench line, boots sinking into loose grit, and the ground trembling beneath his feet from the memory of the blasts. Dust hung thick, veiling everything in a pale, shifting haze.

He dropped to a knee beside the 2-pounder, coughing as the air bit at his throat. He had sprinted the seventy-five yards from his slit trench, shouting to the men to prepare for an attack; his chest heaved as he gasped for breath. The pit was half-collapsed. The parapet was torn open, and sandbags were burst and spilling like entrails. The gunnery sergeant was there, crouched by the trail. His face was white with dust, and his eyes were wide but alert. Another man knelt beside him with a small shovel in hand, swinging it as if he were bailing out water rather than sand. A third had the breech open and was peering down the barrel. "Status?" Archer demanded, leaning in close to be heard over the ringing in their ears.

The sergeant blinked and spat grit. "We're good, Sir. Bit of shrapnel in the shield. She's unlevel, but we'll get her right again."

Archer's breathing eased a little, his heart slowing at the news that the gun was still serviceable. "Good. Be ready, Sergeant. That bombardment means they're coming straight for us."

He moved on, farther down the line, sweeping past men in their trenches with their rifles at the ready. "Stand to, lads," Archer called, repeating the order at each position as he jogged past, hopping over small craters left by the shell bursts. Every now and then, he stepped onto a sandbag or rock, keeping his balance as he went.

He reached Pritchard in the centre of the line, crouched beside the second gun.

"Corporal, how's the gun? How's the section?"

"All good, Sir!" Pritchard's reply came firm and steady, unshakable as ever.

Archer felt his resolve harden, knowing Pritchard was at the centre, and the second 2-pounder was still serviceable.

He continued past the gun position without stopping. "Stand to, lads. They'll be here shortly!" he called as he moved through the centre.

He paused when he saw Jacks coming towards him from the northern end of the line. The sergeant's face was set in a grimace, beads of sweat cutting pale tracks through the sand clinging to his skin.

"What is it, Jacks?" Archer's tone was sharp, expectant. "Section and gun are fine, Sir, but Lieutenant Riley's been killed, along with one other from Company HQ. Their trench took a direct hit."

Archer froze, taking a moment. He had liked Riley even though he hadn't known him well. A pleasant enough chap, diligent, dependable, and he always completed his tasks without fuss. As the news sank in, the distant rumble of engines reached Archer. The sound was coming from the horizon. They were here and as Archer had suspected, they were coming straight for them.

"Jacks, head back to the northern gun. Tell them to wait for my order to fire. We'll let the armour come to within five hundred yards before opening up."

Jacks turned and set off towards the northern gun. Archer broke into a run, moving through the haze towards the central and southern pits, repeating his order: hold fire until the armour was inside five hundred yards. The desert was alive with noise now: engines, tracks, and the deep metallic groan of something vast and moving. He dropped to one knee beside the nearest trench, shouting for the men to keep their heads down.

Pulling his binoculars from his satchel, he focused on the oncoming force. He could make out numerous armoured vehicles. The lead elements were Panzer IIIs, followed by several Sd.Kfz. armoured cars, and a tail of open lorries packed with infantry.

Archer's senses prickled as the reality settled in. Once again, they were outnumbered and outgunned.

He watched as the line of German armour continued to roll steadily forwards, slow but relentless. Through the binoculars, Archer could see the turrets turning with the barrels rising and dipping as they cleared the haze. Black crosses gleamed faintly on their hulls, and the light caught the metal like water. Six, maybe eight, Panzers led the advance. Their tracks tore long, dark scars into the sand. Interspersed among them were four armoured cars, travelling perhaps seven to ten yards behind the tanks. Further beyond, blurred by dust and distance, came the half-tracks and trucks, spreading out in a wide arc across the flats. Archer kept the glasses on them a moment longer, counting without meaning to. This wasn't a patrol. It was a push. He felt the weight of it settle, quiet and certain and knew they were about to be hit properly.

The sound reached him first – deep, rhythmic, growing – a vibration that seemed to come up through the earth itself. It built until it was all there was: a low mechanical thunder rolling closer with each passing second. Archer felt it in his chest: a dull pulse keeping time with his heartbeat. The men in the trenches felt it too. No one spoke. They just watched the horizon and waited.

Archer lowered his binoculars and made his way back to his trench, where Lockett leant against the wall with his rifle held firmly in his hands, and his head low. The lieutenant dropped beside him, dust sliding from his sleeves, and raised the glasses again to monitor the German advance. They were eight hundred yards out and closing steadily.

A moment later, a dull thump sounded somewhere out in the haze, followed by the rising shriek of descent. The first mortar shell landed short, throwing up a plume of sand fifty yards ahead of the line. Another followed. Closer this time. The blast scattered grit across helmets and webbing. The air was alive with the hiss of falling sand, but still Archer held his ground.

The barrage was light, probing rather than punishing. Archer knew it for what it was: just enough to keep their heads down while the Germans made up the ground. He turned to Lockett, voice level despite the blasts.

"Keep your head down! I'll be back!

He raised his binoculars once more. Through the drifting smoke, he could still see them: the Panzers pressing on, steady, patient, methodical, and unshaken by their own fire. Then, in one movement, he was up and out of the trench, running at a crouch towards the northernmost gun.

Lockett was neither bemused nor surprised by Archer's actions, but he still called after his lieutenant, "Sir, I'm not sure this is the time for a stroll!"

Archer paused as a cluster of mortars landed fifty yards to his right, the blasts sending a wall of sand across the line. Pausing to raise his glasses, he peered through the haze. The tanks were nearer now. Their outlines were clear, and the silhouettes of commanders were visible atop the turrets. Sunlight caught on the metal of the tanks, throwing shifting shadows across the sand.

Archer's voice came clear and sharp, deliberately so, to steady his men. "Steady, lads! Hold your fire!" he shouted, the words torn from him against the noise. "Let them come on! Riflemen, concentrate your fire on the infantry!"

This was not Archer's first encounter with armour, and he knew well the terror they inspired. No matter how deep men dug, those machines were killers.

He turned again to his glasses.
The tanks were nearer now.
Their menace was clear.

The gleam of vision slits and gun barrels was visible through the shifting haze. Their paint was still the dark grey of Europe, only slightly dulled by sand and dust. Rommel had thrown them into battle as soon as they'd rolled off the docks, and now they were coming on in deliberate waves. Confident, composed, certain of victory, and driving straight for Archer and his men.

Archer judged the range: six hundred yards, maybe less. The familiar calm settled over him, the same steady calm that always came before a fight. He lowered the glasses and slipped them back into his satchel. Then he unslung his rifle, giving the sights a quick puff of breath. It was more from habit than need. Turning towards the northernmost gun, Archer jogged low along the line, the heat pressing through his sleeves and sand slipping beneath his boots. Ahead, the northernmost gun sat half-buried in its pit. The crew were crouched behind the shield, faces grey with dust. He dropped beside them, breath shallow, eyes fixed on the approaching armour.
"Five hundred yards!" he shouted. "Steady... Fire!"

The 2-pounder fired with a crack that split the air. The blast punched at Archer's chest, and the recoil threw a spray of sand from the pit wall as the barrel slammed back against its slide. Smoke and dust belched forwards, curling over the gun crew in choking swirls.

The corporal in charge of the gun shouted in frustration, "Short! Fifty yards!"

In the distance, Archer heard the other guns fire. It was so close together that their reports merged into one shattering roar.

The loader on the northernmost gun had already fed a fresh brass-cased shell into the breech and was reaching for another from the ammunition box. The spent case from the first shot clattered at their feet, its brass still hot and smoking.

Kneeling and peering hard through the telescopic sight, the gun-layer adjusted the barrel with the traverse wheels and checked elevation once more. He brought the crosshairs square onto the coupler of the lead Panzer which was now about four hundred and fifty yards off, slightly to his right. "Fire!"

Again, the gun sprang into its brutal rhythm-recoil: dust, smoke, flash, bang.

There was a brief pause to see if they'd struck home. The corporal watched as the solid shot slammed into the side of the Panzer's turret, and a bright flash and shower of sparks burst from the armour.

"Hit! Reload!" he barked, his voice rasping but controlled. "Same target!"

The new round slid home with a heavy metallic click.

"On!" the gun-layer called. "Fire!"

The gun roared again. The recoil thudded through the pit, and the smell of thick, bitter cordite lingered. Across the line, the other guns joined in, creating a ragged volley rolling out across the desert. "Hit! Next target. Second tank. Left, five hundred yards!" The fight had begun.

For a few seconds, there was only the noise of the British guns, the harsh rhythm of the 2-pounders, the sharper cracks of rifles and the staccato rattle of the Brens along the line. The thunder of echo and recoil rolled across the line. Then, out in the haze, a different sound took hold. A deeper, heavier beat that made the ground tremble. The Panzers answered.

A flash flared through the smoke and a shell struck short, throwing up a geyser of sand and stone that fell like rain across Archer's position. A second followed. Then another. Each one was walking closer after each impact until one burst near enough to lift him from his feet and hurl him through the air. He hit the ground hard. His ears rang. He struggled for breath. The blast had blown the air from his lungs. The world shrank to darkness, then light, dust and the hammering thud of his own heartbeat.

“Lieutenant!” came the cry. Jacks was already sprinting towards him, shouting for the others to stay down and keep firing. He waved at the nearest men as he passed, but they needed no instruction. Bolts clicked and rifles cracked as fast as hands could work them.

Jacks dropped beside Archer who was shaking his head and spitting grit from a dry mouth.

“Jesus Christ,” Archer muttered, half to himself, brushing sand from his sleeves.

“For fuck’s sake, Sir!” Jacks snapped. “You were just standing there asking for it! I thought I’d taught you better than that!”

Archer’s wide eyes met his through the dust. A grim smile crept across his sand-covered face.

“What the hell are you doing here? Get back to your position!”

He watched Jacks tear himself away. He knew Jacks had come out of admiration. A sign of loyalty more than recklessness, but Archer was furious with himself. Jacks was right, he’d been standing there in the open, asking for it. The anger that should have been directed inwards spilt outwards instead and had landed on Jacks.

The air around them filled with the roar of engines and the shriek of incoming fire. Fifty-millimetre, high-explosive rounds slammed into the earth and among the rifle pits, turning sandbags and men into clouds of flesh, bone, and grit. Further down the line, one of the 2-pounders took a direct hit on its shield. The metal buckled, splintering inwards, and one man vanished beneath a sheet of flying sand. The rest of the crew were torn apart where they stood and what remained fell back into the pit, silent and still.

Tracer rounds streaked across the front, and red threads cut through the smoke. The armoured cars had joined in, their 20mm cannon swept the line in long, vicious bursts. Earth and stone erupted. Fragments of kit and shattered tins spun through the air, and spent cases leapt like sparks from the impacts. One gunner was struck in the shoulder; another man fell back clutching his leg, and his uniform was torn and blood pooled dark in the dust. The other two gunners dragged the wounded clear and had the weapon back in action within seconds.

As he ran back towards his pit, he roared, "Keep firing!" Archer's voice was raw in the chaos. "Keep them back!"

He dropped into his trench where Lockett was firing between bursts of shellfire, ducking as debris rained down.

"Get to Sedgewick!" Archer shouted over the din. "Tell him we need whatever he's got in mortars or artillery on Grid EP 410 370." He tore a page from his notebook. He'd written the grid reference earlier and now thrust it into Lockett's hand. The runner's job was simple but deadly: carry messages between platoon and company.

Lockett swallowed hard, gave Archer a single nod, then was out of the hole and running. Bullets whipped past, and the ground spat up around his boots, but he kept going. A lone figure darting through smoke and fire.

The central gun was answering the German onslaught. Its shots cut low and hard, and the recoil rocked the pit. The loader was caked in dust, half-deaf from the concussion, but still working the breech, feeding rounds as fast as he could.

"Range three hundred!" the gun commander yelled.

With one eye to the sight, crosshairs tracked the advancing tank. "On! Fire!"

The gun barked again. The flash swallowed in the rising smoke. A Panzer's track blew apart, sand and steel flinging wide but the tank kept coming, limping forwards with one side dragging. Its turret swung towards the British line.

Archer saw the muzzle flash and threw himself down as the return shot tore into the trench ahead of him. The explosion showered the position with dust and fragments. He rolled, coughing. Though his vision was blurred, he caught sight of Evans standing up in the trench that had just taken the near hit.

"Close but no coconut, you bastards!" Evans yelled.

Archer couldn't help but laugh. "That's tellin' 'em, Evans. Get stuck in!" he shouted back.

He took a quick look around. Only now did he realise how heavy the pounding had become from the Panzers' guns. Yet he could also see they were slowing. Although they were small and firing only solid shot, the 2-pounders were having an effect on the enemy armour. The crews were well-drilled with ammunition close to hand, and each gun selecting targets, re-aiming, loading and firing in under ten seconds. Six rounds a minute. It was an astonishing rate under such fire.

Across the flats, Archer counted the rising plumes of black smoke, singular columns billowing into the bright blue, cloudless sky. One, two, three... four. Two Panzers and two armoured cars lay burning.

A Bren opened up somewhere off to his right, its stuttering burst cutting through the thunder of the guns. Archer saw the tracers reach out across the flats. They were faint sparks at first; then they became brighter, whipping low over the sand. One of the enemy trucks slewed as a tyre blew, and the vehicle lurched sideways before coming to a halt in a spray of dust. A moment later, it's load of men were clambering out the side and dashing away from the vehicle as it attracted the fire of the Bren.

Another Bren joined in from further down the line, the rhythm of its fire harsh and steady. Archer couldn't see the gunners through the smoke, only the ripple of their tracers and the dull shapes of enemy vehicles jerking to a stop. Webb's shout carried on the wind, half a laugh, half a yell of triumph. Then it was lost beneath the rising roar of the Panzers' guns.

As a shell burst close by, Archer ducked, and the shockwave hammered the trench and filled the air with dust. The centre gun fired again. There was a flat crack that tore through the chaos, and Archer's head snapped up just in time to see the hit. Sparks leapt from a Panzer's side as the round glanced off. The next moment, the tank's return shot came in, low and fast, striking near the gun pit.

The explosion threw sand and men skywards. When it cleared, the gun still stood but the crew did not.

Archer was moving before he'd thought. He vaulted from the trench and dropped into the shattered pit, boots slipping in loose sand and cordite dust. The air was thick with smoke and the acrid tang of explosives. He landed hard, stumbled, and felt his stomach tighten.

The 2-pounder stood where it had fired, blackened but still upright, and the barrel was slick with soot. Archer looked around for the men. One man was simply gone, the blast had taken him completely, leaving only a scorched smear and the twisted wreck of his helmet remained. The other man lay against the cuttings wall, face grey, and eyes wide and wild. His right arm was missing below the elbow, and the sleeve was burnt away to blooded ribbons. The right leg was gone entirely, torn off at the thigh.

He was moaning. It was a sound more animal than human, shallow and rasping. Blood pooled thick beneath him, dark against the sand. Archer froze for a moment, staring at the man. Then he forced himself on.

"Christ Almighty," Jacks breathed, dropping in beside Archer. His voice cracked. "Ok mate. You're ok, mate." It was far from the truth, but Jacks kept talking as if saying it might somehow make it so. t. He turned, shouting over his shoulder. "Bill! Bill Hale! Get over here, now!"

A moment later, Private Hale slid down into the pit, his face white as chalk. A broad-shouldered lad from London, he'd done a few weeks of first aid before arriving in the desert. It was enough to patch wounds and hold a man together long enough for a stretcher but not enough for this. His hands trembled as he fumbled for the field dressing in his pouch.

“Hold him, Sarge,” he stuttered, tying a dressing around the top of the man’s arm, trying to stem the flow.

Archer knelt on the other side, already pressing down on the stump where the leg had been. The warmth pulsed through his palms, hot and slick. The man gasped. His mouth opened and closed as if trying to form words, but only a faint hiss came. Archer leant in, tightening his grip, forcing steadiness into his voice. “It’s alright. It’s alright. Bill here’s got you.”

Hale grabbed a rifle sling and looped it high around what was left of the thigh. He jammed a jagged splinter of wood beneath it and began twisting, using it as a lever until the blood slowed, then stopped.

For a heartbeat, it seemed to work. The gunners moaning eased. The man’s breathing steadied, then faltered again. All sense of the horror around him seemed to fall away as Archer stared down at him. His eyes rolled, and then turned glassy, unseeing.

Hale sat back on his heels, hands shaking, the dressing soaked red through. “I... I can’t stop it, Sir.”

Archer exhaled, slow and hollow. “You’ve done what you can.”

He reached across and rested his bloodied hand on the dying man’s head as the last breath slipped away. For a moment, he stayed there, and then his hand moved, fingers finding the string at the man’s neck. He pulled the tags free, the metal slick with blood.

Archer glanced down at them, reading by instinct more than sight.

“...T Ridley,” he said quietly. “Rest easy now.” The name hung there a moment, before the world began to press back in. Outside, the guns thundered on.

Slowly, Archer wiped his hands on his trousers, smearing the dark blood across the khaki cloth. The gun stood silent. Its barrel was faintly smoking, and the smell of burnt oil loitered thick in the air. He looked at Jacks who met his gaze with eyes that were red from the dust and what they'd just seen.

"Hale, back to your post. We're not done," Archer said quietly.

Jacks nodded once, jaw set, and dragged an ammunition box closer. "Aye, Sir."

Archer stepped over the fallen loader and reached for the traversing gear. The left-hand wheel, used to swing the barrel, was half jammed with grit. He yanked it free, lifting it clear to get to the gunner's seat. Dropping into position, he took hold of the two control wheels – one for traverse, one for elevation – their grips were smooth and shiny, long since stripped of paint after years of use.

He turned the traverse wheel first, dragging the barrel back onto target, and felt the resistance through his palms as the gears bit. With his boot rested on the ground, he started bouncing his knee as he concentrated on bringing the gun to bare on the nearest Panzer. The elevation wheel moved more freely; he wound it sharply, lifting the muzzle a fraction until the target came into the narrow slit of the sight.

"Load!" he shouted.

Jacks rammed a fresh round into the breech, the brass casing ringing as it seated home.

Archer steadied his hand on the firing lever, breath held against the taste of dust and smoke. He leant into the sight. The glass was smeared with grit, and he closed one eye to find the crosshair. Through the shimmer, he caught the Panzer's low, angular shape, crawling forwards with its turret half-turned.

He wound the elevation wheel a fraction. The reticle lifted until it rested square on the Panzer's thin plate beneath the turret ring. Archer was trying to lead the sight to allow for the travel of the shell.

The heat wavered.

The image swam.

Then it settled.

Archer's fingers tightened. For a heartbeat, he felt the world shrink to the faint black cross in the sight, and the pale blur of German armour behind it. He pulled the lever.

The gun cracked like thunder, and the recoil smashed back against its trail. Dust rose, filling the pit in a choking cloud. Archer's whole body jarred from the shock. His ears rung, and the air grew thick with the bitter sting of burnt propellant. Through the haze, he caught the flash of the impact. The shot skimmed high across the Panzer's hull, ricocheting in a shower of sparks.

"Shit!" was all he managed.

"Loaded, Sir!" Jacks was already ramming another round home, the brass casing gleaming dull in the light.

Archer twisted the traverse wheel by degrees: steady and deliberate, and then he eased the elevation down a fraction. The target had crept closer, and its turret was now swinging towards them. "Loaded!" Jacks shouted.

Archer leant into the sight. He focused on shortening his breath to relax into the moment, the crosshair settling on the seam beneath the turret ring. He squeezed the lever.

The gun thumped heavier this time, and the trail bit deep into the sand. Smoke cleared enough for him to see the shell hit true. The Panzer shuddered and halted.

"Loaded!" came the cry again.

Knowing the tank had stopped, Archer only needed a slight correction and almost immediately sent another shell that struck the side of the machine. Then flame, smoke and fire burst from the open hatches as the crew scrambled clear.

Jacks gave a sharp cheer. His voice was raw as the cheer was quickly followed by, "Loaded!"

Archer didn't look away. Lifting his eye from the sight, he took in the deadly panorama, searching for another target. He spun the traverse wheel fast, swinging the barrel to the right.

There. A half-track, no more than a hundred and fifty yards out, racing across their front. Its machine-gun hammered a stream of fire.

He dropped back to the sight, pressing his eye tight against the glass. The vehicle was moving hard, jolting through the sand. Trying to match its speed, he wound the traverse and nudged the elevation by instinct.

"On," he muttered under his breath and pulled the lever.

The gun thundered.

The shot kicked dust into the pit.

The round went wide.

"Again!" he shouted.

"Loaded!" Jacks was already there, slamming in another.

The gun fired.

Then again.

Each recoil jarred through his body.

Each shot walked a little closer.

The fourth round struck home, punching into the half-track's engine block. The impact stopped it dead, the rear lifting as sand and smoke burst from beneath.

Once more, Archer pulled the lever. This time, the solid shot smashed through the armoured visor, and the protective screen folded over what had once been its windscreen and tore through the cab.

Archer held the sight a moment longer. The half-track's wreck stood motionless in the distance. He eased back from the breech. All around, the air was alive with a storm of sand, smoke, and metal. The rest of the platoon was firing flat-out now.

To his left, Pritchard's rifle cracked again and again: the steady rhythm of a man who knew his mark. Each shot carried through the haze, sharp and calculated, the sound cutting through the heavier thunder of the guns. Archer caught the faint flash from his trench: a quick flare before it was gone, and he watched as the silhouettes of his section moved in unison, feeding ammunition, calling ranges, and firing by turn. Somewhere beyond them, a Bren chattered short, controlled bursts that raked the German infantry as they tried to fan out behind the armour.

"Pritchard's section's still holding!" Jacks shouted, half-hearing the sound.

Archer nodded, eyes scanning the smoke-wreathed line. A few figures moved between the trenches – mainly the section commanders who were desperately trying to direct their men's fire. The smell of oil, blood, and cordite was everywhere.

Suddenly, another explosion rocked the northernmost end. Archer glimpsed Webb's Bren was firing from a shallow scrape, Carter alongside him, feeding the magazines. The chatter of their gun mingled with shouted orders, and the deep pulse of the Panzers that continued to press closer.

Archer turned back to his sight, his next target already looming through the dust. "Load!" he snapped.

Jacks was there. He was silent as the round slid home with a metallic click. Easing the traverse wheel to the right, slow and deliberate, Archer tracked the lorry as it rattled through the haze. "Fire!"

The gun roared once more, and the recoil jolted through the pit, lifting sand and smoke in a blinding haze. When it cleared, the truck was still moving - the solid shot had only scored a deep groove along its wooden sideboards.

Archer rose from the gunner's seat, peering over the steel shield. His eyes swept the desert, the air thick with drifting dust and smoke. Shapes still moved out there. They were faint and only broken by distance and the shimmer of heat, but the rhythm was different.

Through the swirling haze, he saw the Panzers turning, their turrets still scanning and firing, but their advance slowing. One after another, they began to pull back. The sound of their engines was deep and uneven. Some limped, dragging their broken tracks. Others trailed thick columns of smoke that hung low and black across the flats.

The armoured cars followed, reversing in jerks. Their 20mm cannon still spit occasional bursts that snapped across the line without conviction. A few scattered infantrymen were running back, and their small, dark figures gradually faded into the haze.

For a long moment, Archer stood at the sight, scarcely believing it. The noise was still deafening, but the rhythm had changed. The steady beat of battle was being replaced by the ragged echo of retreat.

He climbed clear of the pit. His boots sank in the churned sand. Around him, the trenches were alive with movement, men shouting for ammunition, for stretchers, for water. Smoke drifted low and thick with the smell of cordite, fuel, and blood. He saw Saunders crouch over a wounded man. Webb's section was still firing, but their bursts were slower now, scattered and ragged.

Finally, Webb's voice carried above it all, firm but weary. "Cease fire!"

Archer wiped his brow with the back of his hand and looked to the horizon.

The enemy was gone, for now.

CHAPTER 15

The sun climbed hard and white over the flats, bleaching the world to a glare. The air shimmered with heat, rising in waves from the torn earth and the wreckage that littered it. Nothing moved. The desert was silent now, save for the faint pop and crack of burning metal, and the slow ticking of heat-swollen steel as it cooled.

Blackened against the pale sand, the hulks of two German tanks still burnt on the forwards slope. Every few moments, one would cough a dull explosion from within: a ruptured fuel tank or a shell cooking off. This sent a puff of thick, black smoke twisting into the sky. The smell of it carried across the line: burnt oil, cordite, scorched rubber, and something sharper beneath it. The sickly, unmistakable reek of charred flesh. It hung heavy on the air, clinging to the back of the throat. Empty cartridge cases gleamed like brass beads across the sand. Sandbags lay torn open, spilling their contents into small, uneven drifts. A shattered water can slowly dripped beside a trench, each drop hissing into the hot dust.

Somewhere among the debris, a wounded man called out. His voice was hoarse and thin, and it was answered only by the low rattle of a stretcher being lifted. A breeze stirred, carrying the fine grit that never quite settled, coating faces, lips, and eyes.

Archer stood amid it all. His shirt was stiff with baked sweat and dust; the cloth was marked dark where blood had soaked through. Around him, men were moving again. Slowly and mechanically, they were clearing weapons, fetching water, and counting what was left. Archer watched them for a moment, the motion distant somehow. He wasn't sure yet how many weren't moving. Not yet.

He looked out across the flats. The enemy had gone, leaving wreckage, smoke, and silence. But the horizon to the north was already blurring with dust again.

Archer moved along what was left of the line, his boots crunching over cartridge cases and bloodied field dressings that fluttered where they lay having been discarded. The trenches were half-filled with sand and spent casings. The men were hollow-eyed, and their faces were blackened and drawn. Someone was brewing tea on a battered petrol tin, and the faint sound of it felt unreal amid the ruin. The lieutenant watched it for a moment, unsure whether it was habit or something else – a small, stubborn act against what had just happened.

He counted the fallen without meaning to: one here, two there. Each of them were in the process of being covered with a blanket or groundsheet. Most lay where they'd fallen, half-buried by the blast. Jacks moved among them with a notebook, writing down names when he could, initials when he could not.

The company had been hit hard. Nearly a third were gone, and out of the rest of them, too many were bandaged, limping, or staring blankly into the distance, the shock of it settling in now the noise had fallen away. The 2-pounder they'd fought from was silent now, its barrel still.

Lockett came up the line, sweat and dust streaking his face with his rifle in his hand. He stopped beside Archer, shaking his head.

"Under the circumstances, Sir, we had it easy," he said quietly. "Most of the tank fire went straight into the centre. Company HQ caught the worst of it."

Archer turned to him, eyes narrowing against the glare. "Casualties?"

"Bad," Lockett replied, voice rough. "You know Second Lieutenant Riley's gone. CSM Rudge with him. Took the Boys rifles forwards to have a crack at one of the tanks, and the armoured cars. Never got close enough. They reckon he was blown to pieces by a high explosive shell."

He hesitated, glancing down. "The mortar group they'd put together, that's gone too. Their pit took a direct hit in the first bombardment. Nothing left but twisted tubes."

Archer looked past him, over the trenches and out to where the sand had been torn open by shellfire. Smoke still drifted in slow, dark ribbons from the centre of the line where the company command post had been. "Captain Sedgewick?"

"He's alright, Sir. Says you're to prepare for another assault. He'll be up to see you soon."

Archer said nothing for a moment, only nodded once. "All right, Lockett. Well done. Go check on your mates. Then see about a brew, will you?" he said quietly.

Lockett moved off, slinging his rifle and calling softly to one of the stretcher-bearers – a mate of his from one of the sections - as he went. Archer watched him go and then turned back toward the line.

Limping slightly, Jacks was making his way along the trench. His face was streaked black with smoke. His helmet was gone. His shirt was torn at the shoulder, and his webbing belt hung loose. He paused beside Archer and gave a nod. "Sir."

Before he could speak, Archer exhaled. "The centre took the brunt. Riley and Rudge are gone. Mortar pit's finished."

Jacks grunted, rubbing the back of his neck. "Aye. That explains the mortars."

He paused, then added more quietly, "Riley... decent sort. Bloody waste."

"They're all a waste, Jacks." Archer's tone was almost reflective.

For a moment neither spoke. The silence settled between them, heavy and close. Their gaze drifted across the ground: the scattered kit, the still shapes, the thin smoke rising where the wrecks burnt. The constant sound of flies buzzed faintly around them and blended with the distant hiss and crackle of the burning wrecks.

Jacks shifted his weight. "We came off better than most, I guess. Lost one gun crew. One badly beaten up. Two still fit for duty. I've put them on the centre gun. The gun to the south's wrecked, so we're down to two. They've twenty rounds each, and another thirty in their wagons. Plus whatever they can scrounge from the third."

Archer nodded slowly. His eyes followed the wavering smoke across the flats. "And the platoon?"

Jacks exhaled through his teeth. "Could've been worse. Beckett, Donnelly, and Wilkes didn't make it. Skinner caught some shrapnel, but he'll live. Groves took a nasty knock to the leg. Hale's patched him up and sending him back to Battalion. Not sure that's any better for him, but he's too hurt to keep round here. Joyce's got a crease across his scalp. It's deep, but he wants to stick around. Says Hale can stitch him."

Archer didn't speak for a moment. The names hung between them. Each one was a face he could still picture in the half-light of the trenches.

"Three gone," he said quietly. "Three more wounded. Not bad, considering what we took."

"Not bad," Jacks echoed, though his tone carried no conviction. "Doesn't feel that way when you see the stretchers go past."

The two men continued to stand in their own silence while the air hummed with heat around them. Flies were everywhere now, clinging to sweat, eyes, and lips. From somewhere down the line came the scrape of a shovel biting into sand. Men were already digging to improve what little cover they had.

Archer drew a slow breath. "See to the lads, Jacks. Water, rest, whatever we've got left. We've orders to prepare for another assault." He paused, then added, with a faint attempt at levity,

"And get yourself a helmet. It's not right to be turned out improper."

Jacks gave a tired grin, slinging his rifle over his shoulder "Aye, Sir."

The heat had slackened only slightly. The air still hung thick with grit and the sour taint of cordite. Archer had returned and was sat low in the trench, his back against the wall, mug cradled in both hands, Lockett had passed the tin cup the moment he was seated. The tea was strong and half-gritted with sand, but it did its job.

Across from him, Lockett crouched over the Benghazi burner, coaxing the last of the flame to lick the blackened tin. The faint hiss of it filled the heavy silence between them. The only other sounds were the scrape of shovels farther down the line and the dull, constant buzz of flies. A few men were asleep where they sat with their heads slumped forwards, and their rifles across their laps.

Archer took a slow sip. The tea scalded his tongue, but he didn't mind. He stared over the lip of the trench at the baked horizon. The heat-haze made the wrecked armour to their front shimmer as though it were still alive. He turned back and saw Lockett staring aimlessly into his white enamel mug.

"You know, I'm not so sure I'll ever get used to losing lads, Sir," Lockett muttered.

Archer gave a weary smile. "I hope not, Lockett. If we ever do, it'll mean we've lost something of ourselves."

The words were meant honestly. Yet even as he spoke them, Archer felt that familiar unease rise again. The way he took news of a man's death with quiet acceptance, almost by habit. He knew it was the price of war, but the thought of becoming remorseless about it always sat heavy in his mind.

Lockett's forehead was wet with sweat. He wiped a forearm across his brow and glanced at Archer while offering him a cigarette. "Jacks says we're down to what, two serviceable guns now?"

Taking the short, stumpy tube of tobacco, Archer replied, "Yes. Two still firing."

They drank in silence for a while. A distant hammering came from where Evans and Pritchard were rebuilding a slit trench, and the normality of their quiet curses carried faintly on the wind.

Before any conversation could continue, a voice called along the line, asking for the whereabouts of Lieutenant Archer.

Archer rose to his feet. "Over here, Sir."

Sedgewick's figure appeared moments later. His uniform was streaked with dust, his collar was open, and his face was drawn with fatigue. Carrying his map case under one arm, he paused to steady himself on the trench lip before dropping down beside Lockett and Archer. Checking his watch, he started.

"Morning, Archer," he said, voice low and hoarse. "You look as if you've been here a lifetime."

"Feels that way, Sir. We were just taking a brew. Can I offer you one?"

Lockett was already there with a mug of warm tea held out to the captain.

"Thank you." Turning to observe the carnage to their front, he added, "You look like you did your bit here."

"The gunners were outstanding, Sir. Their rate of fire made the difference."

Sedgewick took a breath, handed the now empty mug back to Lockett, and motioned for Archer to climb out of the trench and follow him. Moments later, the two men stood facing each other, and the captain rubbed his chin before he began.

"I've just come from Battalion HQ. Bad business. Major Markham's gone."

Archer straightened slightly. "Gone, Sir?"

Sedgewick nodded. "Mortar landed right among him and the mortar team. Killed them all outright, destroyed our tubes. He took the blast square on."

The words hung between them. Lockett had stopped tending the burner, straining to catch the officers' conversation from inside the trench.

Archer lowered his gaze to his boots. "Damn shame. He kept things steady."

"He did," Sedgewick said quietly. "He was one of the good ones. Always managed to keep Blackstone calm and effective." He rubbed a hand down his face before continuing. "So, I've been ordered to act as Battalion second-in-command until they can send someone up from brigade."

Archer said nothing at first, watching the wind lift a small wave of sand over the trench lip. "Coming up from brigade... that'll be no time soon. Christ, we won't hold long enough to..." He stopped himself, then asked, "Who's taking the company?"

"D Company's been mauled, Tom. Captain Denholm's wounded," Sedgewick said.

Archer felt the news hit harder than he expected. Although he had not known him well, Denholm, the battalion's quiet intelligence officer, had always been polite and quietly supportive since Archer's arrival in the desert.

Sedgewick met Archer's eye. "So, I'll need you to take on D Company from me, Tom."

Archer's gaze held on Sedgewick.

Sedgewick looked towards the shimmering line of wrecks. "The enemy's quiet for now, but that won't last. We hold this ground until someone tells us otherwise. I'm not convinced reinforcements will come."

He took a breath, then added, "I'll be with Battalion HQ from here on. Get yourself to the Company HQ and take charge from there. With the death of Rudge, I would have had Jacks as

CSM, but you'll need him to take one platoon for now. Speak to McBain. See if he can spare Sergeant Anderson if you need to."

Archer nodded. "Understood, Sir. I'll do my best."

"Keep your head. I know you'll be alright with the company." Sedgewick's voice was steady and sincere.

He outstretched his hand, and after a firm shake, he turned away, dust trailing from his boots as he headed toward Battalion HQ.

Archer watched him go, then turned back to Lockett. "Grab your gear. We're heading to company HQ." He paused for a moment before calling out with a bellow, "Jacks! Jacks, on me!"

Lockett was already packed, rifle slung to his shoulder and ready to move by the time Jacks arrived.

"Yes, Sir?" Jacks' voice was inquisitive.

"Jacks, Sedgewick's been bumped up. He wants me to take on the company which means you're taking the platoon."

Jacks' face screwed a little, but his focus never wavered.

"Brief the men. Then meet me at Company HQ with the other platoon commanders. Lockett, find Mr McBain and Kingsley and tell them to join me there."

The walk to Company HQ took Archer across a shallow dip where sand had half-filled the trenches. Men were still digging, shoring up collapsed sections with ammunition boxes and broken timbers. The air was heavy with the smell of oil and burned paint, and each gust carried fine dust that stung the eyes.

Looking ahead, Archer could make out the squat, sun-bleached Italian blockhouse; its concrete was cracked and scabbed with bullet scars. The roof had taken a direct hit; one corner sagged, and the reinforcing rods twisted out like ribs. The front wall was peppered with the marks of solid shot, and the whitewash had flaked away in rough circles where tank rounds had struck and spalled across the surface. A section of the wall had been blown open where a high explosive shell had landed, and the edges were blackened and still crumbling.

Through these gaps, Archer could see the ruin inside the building. There was a tangle of splintered crates and twisted metal, and torn webbing and clothing scattered across the floor. The blast had ripped through the centre of the room, shearing a supporting beam clean in two. He could just make out a field table lying on its side with its legs shattered; cups and papers seemed to be fused together under a crust of sand and blood. The air carried the stench of blood and flesh.

A Bren carrier sat half-buried behind the ruins, one of its tracks shattered and spread along the length of the twisted frame. The gunner's seat was gone as was most of the vehicle's innards. Empty cases lay everywhere, scattered in the sand like brass pebbles. Two men crouched nearby, bandaging a third who sat propped against the wall. His eyes were half-closed and dried blood had stiffened his uniform.

Lockett slowed as he advanced towards the lieutenant, glancing about in silence. Archer and Lockett both took in the scene without a word. The blockhouse was in the heart of the company line, and its prominence meant it had taken the brunt of everything thrown at them.

Slowly, Archer stepped through the shattered opening, ducking beneath the hanging beam. Inside, the air was heavy and close: thick with dust and the familiar sour smell of battle. The blast had torn through everything. A dead telephone lay half-buried under sand, and its cord snaked towards the corner where a small table was now no more than kindling. The only sign of the men that had been in there were dark stains across the floors and wall. The odd piece of shredded uniform and fragments of kit scattered across the room.

Across one surviving section of wall, there were scrawled grid references with streaked letters that had been half-erased by smoke. Beneath it, a twisted steel helmet lay upside down, its liner stained in fresh blood.

He paused a moment, drawing a breath, and then he stepped back from the shattered doorway.

"Lockett, find us a trench outside. I won't be putting anyone in here. It'll only draw fire again."

Lockett gave a short nod and left the ruins without a word.

Moments later, the first of the platoon commanders arrived. Archer met him with a tired grin and an extended hand. McBain's helmet was pushed back, his face lined with fatigue and streaked with grime. A thin trickle of blood ran down his left arm, half-dried in the heat. His expression lifted at the small gesture of Archer's hand.

"Tom," McBain said, his voice low with the hint of a tired smile behind it. "Alistair, how are you holding up?"

McBain gave a weary shrug. "2nd Platoon's still on its feet, just. Six killed, four wounded. Ammunition's short, water worse, but the lads are steady."

Archer nodded, a brief flicker of respect in his eyes. "Six? Christ. We lost three dead and three wounded."

Just then Kingsley arrived, still managing to look the immaculate officer despite the dust and grime. Even with a few tears and holes in his shirt, he was buttoned up and squared away.

"Shame about Riley," he said quietly. "He had the makings of a fine officer." There was a genuine sorrow in his expression.

"It is," Archer replied. "How's 3rd Platoon?"

Kingsley exhaled through his nose before answering. "Rough, I'm afraid. We caught it early on when the Panzers opened up. The first volley tore right through our forwards trenches. Sergeant Cooper and two others were gone before we knew it. We put up a lot of fire with rifles until one of the Brens jammed solid."

He paused, brushing dust from his sleeve almost absently. "We managed to knock out one armoured car with a Boys, but it cost us half a section. Corporal Welling among them. The 2-pounders did an excellent job once they got the range, but all told eight dead, two wounded; one of the wounded won't see the day out."

There was a short silence between the officers as the losses sank in. Kingsley continued. "We're digging deeper, but ammunition's down to half and the men... they're steady enough, though. Just concerned if we've got to face another assault by armour."

Archer gave a small nod, his voice even. "You did well to hold them, Phillip. Make sure the lads get water and what shade they can."

"Okay, here's the situation. Major Markham was killed, so Sedgewick has gone up to battalion to act as second-in-command. I am taking on D Company. Sergeant Jacks will take charge of one platoon for the time being." Archer let that sink in, then continued. "We were thin. Now, with the losses, we are even thinner. We still have two of the 2-pounders in action. They've got about thirty rounds each, so enough for another assault. I don't think they'll split their force this time. If it were me, I'd expect a single thrust at one point. The question is where."

Archer took a moment. His gaze swept the burning wrecks to the front of their position. He fixed them both with a stern look. "Right. I'm going to pull one 2-pounder in from a platoon's position on the flank and place it here in the centre. That will weaken the flank, but it will give better support to our right."

McBain frowned, shifting his weight. "If they swing wide again, won't the flank be open?"

Archer gave a slow nod. "It won't be as strong, but if they do swing fully to the left, we can offer support from the centre. If they come a little further north though, we'll have nothing on our front that can help."

Kingsley glanced towards the southern sector. "It's a risk, but I reckon you're right on this, Tom."

"Now. chaps. It's been a rough one, but you've all done well. Let's keep it up, keep the lads sharp." Archer took a breath, "Back to your positions. Lockett!"

Archer moved away from the ruins of the blockhouse, stepping down into a shallow. The ground was churned and pitted. Slit trenches zigzagged through the sand, half-collapsed from shellfire. Broken rifles, ration tins and the blackened frames of water cans lay scattered where men had dived for cover. The air was thick with grit and the sharp tang of burnt powder, a dry heat that clung to the throat and stung the eyes.

He stopped beside a trench where two riflemen were crouched. One was working the bolt of his Lee-Enfield where sand scraped in the action while the other poured a few inches of brown water from a canteen cap into his hand to wash the grit from his eyes. They looked up as Archer approached.

"All right, lads," he said quietly. "How you holding?"

"Bit light on rounds, Sir," one of them replied. "But we're fine."

Archer nodded. "Make sure you keep that clean," he said, pointing to the soldier's rifle. "I have requested ammunition and water. Hopefully, it be up here soon."

Archer realised he didn't know the two men's names. Reaching into his trouser pocket, he pulled out a crumpled cigarette packet, took one, split it in half, and offered each man a share.

"What are your names?"

"Lance Corporal Compton, Sir!"

"Private Albert, Sir, and thank you!" The man took his half eagerly and struck a light, offering the match to his mate.

"We gave it to 'em good, Sir."

"We did, Corporal," Archer replied quietly. "That we did."

He drew on his cigarette, his thoughts already drifting. The two soldiers, realising the officer's mind was elsewhere, turned back to their work, shifting sand and cleaning their rifles.

Archer walked on, murmuring under his breath, "McBain - ten. HQ - six. Kingsley..." He paused, doing the numbers in his head. "Can't be many more than eighty of us left." The figure sat heavy on him.

As he moved among the men, he saw the weariness etched into every face. He knew that look, knew how far a man could go on sheer will. If eighty was all he had, then eighty would have to do. He would hold with what remained.

A sudden stillness fell over the position: the kind that comes before sound. Then it began: a deep, rolling murmur that grew into a steady, rising thunder. Archer turned west, eyes narrowing on the horizon. The rumble built until it pressed against the air itself. Engines. Several of them, carrying low and fast. "Aircraft," someone shouted.

Archer reached for his satchel and drew out his binoculars. Lifting them to his eyes, he scanned the sky, the glass catching the glare. Against the hard blue, he picked out several dark dashes that were moving fast and steady in formation. At first count, he made it eight, maybe more, were behind.

They came on in a shallow vee. The sun glinted off the wings and fuselage as the faint hum of engines grew to a steady drone that rolled across the desert like distant thunder. As they drew ever closer, he saw the shape more clearly: broad wings, long noses, the glimmer of three propellers turning as one. Tri-motored, he realised, though the type meant nothing to him.

"Bombers," he muttered, lowering the glasses. "Eyeties, by the look of it."

Locket, who had returned with the gun crew, stood a few paces away, shaded his eyes with a hand. "They're coming in low," he said quietly. "Can't be ours."

The drone swelled. It was uneven but heavy, the kind of sound that made the gut tighten before the mind caught up. Archer felt the vibration more than heard it now. It rose through the soles of his boots and through the ground itself.

He steadied the glasses again. The formation had begun to spread. Pairs peeled slightly wide with the lead holding straight and true. Sunlight flashed from their wings as they banked. Then, from the bellies of the lead aircraft, he saw small dark shapes tumble clear. First one. Then several more. Each one dropped lazily before gathering speed in their fall.

"Down!" he shouted. "Take cover!"

The first explosions tore through the stillness: a hard rolling concussion that thumped through the air and into the chest. Dust and sand lifted in thick, rippling clouds as the northern horizon bloomed with orange flashes. The sound followed an instant later: heavy, raw, deafening. Archer's glasses shook in his hands as he crouched behind the lip of a trench, watching the bomb bursts walk their way across the northern sector. "North end's catching it!" Lockett shouted over the din.

Archer lowered the glasses just long enough to wipe grit from his face. Through the haze, he could see the plumes rising, thick, oily columns clawing at the sky. The aircraft were already turning. Their silvered wings banked sharply, climbing away into the sun.

Then came the second sound. Deep, rhythmic, deliberate. Artillery. The first shells landed short and great fountains of sand were thrown up along the northern ridge. Moments later, heavier impacts followed, pounding the same ground the bombers had struck moments before.

Archer's stomach tightened. He turned his view to the distance where he could see the German assault forming up and moving towards the British line, probably a thousand yards out. They were small dark dots, but the dust trail was clear. He swung the glasses back to his own front. Nothing. The horizon was clean. No movement, no dust, no shapes.

Archer steadied the glasses. "They've picked their spot," he muttered. "North side... they want to break us and drive on down the road."

He could see their plan as if he'd drawn it himself: punch through and drive hard. There was a weakness in it. Their flank hung open, and it was ripe for a counter. But it was an opportunity wasted. Without artillery, without armour, all the British could do was to try and hold. No clever out flanking manoeuvre was available to cut their line.

The artillery barrage intensified as the German assault drew closer. Unlike the first attack, they were using the guns to cover their advance. From his position, Archer could see only the tops of the explosions, smoke rising into the brilliant blue sky. He turned again to his front, still nothing. Only silence beneath the roar.

CHAPTER 16

Archer had heard bombardments before, but never like this. The sound didn't just echo. It pressed in, swallowing every other noise until the desert itself seemed to tremble. The thunder of engines, the flat hammer of guns, and above it all, the shriek of metal tearing air. He stood beside McBain on the lip of a shallow rise, binoculars fixed on the plain ahead where the German armour rolled six abreast, staggered in three glittering lines.

Through the haze of dust and smoke, he could see the Panzers moving with ruthless precision, spreading out as they came. From his rise, the vista looked unreal, distant, as if seen from some higher perch: a god's view of men tearing the world apart. The sun caught on the Panzer hulls, sharp and pitiless, turning each tank into a fragment of blazing metal. With every flash, Archer knew it was probably marking another life that was about to end.

He swung the glasses north. There, the full scale of the assault was laid bare. More than fifty tanks made this much greater force than they had faced earlier in the day. Maybe closer to seventy of them, he thought as he reassessed them surging forwards in waves. The first line of Panzers had already punched through the British forwards positions. Their turrets snapped left and right as they fired on the move. Beyond them, came another wave of destruction: half-tracks and gun carriers keeping perfect spacing, and columns of dust rose behind like the wake of ships at sea.

Shell bursts danced among them, and white flashes erupted against the dune horizon, but the rounds were falling short or wide. British gunners were firing blind now. Their positions were smothered by smoke. Archer could just make out the silhouettes of the northern companies, tiny figures moving against a wall of fire, and then even those were lost as the barrage rolled over them. "God help the poor sods in front of that lot," McBain muttered, lowering his field-glasses.

Archer said nothing. He could see what was coming and what it meant. The line ahead was folding. Not from panic, but from sheer weight. Every few seconds, another shell landed among the trenches: a slow, methodical pounding that crept closer with dreadful regularity.

"They can't hold there much longer," Archer said. "If our lot break through, they'll swing round on our rear and be on top of us in minutes."

McBain lowered his glasses and turned towards Archer who was still transfixed, watching the defeat through the binoculars.

"Start getting your platoon ready to pull back. Get word to the other platoons. Drivers to the vehicles. We may have to move fast."

McBain hesitated, glancing again at the rolling tide of armour. "And if we're told to stay?"

"Then we stay," Archer replied quietly. "But I'm pretty sure that won't be an option."

He dropped the glasses, dust clinging to his cheeks, and dirt was ingrained in the corners of his eyes. Sweat had cut pale streaks through the grime. He wiped at his face before bringing the glasses up towards the north where the assault was hitting hardest. He scanned the smoke for what was left of the line. It wasn't crumbling, more bending to the onslaught. No panic, but it cracked and crept as a wall may do once its foundations are gone. Smoke and dust blurred the horizon. Black shapes moved through the gaps where the trenches had been. He knew the northern flank was finished.

He turned sharply to the right, scanning the ground beyond their own position. The land fell away in a shallow curve before it rose again to a low ridge. A faint depression ran between them. It was dry now but deep enough to break the line of sight. It wasn't much, but it was cover. From there, they might still bring the 2-pounders to bear across the road and the open flats beyond.

"That's it," he said under his breath. "That's where we'll make our stand."

He lowered the binoculars and shouted over the din. "McBain! Get the gunners mounted up. We're moving!"

McBain turned, already running for the nearest gun, voice bellowing through the smoke. "Right lads, you heard him! Get the guns moving!"

Engines coughed to life all along the line as Archer broke into a run, shouting over the din.

"Mount up!" he called out to the infantry and gunners. "Get those guns moving! Now!"

He dashed between the trenches, waving men forwards, his voice carrying above the thunder. "Drivers, get your engines started! Section Commanders, count your men!"

Men spilt from slit trenches, holding rifles and kit, helmets knocked askew as they sprinted for the Bedfords. Sand kicked up around their boots, blending with the rising dust of the bombardment.

The gun crews were already at work. Their hands were black with oil and grit. One 2-pounder's barrel was still warm to the touch as its team broke it down, their muscles straining as they swung the carriage up onto the Morris. Chains clattered, bolts slammed home. The sound sharp and metallic against the background roar.

Engines revved, gears grinding. Drivers shouted to each other through the smoke. The clang of steel on steel merged with the churn of tyres and the distant crash of shells walking steadily closer.

Archer turned. His breath was raw in his throat as he scanned for Jacks. The sergeant appeared through the haze, waving the last section forwards towards the waiting trucks.

"That's all of one platoon, Sir!"

"Head to the slight rise," Archer's arm was outstretched, pointing at his chosen position. "Move out!" Archer called back.

Various vehicles began to roll. Moving slowly at first, they quickly picked up speed as the line of vehicles nosed through the desert dust they were spewing.

Still running along the line, Archer spotted Lockett sprinting towards him with his head low, and his breath ragged. Archer caught his arm and pulled him close so the words would carry.

"Get to Battalion HQ. Tell them what we're doing. We're moving to a low-rise south-east of our present line. About seven hundred yards. I'm shifting the guns there to cover any withdrawal to the road. Make sure they understand it's a deliberate move, not a retreat and emphasise that I don't have time to wait for orders."

Archer pulled his map from his satchel, estimating the position before circling it with a stub of pencil. He handed the map to Lockett. "I want that map back."

"Yes, Sir!" Lockett was gone before Archer finished the last word, weaving through the haze towards the battalion position.

Archer turned back to the ridge. The horizon shimmered under the weight of heat and smoke. It wasn't much of a plan, but it was ground they could fight from and right now, that was all that mattered.

The lieutenant took one last look around, realising that he was the last man headed for his carrier. He climbed into the back, and with his head down, he called out to the driver "Let's go!"

The company's vehicles stopped close to the rise in a haze of dust and exhaust. Archer leant out of the cab, shouting to the lead Bedford to slow as they swung into a shallow depression beyond. The ground here was softer: a stretch of pale sand broken by low scrub. Not ideal, but it would do.

Archer leapt from his carrier, and ran up the shallow rise, signalling for the vehicles that were towing the 2 pounders to follow him. "Here!" he called, gesturing with his arm. "Guns along this line."

Engines cut out one by one. Their drone faded into the thunder of war to the north. Men spilt out from the vehicles, rifles slung and shovels and picks in hand. The first strikes of metal hitting into the sand gave off a dull, muffled sound. The surface crust broke easily, and within minutes, the air was full of dust and grit. Their bodies were soaked with sweat as the rising heat made their toil more exhausting.

"Keep it tight!" Jacks shouted, guiding a section of infantry to the left flank. "Dig fast. They'll be on us soon enough."

Archer moved among them. His sleeves were rolled like the rest of the men trying to relieve the heat and he kept his voice low but firm. The men knew their work; slit trenches took shape along the curve of the rises' lip. The sand shifted too easily, falling away in dry sheets. They could cut perhaps a foot before it started to crumble back on itself. The men were forming small shallows rather than a protective trench.

Near the centre, the gun crews wrestled with the first 2-pounder. The barrel was dull under its dusting of sand, and the weapon's small, neat shape seemed at odds with the violence it could deliver. The Morris backed into position with a cough of exhaust, and Sergeant Blake, a, steady man with a half-chewed cigarette between his lips, was already barking orders.

"Unlimber! Get her round. Trail in the sand! Number two, sight's clean?"

"Clean, Sergeant!" came the reply.

"Then get those legs locked, and the shield down. If they show themselves over that ridge, we'll give 'em something to think about."

Archer stepped up beside him, wiping the grit from his face. "How many rounds have you got left, Blake?"

"Seventy-five between the two, Sir. Enough for a proper go at them. Maybe two if we're lucky."

Archer gave a short nod. "Make the first count, then. We'll have company before long."

He paused a moment, watching the gun crew work with swift discipline, each man knowing his job without a word being said. They'd been fearless in the earlier engagement, and once again, they were showing their professionalism.

"You and your lads did fine work this morning, Blake," he said quietly. "The rate of fire was something else. It turned them back, no question."

Blake spat into the sand, eyes narrowing against the glare. "Aye, well, you weren't much of a slouch yourself, Sir, the way you took over that centre gun. You looked like I'd trained you myself."

Archer allowed himself the faintest smile. "Keep it up, Sergeant."

The lieutenant glanced back along the line. Men were still digging hard. Trucks were half-hidden behind the rise, and the scene was alive with purposeful movement. Not panic but preparation. Beyond them, the desert shimmered, and the faint rumble of engines rose again on the wind.

Jacks yelled out pointing through the haze. "Vehicles approaching! Looks like our lot."

Archer turned as a line of Bedfords and a pair of portee lorries appeared through the desert shimmer, moving fast, tarpaulins flapping. The portees caught his eye first. They were lorries that had been stripped of their sides, and each carried a 2-pounder gun bolted to the flatbed so it could be brought into action with ease and speed. Crude, but effective. The barrels jutted over the rear of the flatbed like scaffold tubes, stark against the glare. Dust billowed around their tyres as they bounced across the rise, crews clinging to the rails.

At their head, a Humber utility approached. Its windscreen was scarred with scratches, and the driver was hunched low over the wheel. The little truck was crammed with men and helmets, and rifle barrels jutted from the open sides. Every face was streaked with sweat and sand. The suspension sagged under the weight as it bumped and slewed across the rise, engine labouring in the heat.

"Reinforcements?" McBain asked, squinting against the glare.

"Maybe," Archer replied, already lifting his binoculars. "But we'll know soon enough."

The Humber swung to a stop in a cloud of dust with its engine still running. The passenger door was thrown open before it had settled. Captain Sedgewick climbed out, pulling off his goggles and brushing the grit from his face. His tunic was caked with sand, and his expression was darker still.

Lockett came running past Archer, breathless, head low. "Sir, Captain Sedgewick's not happy," he panted. "Says you've jumped the gun."

Archer gave a short nod as his eyes were fixed on the approaching officer. "I gathered that."

A moment later, Sedgewick reached them. "You've moved without orders, Archer," he snapped, raising his voice over the engine noise.

Archer stepped forwards, sunburnt forearms resting on his ammunition pouches.

"Yes, Sir. The northern flank's wavering. Our own front on the southern end was quiet, doing nothing." He paused, searching for the right words to frame his instinct. My thinking was this, if we'd stayed where we were, the whole battalion would've been boxed in. Moving here gives us room to support a withdrawal, and if the Germans swing south, we can still turn and cover it from this position. A little further east, but still possible."

Sedgewick glanced about him. Men were still digging, the gun crews sweating over their portees, and engines idled behind the rise. He took in the ground. The ridge fell away into a shallow cut and then stretched into an open field of desert. The smoking port of Mersa Brega was visible in the distance.

"Well, Lieutenant, you've guessed the General's mind, then," he said at last, lowering his voice. "Fortescue's ordered a fighting withdrawal. The armour's pulling back east to form a new line. We're to hold here until they're clear."

"How long?" Archer asked.

"Until I tell you otherwise." Sedgewick's tone was firm and still carried irritation although a grudging respect was creeping in. "Your move has saved us time. The ground looks good. You've done well there."

He turned and gestured to the arriving trucks. "The rest of the battalion's forming on your right, stretching towards the coast road." Sedgewick took a long look across the line and then turned back to Archer.

"Here's the situation. The whole Brigade's pulling out eastwards – 3rd Armoured first, then the support group and the artillery. Fortescue's orders are clear: we hold this line until they're clear. We're the last wall between them and the Jerries. The King's Royal Rifle Corps are already falling back from the north. The Essex Yeomanry are limbering up their guns, and the tanks are moving through behind us. Once they're past, we move. 3rd Armoured will then take up a holding position. As a battalion, we'll withdraw company by company. Tom, you'll lead us off, followed by HQ, then B and A Companies. Understood?"

Archer nodded. "Understood, Sir."

Sedgewick gestured towards the smoke drifting across the flats. "Here's what we've got to work with. The two 2-pounders you've got here, the two mounted on portees, and another pair coming up from the divisional anti-tank lot. I'll place that pair to cover the road. The Essex Yeomanry have a troop disengaging now.

They'll set up just behind us with four 25-pounders.

They'll give us some weight although ammunition's short.

I've also borrowed a Vickers section from the Northumberlands. They'll take a post to your north. It's not much, but it'll have to do. I expect Jerry will try to drive along the road and then find a way to turn our flanks once he's through Mersa Brega. We hold long enough for the armour and the others to get clear and fall back on their new line."

He looked Archer straight in the face. "Make every round count. If needs be, expend every round."

Archer hesitated, glancing towards the first of the 3rd Armoured vehicles rumbling down the road, dust billowing in their wake. "And Blackstone, Sir?"

Sedgewick gave a thin smile, the kind that carried more fatigue than humour. "He's moving with 3rd Armoured. Wants to get ahead, see the ground and get a start on the next defensive line."

Archer held his tongue. The words hung between them for a moment, lost in the distant thunder of guns. "The next defensive line?" His tone was incredulous. "What's that mean? We're here!"

Sedgewick adjusted his helmet strap, straightening his shoulders before he narrowed his eyes.

"His job's back there. Ours is down here, or that's the way he sees it."

Heat surged through Archer. Rage flashed in his chest as if his blood were on fire. Sedgewick caught it immediately, and his tone cut in fast.

"Lieutenant, now's not the time. Concentrate on your men and the task in hand."

Archer nodded once, set his jaw tight, and didn't bother to hide his contempt. "Yes, Sir."

"Right, I'll be with Battalion HQ. I've placed it just on the northern side of the road, with A company." Sedgewick held Archer's gaze a moment longer and then turned sharply away. He strode back toward the Humber, shouting for the driver and the other men to get back in the vehicle. Moments later the vehicle jolted into gear and began to bounce across the desert.

Archer watched it go. The sound of the engine faded into the steady background thump of artillery. His anger ebbed and was replaced by the familiar weight of duty pressing in around him. He turned to where Jacks was directing a section of men into position on the crest of the rise.

He turned to call him and stopped.

For a second it didn't register, he was so used to the man's voice somewhere in the noise, keeping order and chivvying the sections along. The space beside Archer where Jacks should have been, felt oddly silent. Then he remembered.

Archer swore under his breath. The company was half in position, men digging, shouting for tools, one of the portees slewing its gun into line. They needed direction, and they needed it now.

He'd always relied on men like Mallory and Jacks. Not to carry the weight but to keep the men steady, to spread orders when there wasn't time to reach every section himself. With Jacks now leading 1st Platoon, that link was gone, and the noise of half a company trying to find its footing pressed hard against him.

He scanned the line again, gauging what needed doing first. The platoon commanders were fine. He had complete confidence in each of them to hold their ground: McBain on the right, Kingsley anchoring the centre, and Jacks driving his platoon into position on the left.

The real concern was getting word around. He could use Lockett, the company runner, but the man would likely be needed between company and battalion. Orders might also need a touch more weight behind them. When Jacks relayed an order, everyone knew it carried Archer's full authority.

He needed that again.

He decided that Sergeant Anderson would serve well.

He was a man with presence and had experience as well as the right sort of tone to carry his word with gravitas.

He caught sight of McBain, helmet askew, waving a group of riflemen towards a stretch of shallow ground.

"Lieutenant McBain!" Archer shouted, striding across. "Where's Kingsley?"

"With 3rd Platoon." McBain's voice carried a quizzical tone, surely Archer knew that?

"Of course. Go get him. Then bring yourself and Sergeant Anderson to me. I'll be with 1st Platoon."

McBain acknowledged his orders with the briefest of salutes and ran in search of Kingsley and Sergeant Anderson.

Archer made his way over to Jacks, stepping around a trench where two men wrestled with pick and shovel inside.

"Jacks," Archer called, keeping his tone level.

Jacks turned, dust on his face, sleeves rolled, expression already asking what next.

"I'm putting Anderson up as Acting Company Sergeant Major," Archer said. "He'll keep the men moving while you hold 1st Platoon together."

Jacks nodded without hesitation. "Good call, Sir. Anderson's solid with a steady head. The lads listen to him. He'll take the load off you."

Archer allowed himself a brief nod. "That's what I'm counting on. And for what it's worth, there's no one else I'd trust with 1st Platoon. You know their ways better than any man here."

A faint smile tugged at Jacks' mouth. "Aye, well, they're a rough lot, but they'll do as they're told."

At that moment, Kingsley, McBain, and Anderson appeared together, each one damp with sweat. The desert heat was still rising fast, and the air hung thick, and sand clung to their skin. It was an irritation they all carried but had long since stopped complaining about.

They gathered by a shallow scrape that a couple of riflemen had hacked into the earth. Each man took a knee, helmets pushed back. McBain offered a half-burnt cigarette to Archer, who took it and placed it to his dry lips before leaning into the blue flame of McBain's brass lighter. The air shimmered between them, and the blue-grey smoke curled from Archer's mouth and twisted in the heat.

"Anderson," Archer began without ceremony. "You'll act as Company Sergeant Major while Jacks takes 1st Platoon." He neither waited for a reply nor wanted one. "You'll stay with me in the centre."

He drew once on the cigarette, exhaled slowly, and continued. "Gents, I don't need to tell you the situation's dire. The Germans have hit hard, and brigade's called for a fighting withdrawal. Along with the rest of the 7th, were the first line of defence while the brigade pulls east."

The mood was solemn. Each man listened in silence as Archer went on.

"Again, we're the extreme left of the new line. Captain Sedgewick's leading the battalion; Colonel Blackstone's falling back with 3rd Armour to form the next position."

He paused deliberately, letting that sink in. Each man needed to draw his own measure of what that meant.

"I want the two portees moved further right. One either side of 2nd Platoon. Anderson, see to it when we're done here." The sergeant nodded once.

Archer took another drag and flicked ash into the sand. "They'll likely come straight up the road. The force that hit us this morning was just a probe. This one's heavier. We've got maybe thirty, forty rounds per 2-pounder. Our intention, gentlemen, is to spend every single one before we move."

"I think we've been here before, Sir," Jacks said, his voice a mixture of confidence and resignation. "We have, Sergeant," Archer answered quietly.

He turned to Kingsley and McBain. "We know what it'll take, and we'll do it again. Keep your heads. Keep your men tight, and we'll get through it."

CHAPTER 17

Engines growled along the road, low and constant like a dull mechanical heartbeat that rolled across the desert. It was not one long, unbroken column, but a series of them, each a sign that another element of the brigade had disengaged and was now heading east. Shimmering threads of trucks, carriers, and guns wove through the haze, and dust hung over them like a thick and unbroken veil, softening the shapes until men and machines blurred into one endless smear of movement.

With each new wave of motion, the noise never ceased: gears grinding, and engines straining as steel tracks bit into the hard-packed earth and carved grooves that immediately filled with powder-fine sand. Every few minutes, a dispatch rider tore past with their goggles grey with dust, and scarf whipping behind them as the motorbike's growl rose and faded into the glare.

It was an ordered withdrawal, steady, deliberate but to Archer's eye, it looked like flight. Men were hunched low in the backs of open trucks with their helmets tilted against the sun and faces blank with exhaustion. The great machines that had carried them forwards now crawled back the way they had come, each leaving its own faint trail of defeat.

Above it all, the desert shimmered and pulsed with its deadly heat, a weight that never lifted, pressing down through cloth and skin until it felt as though the sun itself was grinding them into the sand. The air smelt of fuel, hot metal, and as always, there was the faint, bitter tang of cordite carried east on the wind.

Archer sat crossed legged on the edge of a shell scrape Lockett had scratched into the ground. Anderson sat beside him with Lockett sitting in his scrape packing up the brew kit. Both Archer and Anderson watched in silence, sipping sweet tea as the brigade had withdrawn piecemeal. The afternoon sun was high now, flattening every shadow.

Anderson shifted his stance, the brim of his helmet catching the light. "I have to say, it's a sorry state, Sir."

Archer's eyes stayed on the passing line. "No, Sergeant. Believe me, this isn't sorry. I've seen sorry." His voice trailed off as his thoughts flickered back to France.

Archer continued. "Just once, it'd be nice not to be retreating."

He said nothing more, just lifted his cup and stared into the warm liquid as if trying to find the answer there.

"There can't be much more of the brigade to pull out now can there, Sir?" Anderson's tone was more statement than question.

Archer didn't reply. He passed the cup back to Lockett, unfastened his satchel, and reached inside. His fingers brushed the familiar shape of his binoculars, but beside them, he felt the edge of a small frame. He drew it out carefully.

For a long moment, he simply looked. Charlotte, smart in her Wren's uniform with her faint smile, and the soft curve of her fair hair. His thumb traced the glass lightly as he stared into her hazel eyes, and for a heartbeat, the noise and heat fell away. He was back in a quiet West End restaurant with a glass of Scotch in hand, lost in the warmth of her gaze.

Archer was suddenly pulled from the moment, and it collapsed as Sergeant Anderson tapped his shoulder and nodded towards a battered open Morris 1500 weight, the same type the gunners used to haul their 2-pounders. Half the bonnet was missing, exposing one side of the six-cylinder engine. Its panels were streaked with sand that had formed a second skin, baked hard where it mixed with the grease and oil that were smeared across the bodywork. The truck lurched to a halt, the engine coughing in protest. Men jumped down at once. The driver went straight to the hot engine, probably clearing grit from the exposed engine parts, while others moved to the rear with their weapons slung and eyes scanning the horizon. From the cab, one figure stepped down with measured ease.

He was tall and spare. The creases of his lightweight service tunic was darkened by sweat. A worn Sam Browne belt cut diagonally across his chest, its leather dulled by time in the field, and the brass buckle barely catching the harsh light. Archer noticed the red tabs on his collar, almost lost beneath the grime, and for a moment, the man simply stood, taking in the line of scrapes and the weary faces within them.

"Sir, is that the General?" Lockett called, instinctively straightening his uniform and tightening his webbing.

The tall man, accompanied by a Sergeant Major, was already making his way towards them. Archer and Lockett scrambled to their feet, brushing dust from their clothes and immediately coming to attention. General Fortescue waved the salute aside with a small motion.

"Don't stand on ceremony, men. I just wanted to see who's still holding the shop together."

Now closer, Archer saw him clearly. He was a tall, lean figure in his mid-fifties, greying at the temples, and the lines of his face were carved deep by sun and fatigue. There was no polish about him. No hint of headquarters ease. His tunic was stained in grime, the sleeves rolled back on sinewed forearms, and his boots had long since lost their shine. The Sam Browne belt sat comfortably on him: the mark of a man used to its authority rather than one who wore it for show.

His expression was calm, yet his eyes were watchful and steady beneath the brim of his hat. There was authority there, but not the kind that shouted. It was the sort that came from years of hard service, the kind that made men listen without being told. He had the look of someone who had seen it all before and still believed in doing the job.

When he spoke again, his voice carried that quiet rasp of age and experience.

"You're Archer, aren't you? Captain Sedgewick says you're the end of the line. So run me through it, Lieutenant." Fortescue nodded once.

"Sir, we're a bit thin on the ground. D Company's down to eighty-two, all ranks. I have two emplaced 2-pounders and two 2-pounder portees." Archer's outstretched arm indicated the portees to the right where their crews sat low in position behind the tilts.

"My thought, Sir, is that the Jerries will drive on down the road with only a limited flanking move. I think it'll be a broad assault across the road." Archer paused, half expecting Fortescue to tell him he was mad. The pause went unbroken. The general's face stayed stern; he was taking it in.

"If that's the case, sir," Archer continued, "we can influence the German drive from here. At the least, we'll give them something to think about on their right. If we can make them hesitate, you never know sir we might get them to bugger off!"

The general gave a tight grin but said nothing at first. His gaze moved from Archer to the ground in front of them, and then back again, weighing every word as he absorbed it.

"Lieutenant, that's not a bad assessment. Sedgewick tells me you withdrew early to take up this position."

Archer's stomach tightened; he started to frame his explanation, ready to defend the decision, but Fortescue cut him off with a raised hand.

"Well, that was a wise move, Archer. This rise is the only real high ground worth the name around here. It gives you an excellent field of fire across the road. The only flaw in your plan," he paused, eyes narrowing toward the horizon, "is that I think they'll try to flank us at the same time as they strike up the road."

Fortescue turned back to Archer. His tone was steady, almost encouraging. "What you've done is right. If they do try to flank us, you still hold the best ground available. You'll just have to deal with a frontal assault."

He glanced once more along the battered line, the corners of his mouth tightening into what might have been a smile. "You've done well here, Archer. I'm afraid I can only offer words of encouragement at this stage, not good, but it's all we have."

Before Archer could reply, a low, distant thump rolled across the desert. Another followed. Heavier. Then two more in quick succession. The sound grew. It wasn't sharp like rifle fire, but deep and deliberate, the kind that carried in the chest.

Fortescue's head turned slightly, eyes fixed back on the horizon. "Artillery," he said quietly, almost to himself.

The first rounds fell short of where the two were, and plumes of dust and sand rose in the distance. A moment later, another salvo came in closer. The shriek of shells tore through the air, ending in concussive bursts along the forwards slope. Within seconds, the British line was alive with movement, geysers of sand leaping skywards; flashes punched through the haze, and the dull, rhythmic hammer of the guns rolled across the desert like distant thunder.

Archer felt the ground tremble underfoot. Each impact sent a puff of grit through the trenches, fine dust settling over helmets and rifle bolts. A man sprinted past Archer, head low, making for the nearest scrape as fragments hissed across the surface of the rise.

The barrage wasn't random. The pattern was clear, deliberate, and measured. The road took the worst of it with shells bracketing either side of it before more shells walked outwards along the line. The shorter the British front had become, the more concentrated the fire now seemed, tearing at their positions with increasing precision.

Fortescue watched without flinching. His eyes followed the rhythm of the bursts. "They know where we are," he said at last, his voice steady, almost conversational. "There goes our element of surprise."

Archer managed a thin smile despite the roar of another detonation nearby. "If it's any consolation, Sir, I'm not sure we ever had one."

The general gave a brief, dry chuckle as he witnessed the sergeant major and the men accompanying him rushing around for cover. "Quite so, Lieutenant."

Another shell landed closer still. The blast hurled a sheet of grit over them both. Nearby, men ducked, cursing, helmets rattling under the hail of debris. Fortescue merely stepped aside, calm and deliberate, as if avoiding a puddle on a parade ground.

"Sir," Archer called over the ringing in his ears, "Might I suggest you drop in here with me and Lockett? It'll be a squeeze but probably safer than standing about at present."

Fortescue glanced down at the shallow scrape Archer and his runner were crouched in, then back towards the horizon where the next salvo was already falling. A faint smile touched his face. "I've stood in worse spots, Lieutenant," he said mildly.

Archer wasn't having it. "Sir, with respect, you're in my charge for the moment, and I'd rather not be explaining to division how I got their general killed."

Fortescue gave a short nod. Not reluctant, merely understanding the predicament he'd placed on a young officer. "Apologies, old chap. Quite right."

He dropped into the shallow scrape beside them, boots knocking against the others as the rain of steel and sand continued to fall. Shoulder to shoulder, the three men crouched, pressed close, and their helmets tilted against the grit that swept through with each blast.

Archer reached into his satchel, thumbed around until he found what he was looking for. Pulling out the slightly dented silver metalled flask, he unscrewed the cap and held it out.

"Might as well make the most of it, Sir. Lockett swears it keeps the nerves steady."

Fortescue took it with a faint grin, wiped the rim with his thumb, and took a short sip before passing it back. "I'd say your man's a good judge."

Without a word, Lockett accepted his turn, and then he handed it back and hunkered lower as another salvo fell further up the line.

Suddenly, there was something different. It was hard to place at first, but it was distinct. Archer cocked his head, straining to catch it through the fading thunder of the guns. A new rhythm, deeper, more deliberate. The realisation came at once: the 25-pounders had opened up. Was it a counter-barrage? Or were the Germans beginning their attack?

Without thinking, Archer was on his feet. The incoming fire was lighter now but still walked up and down the line, the blasts thudding closer as he moved. He climbed from the scrape and ran towards one of the gun positions. From the crest of the rise, he could already see it: a spreading haze of dust above the desert, rolling and swelling in the heat. Beneath it, faint shapes moved en masse, the familiar silhouette of German armour.

Immediately, he called out to the men, "Stand to!" Many were reluctant as the shells still fell among their positions. Staring at the line of vehicles churning up the sand and heading straight towards them, Archer repeated the order more sharply. "Stand to!"

Seeing that some still hesitated, he ran along the rise, shouting and dragging men to their feet. Despite the pounding of the barrage, he knew this was the moment to show the leadership they needed. By exposing himself along the line, he gave the riflemen something to rally around. His usual words of encouragement were mixed with the odd blasphemy, each one cutting through the chaos.

He reached Jacks, who was already moving among 1st Platoon, urging his men into position and shouting orders above the noise. Amid the din and the smoke, Archer felt a strange sense of comfort being back among his platoon. It was a familiar steadiness even though fire raged down around them.

There was the briefest of acknowledgements between Jacks and Archer: men who knew each other too well to need more than a quick nod or half a smile. Archer trusted 1st Platoon. They would hold. He turned and moved back along the line, still calling out, "Steady lads! Wait for my word!"

Passing McBain's position, he saw the platoon ready. Men were crouched low in their scrapes, their rifles and Brens laid out, waiting. Archer knew that rifle fire would do little against armour. This fight would come down to the guns he'd been given. He reached the first of the static 2-pounders which was dug into the shallow rise. Its barrel was barely a foot above the sand. The crew were already in place with the layer turning the crank gently as he brought the sights onto one of the advancing vehicles.

Archer dropped to one knee beside the crew and raised his binoculars. The German barrage had slackened. The desert air was now filled with the dull growl of engines. Through the drifting haze, he saw them. Armour was pouring out of Mersa Brega just as he'd expected, straddling the road. The lead elements were pushing a hundred yards ahead of the flanking groups. The attack formed like the head of a spear.

Further north, the British 25-pounders opened fire again. For a moment, their shells walked neatly across the German advance, and to many a man's surprise, found their mark. Two tanks halted mid-stride, fire licking from their hatches. Thick black smoke twisted upwards like twin signals to the heavens.

A voice came from just behind him, steady, unhurried. "What have you got, Archer?"

He turned slightly. Fortescue was crouched at the edge of the gun pit, dust clinging to his cap. The General must have followed him up from the scrape. Archer passed him the binoculars without a word. Fortescue raised them. He knelt with one elbow resting lightly on his knee as he studied the view.

"Armour and halftracks," Archer said, still watching with the naked eye. "At least a dozen moving on the road. More fanning out on either side. They're coming on as I thought. 25-pounders are working well."

Fortescue grunted softly, still looking through the glass. "Archer, we'll open up at a thousand yards. Pass the word."

Archer hesitated, instinctively biting back his reply before speaking. "Sir, if I may, the 2-pounder's most effective inside eight hundred. If we open at a thousand, we'll give them more time to spot the guns."

Fortescue lowered the binoculars and turned, eyes narrowing slightly. Not in irritation but thought.

Without emotion, the general replied, "Mr Archer, engage at 800 yards."

Archer turned to the gunners nearest him, "800 yards gents."

The general lowered the binoculars and passed them to Archer with a brief smile. His eyes lingered for a moment as if taking the measure of him. There was something in Archer's composure that surprised Fortescue for such a young officer, the unhurried calm or his quiet confidence to voice his own judgement to a superior. Soon enough, the general would see him under fire and that would speak louder than any formal introduction.

Another explosion flared along the road, and a third tank slewing sideways as its tracks bit into the sand. Somewhere to the north, the 25-pounders were still hammering away, the thump of their fire drifting across the plain.

Fortescue shaded his eyes against the glare, watching the 25-pounders. "Those gunners have got their range," he remarked.

He squinted against the strain. The distant flashes were clear even through the shimmering haze. Each of the four guns fired in disciplined sequence. They were well-trained crews achieving nearly ten rounds a minute. Every shot was adjusted like a reversed creeping barrage to maintain their assault on the lead tanks.

It wasn't long before the third tank to be hit slewed across the road, forcing those behind to veer off onto the sand. Fortescue watched as each vehicle dropped from the raised roadway and then straightened to continue its advance. The four guns were mightily impressive; each crew, in rapid-fire mode, laid down an almost continuous barrage on the lead vehicles, stalling the enemy's progress but not halting it.

Archer's attention was fixed on the left of the road. Advancing on that flank, the tanks had closed the distance and were now within eight hundred yards. Trying to judge the most effective moment to open fire, Archer called out, "Hold! Wait for it!"

At eight hundred yards, they could be deadly but not yet decisive. He repeated his order as loudly as he could, ensuring all four of the gun crews and the company heard him.

Fortescue turned his gaze on the young lieutenant, aware that the oncoming armour was now well inside the eight-hundred-yard mark he'd been corrected on. He watched as Archer, one hand gripping his binoculars, the other slowly rising aloft, bent at the elbow - the sleeve of his shirt sliding down as his arm lifted higher. "Steady... steady..."

It was all the general could do to stay silent and not bellow the order himself. Yet he held his tongue, taking in the sight before him: a young officer on one knee, four men at the 2-pounder straining in anticipation of the command with the sun gleaming through the dust and sweat and fear plain to the naked eye. The word struck him like a release. "Fire!"

The flash came first, followed by the sharp, unmistakable crack from the barrel: loud and violent in its precision. Within moments, another followed. Each solid shot tore from the muzzle at over 2,600 feet per second, striking home before the next round could be slammed into the breech and sent on its deadly way.

"Great shot!" the general called out, his voice carrying over the din as if he were watching a sporting event. He could not help himself; the precision and power of the display stirred something deep within him. He watched as the men worked with practised urgency; one man stripped a round from its container as another passed it forwards; the loader slid it into the breech and slammed the block shut; and the layer traversed the gun onto its next target before the command came again. Each sequence took no more than ten seconds. The teamwork was flawless. Mechanical yet alive, and Fortescue felt a surge of pride rise unbidden in his chest.

His words were still hanging in the air when Archer stepped forwards, giving a brief nod. "With your permission, Sir, I'll check on the other guns."

"Carry on, Archer," the general replied, his voice still edged with excitement.

Archer set off at a run along the low rise, ducking instinctively as a shell burst somewhere off to his right. The Germans had answered. Within moments, the high whine of incoming rounds cut through the thunder of their own guns. The air grew thick with the roar and concussion of near misses.

Sand and dust rained down as Archer dropped beside the next crew. The No. 1 gunner was shouting corrections over the din, his voice hoarse. Archer caught his breath, scanned the line, and gave a quick thumbs up. The men were steady. Their discipline held even as enemy fire began to find the range. Another explosion rocked the earth behind them, closer this time. Archer felt the tremor in his boots and the sting of grit across his face. "Keep them firing!" he shouted, his words snatched by the wind.

The reply was fast, brutal and precise. The first German shells landed short, flinging stone and sand high into the air but within seconds, they were walking the barrage onto D Company's line. The air filled with a rising shriek, each incoming round tearing the sky apart before slamming into the desert with a savage, hammering concussion. Archer felt the blast punch through his chest as a detonation sent a wave of heat and grit cascading over his head. He ducked low, shouting for the men to stay down. Another shell tore into the rear area where the trucks were parked; a Bedford OY truck vanished in a sheet of flame, its canvas canopy erupting as fuel and ammunition cooked off.

"Get down!" someone screamed, too late. A near miss hurled two men from their gun pit, their helmets spinning away into the dust. Archer tried to see through the smoke. The once-clear gun line was now a storm of smoke and flying debris.

Behind him, the battered Morris that Fortescue had arrived in took a direct hit. The blast lifted it clean off the ground, and the vehicle vanished in a fireball that sent shards of metal whining across the position. For a heartbeat, Archer could only stare. The two men who had taken shelter beside it were gone, vaporised before his eyes.

Another explosion followed. This time, it struck one of the portees, the open-backed truck mounting a 2-pounder gun. The vehicle buckled. The weapon was flung sideways as one man was blown clear. A gunner scrambled up, blood running down his face, and his shirt soaked dark with it as he tried to drag his mate free of the wreckage. Flames from the burning tyres spread fast around the vehicle.

The German barrage was merciless. Men and machines alike were swallowed by fire and dust. The once-orderly line had broken and writhed under the storm. Archer pressed himself flat as another explosion tore nearby. The percussion rippled across his back. Everywhere was thick with that all-too-familiar stench: flesh, blood, sweat, all laced with the bitter tang of cordite.

Archer lay prone. His cheek was pressed into the sand as his heart hammered. He knew he had to act. But how, and with what? The guns were faltering. One was already lost, and the rest had been smothered in dust and smoke. He lifted his head just enough to take stock of the line. What had once been a tight, disciplined position was now half-obscured by fire and ruin.

Archer pushed himself up from the sand and forced his way back towards the shattered gun line. The heat and dust clawed at his throat, and every breath filled with the bitter tang of cordite and smoke. Ahead, through the drifting haze, he could make out Fortescue - not sheltering, but standing amidst the chaos, shouting encouragement to the nearest crew. He was waving his arm, urging the gunners on, his voice hoarse but steady. “Keep them firing, lads! Make every one count!”

Archer dropped beside the gun. The crew were drenched in sweat and grime. Their movements were mechanical now: load, fire, load again. The ground trembled with each discharge. He glanced towards the horizon and saw black columns of smoke twisting skywards. Several German tanks were burning, two more stood motionless with their hatches blown open. The gunners had done their work well. The desert was littered with the wrecks to prove it, but Archer knew it wasn’t enough.

For every vehicle knocked out, more pushed forwards through the smoke. Archer wiped a sleeve across his eyes, trying to make sense of the movement to the north. Then he saw it. There was a gap opening in the line, and men were falling back in disorder. The enemy armour was exploiting the breach. His stomach tightened.

He turned and clambered towards Fortescue, ducking as another round screamed overhead and burst behind them. “Sir! They’re breaking through to the north!”

Fortescue turned sharply, eyes narrowing against the smoke. He didn’t need binoculars to see the truth: the line was breaking.

He watched for a moment longer, his jaw set, and then he gave a single nod.

"Well, I think we have done all we can here, Archer. I think it's time we used our discretion and left."

Archer hesitated only a moment before replying. "Yes, Sir." He turned sharply, scanning the shattered line. "Anderson!" he shouted.

The sergeant appeared through the drifting smoke. His helmet was askew, and his face was streaked with dust. "Sir!"

"Get word to Jacks. We're pulling out! We'll start with the lads, then the statics. I'll head down to the portee and have them cover the withdrawal. Let's try and keep it as orderly as we can."

"Aye, Sir!" Anderson vanished in the distance although his voice carried above the chaos as he called for platoon leaders and section leaders to get themselves moving.

Archer left in the opposite direction to do the same, stooping low but moving fast. "C'mon! We're moving. Back to your vehicles."

The order spread man to man, shouted above the din. Men grabbed their rifles and Brens. The gunners were now silent and going through the arduous task of getting the gun ready for towing. Archer paused, admiring the effort of these men to carry out a drill they had done a thousand times before, even under heavy and sustained fire. It brought home the real benefit of training and training hard.

Archer ran low through the smoke towards McBain's platoon. His men were still firing short bursts at shifting shadows. "McBain!" he shouted.

The officer turned at once. His face was streaked grey with dust and sweat. "Sir!"

"Get your men together and back to the vehicles. It's time we got out of here."

Another explosion tore into the line, the blast sending wild, agonised screams through the air.

Archer leant closer to McBain. "Alistair, I need you to get the general clear. I've a feeling he may prove a little... difficult. You need to get him out."

"Aye, Tom. Understood." McBain's Scottish burr, faint though it was, seemed to cut through the din. It steadied Archer, lending a quiet confidence he hadn't realised he needed.
Archer tapped his shoulder. "Good man."

He was up and moving again, knowing McBain would not let him down.

As Archer reached the portee, he intended to use to cover the retreat, he glanced back along the line. One of the gun crews had already managed to limber a static 2-pounder. The towing bar was locked, and one man scrambled into the cab of the Morris while the others heaved themselves into the back. Their NCO waved an arm and leapt aboard just as the truck lurched forwards. Then it happened.

A white flash tore through the cloud of dust and grit. The blast punching the air like a hammer. The Morris vanished in a storm of dust and fire. When it cleared, there was nothing left but a burning chassis and blackened shapes strewn across the sand. For a heartbeat, no one moved.

The crew manning the gun on the nearest portee stood frozen, stunned by the sight of their comrades simply gone, several of them. The stillness broke at once as their NCO snapped them back to reality.

"No one told you to fucking stop firing!" he roared. The shock and anger were plain in his voice but beneath them each word lay the hard knowledge that he had to drive his men on even through the horror of losing mates in such a brutal death.

"Corporal!" Archer shouted, waving his arm towards the remaining gun.

The surviving crew were already working like men possessed, muscles straining, faces blank beneath the sweat and grit. Another shell struck short. It threw up a wall of sand that rained down over them. One man stumbled, another hauled him upright, and still they pushed.

Archer caught the corporal's arm. "We'll cover the retreat. Get your lads firing three or four rounds, no more. Then be ready to move the instant I call it."

"Yes, Sir!" The corporal turned sharply. "Load!"

"On!"

The gun kicked. The shot cracked across the desert. "Again!"

A second round slammed out.

A third.

A fourth.

Archer looked back along the ridge. The company were already mounting up: lorries grinding into gear: a carrier jolting forwards with smoke pouring from a damaged mudguard, and men clinging to sideboards or crouching low in the backs. McBain had the general aboard one of the Bedfords. Anderson was signalling the last vehicles out, and Jacks was waving his platoon onto anything with an engine.

Further out across the flat, German tanks were closing. Their guns flashed white through the drifting dust.

A near miss tore the sand open beside the portee, spraying the crew with grit.

"That's it!" Archer roared. "Move!"

The driver dropped the clutch, and the lorry surged forwards while the men bounced as they clung on. Archer ran beside it for a few paces. Then he grabbed a handrail and hauled himself up as another shell burst behind them. The concussion slammed into his back like a fist.

CHAPTER 18

The desert blurred into streaks of dust and smoke as the battalion tore itself free of the line. Trucks lurched in ones and twos across the broken ground. No formation yet, just the urgent instinct to move. Engines revved high, gears clattered, and each vehicle bounced wildly as drivers fought to find any track that might carry them west.

To the north, where the line had been hit hardest, the whole position had folded in on itself. The first ripple of collapse had begun there. German armour had punched through from the coastal side of the road and pushed through the British bombardment, reaching the thin line and rolling up the flank before anyone could react. Now that breach had spread, tearing open the centre and sending B Company, who had been holding that sector, into full retreat. Men ran in small knots, bent low under the weight of their kit, helmets slipping and rifles clutched tight. A few were dragging wounded comrades between them, stumbling through the smoke while the air around them erupted with dust from bursting rounds.

A burning Bedford slewed across the flats. Its tilt was alight, and flames licked along the canvas. The driver bailed out and fell rolling across the sand. Behind him, the rear axle gave way with a metallic shriek, and the vehicle collapsed onto its side. Another lorry ploughed on towards it, tried to veer clear and clipped the wreck. It pitched violently before righting itself, the men in the back thrown bodily against the sideboards.

Further still, the thin silhouettes of a pair of two-pounder portees were visible through the shifting murk. Both were driving hard, one already firing off hurried shots as its crew struggled to aim the gun while it bumped and slid along the desert ground. The second was less fortunate. A shell struck it, shearing the tyre and flipping the portee almost neatly onto its flank. Men leapt clear. One limped, and another crawled on elbows as the sand around them erupted with machine-gun fire.

But D Company held if only by instinct. Not tidy, not calm but recognisable.

Archer's world was a blur of heat and vibration. He stood braced on the running board of the last portee, wedged between the cab and the two-pounder. One hand gripped a steel grab rail welded beside the gun mount, and the other clung to the rough edge of the gun shield, knuckles white under the grit. Every jolt threatened to throw Archer clear. The portee bucked like a living thing beneath him. The two-pounder juddered violently behind his shoulder. The barrel kicked with each impact, bouncing on its travel clamp while the frame shuddered as the suspension fought the broken desert floor. Sand hammered Archer's face and shirt, stinging like shot.

On the same portee with Archer, the gun crew were scattered across the vehicle in whatever positions they could cling to. Two men had crammed into the cab beside the driver, wedged shoulder to shoulder, helmets thumping the roof every time the portee lurched. One more clung to the grab rail above the passenger door, half in, half out, boots skidding across the running board as he tried to keep his balance.

The last two stayed with the gun in the rear. They crouched low on the rear platform. One hand gripped the side rails, and the other steadied the breech as though their touch alone might stop it smashing itself apart. They weren't firing. No one could have fired with the portee hurtling across the flats at this pace, but instinct kept them close to it, ready and waiting for the moment the driver slammed to a halt, and they would be needed.

One of the gunners shouted something at Archer. His words ripped away by the wind. Archer only caught the look: wide-eyed, teeth clenched, sheer bloody determination forcing him to stay on the platform rather than dive for the cab.

The portee hit another hollow, and the men in the back were thrown inches from the side. One scrabbled for a lost grip, caught the trail with both hands, his boots sliding until another gunner hauled him back in by grabbing a large portion of his shorts.

Another violent jolt tore through the portee. The whole vehicle shuddered as the front wheels slammed into a patch of churned, uneven sand. Archer felt the impact thump through his legs and spine. The two gunners on the rear platform hunched instinctively, arms locked tight around rails, their helmets clashing together as they fought to stay aboard.

A burst of black smoke rose to their right. A Bedford from C Company had been hit. Its radiator blew apart in a hiss of steam, and the lorry slewed wildly before tipping nose-first into a shallow depression. Men tumbled from the back in a flurry of limb. Some scrambled clear. Others didn't rise at all. The portee roared past and vanished into drifting dust. Archer dragged his gaze forwards. The driver was a dark outline behind the bouncing windscreen, fighting to keep to what little track he could see. The corporal braced himself in the cab, both hands hardened around the dash.

For a heartbeat, a carrier surged alongside tracks hammering the ground. With his mask pulled up to his dirty goggles, the Bren gunner crouched low, clinging to the sides and riding every rise and fall of the unforgiving ground.

The portee struck a rise in the dunes at an angle and heaved skyward. Archer's boots left the deck, and he clamped both hands on the rail, knuckles white with the effort. One of the gunners slid with the motion, boots skating on empty air before he caught the gun shield. The portee crashed down, slewed left, and its tyres bit into loose sand before it steadied. The gunners hung on grimly, faces stiffened by dust. For an instant, Archer caught their gaze. No fear, only the hard recognition of how close death travelled with them.

The convoy began to ease at last. Engines that had been roaring now juddered unevenly as drivers throttled back to coax overheating motors away from the red. Dust settled in slow sheets over the backs of the men who were crammed into the trucks. Each face was coated with the same thin film of sand and sweat that had become a second skin.

At the head of the convoy, the pace eased a fraction, engines settling into a steadier rhythm. In the back of one of the lorries, a few of the lads slumped against the wooden sides with their chests heaving and rifles propped between their knees. Saunders sat with his head forwards, and his eyes half closed, drawing on a cigarette cupped carefully to keep the wind from robbing it. His fingers trembled slightly. It was the same familiar shake that took hold of him before a fight, but it was easing now. He had been sick in the sand not an hour earlier, yet he had stood firm when the rounds were coming in. The shooting was over. What lingered was not fear, but the dull shock of still being alive.

As he exhaled a thin stream of smoke, the tremor eased, and he passed the cigarette to Corporal Matthews who sat beside him - the former Royal Engineer who'd forced a transfer to the Greenmoors after France. The shakes would go soon enough; they always did once the adrenaline bled away.

Further along the truck, Evans picked grit out of the working parts of his Bren with impatient thumbs, blowing little clouds of dust from the mechanism. He paused to rub at a raw patch on his forearm where the jostling had battered him against the gun mount. The grin he usually wore had slipped; his face was pinched, his jaw tight, and eyes flicked to the horizon every few seconds.

Matthews shifted position, steadying himself as he crouched next to Saunders. Beyond them, Fry, Murgatroyd and Eddie Pike sat shoulder to shoulder, helmets tilted back, each man hollow-eyed but upright. Three others, strays from one of the other platoons, were wedged near the tailgate, their uniforms dulled to a pale, desert-worn shade, one of them clutching a blood-stained bandaged arm.

Matthews gave Saunders a once-over. "You still with us, Harry?"

Saunders managed a tired grin. "More or less."

"Good." Matthews lowered his voice. "Still got all five of us. It got a bit tasty back there."

Saunders glanced at Fry and the others. Fry raised two fingers in a weary salute; Murgatroyd just nodded, lips pressed tight.

"We're scratched up, but we're here," Saunders said. "Could've been a lot worse."

Matthews exhaled through his nose. It was a small breath he'd clearly been holding for far too long. "We'll stop in a bit, get a brew on. That'll sort us out."

Saunders smirked. "Not sure about that, Corp. Water's short. We never got the chance to refill this morning."

Matthews' gaze lifted automatically to the pale shimmer above the desert.

"I'm sure we can magic summat up, Lance Corporal," he said, the optimism loud in his voice. Then, with a big, naughty smile as he changed the subject, "Did you see Lieutenant McBain virtually manhandle the general into that lorry?"

Saunders' youth showed again as his broad smile broke through, a chuckle shaking his shoulders up and down. "Christ, Corp, not sure McBain'll be promoted for a while!"

Both men sniggered at the thought. The brief moment of relief lifted the troubles from their faces. But it faded as soon as Matthews caught sight of a figure in the next truck as it drew level, waving sharply to them. "It's Archer."

Matthews snapped out of the humour at once. He turned and banged on the cab roof, leaning over the side boards to reach the driver. "Pull up! Stop the truck!"

The lorry slowed to a halt. The rest of the convoy followed suit – a ragged mix of Bedford lorries, several carriers, a couple of battered Morris 1500 weights, and the lone portee, Archer still riding on its rear as it jolted to a stop. He dropped down on to the sand at once.

Archer strode through the sand, signalling the next trucks to halt, keeping their spacing as the last of the group ground to a stop. Men were already climbing down, stretching stiff legs, checking weapons or simply standing still, trying to catch their breath. "Platoon leaders with me!" Archer called.

Jacks, Kingsley, Anderson all moved towards Archer. The general arrived a moment later with McBain close behind, still looking a little embarrassed at having to move the general and almost physically shove the senior man into a lorry.

Archer gave them a quick nod. "Right. Quick state of play. Jacks?"

Jacks pushed his helmet back. "One truck's radiator's near gone, but it'll limp. Carrier's running hot but still serviceable. We were lucky – all twenty of us made it."

"Kingsley?"

"I've lost seven. Four dead. Three wounded. Vehicles are fine. Ammunition and water are low... very low." His tone made the point clear enough. "McBain?" Archer asked.

"Similar, Sir. Eight casualties. Three walking wounded. Four confirmed dead. One missing." McBain paused as he watched the general tamp a generous plug of tobacco into his worn brown pipe. "And one of the 1500 weights won't last much longer, Sir."

The general raised his head, fixing McBain with a faintly disapproving look as he lit the pipe. "What does that leave your strength at, Archer?"

Archer was already scribbling in his little black notebook where he kept record of the fallen. "Fifteen casualties... eight dead, six wounded, one missing. Fighting strength."

Anderson interrupted him. "Sir, Company HQ lost four men killed, no wounded. Hit as they were boarding the carrier. Also, Sir... we've one portee and one static gun position with four gunners on each. Twenty rounds in total. Ammunition state is bad, Sir. If we spread it evenly, we'll have about fifteen rounds per rifle and roughly the same number of Bren magazines across the company."

Archer paused, amending his notes. He realised, with a pinch of embarrassment, that he'd overlooked HQ in the chaos. They'd taken a hard knock and deserved to be counted. He looked up. "Sir... apologies. Company strength is sixty-three."

The general drew on his pipe and fixed his gaze towards the coast road where the remnants of the 7th Battalion streamed east. The Via Balbia ran straight and pale across the desert. Its metalled surface caught the sun like a strip of bleached stone. The centre of the road was still firm enough, but the verges were broken and scored where lorries had swung out to overtake with their tyres biting into the loose grit at the edges. Dust had risen, not from the road itself, but from the shoulders, drifting in long, dirty plumes behind each passing vehicle. Here and there, gouged potholes and cracked sections showed where tanks, carriers, and overloaded trucks had torn at the surface during the divisions retreat. Still, it was the only reliable line east, and every surviving vehicle clung to it, engines labouring as they pressed eastwards.

"It's a bloody shambles." The general took the pipe from his mouth and gestured towards the retreating columns. "Had we not been stripped bare for that Greece business, we would have kicked the Italians out altogether. Now look at us. We're in for the fight of our lives against Jerry."

Archer and the others held their silence, letting him speak.

The general continued. "We need to move, and move fast, Archer. I'm not convinced we've slowed Jerries advance at all. It will not be long before he is steaming down this road." He drew on his pipe again, the bowl glowing briefly.

"Agedabia." He said it as if the name had simply broken the surface of his thoughts. "The Rifle Brigade are digging in there.

Ten miles to the east along the coast road. They're meant to hold the next line although I would not wager on how long they can stand."

He paused, eyes narrowing on the haze where the road behind disappeared into the heat. "If Jerry punches through here before Rifle Brigade's ready, the whole position will fold."

"Sir, if France taught us anything, it's that Jerry isn't half as frightening once you stand up to him. Odds or no odds, a line will hold if the men believe it must. Mine do. We'll beat him in the end... just not today."

"Damn right, Archer. Now we need to be on the move!"

"Yes Sir!"

Engines once again kicked and coughed into life one by one, and the sound rolled across the shallow rise like a tired groan. Archer climbed up onto the Bedford's step, steadying himself with a hand on the hot metal of the cab. Anderson was already settled beside him, giving a quick nod to the driver who released the brake with a clank. Around them, the remnants of the company were mounting up, boots on tailboards, men hauling one another aboard with weary hands and mumbled curses.

"Keep tight," Archer called across the racket. "We head straight for the road and slot in behind the rest of the battalion traffic."

Lockett tapped the side of the Bedford as it lurched into motion. Dust rose immediately, hanging in the still air before drifting across their line like a low cloud. The small convoy began to snake its way across the flat, featureless desert, the rise of the road clearly visible to all as was the last of the battalion vehicles a few hundred yards ahead.

As they reached the low sloped ground, Archer leant out the cab window, bracing himself on the Bedford's window frame. To the north and heading east, the coast road gleamed like a pale ribbon. The metalled road - laid by the Italians several years before - shone pale and hard against the sand. The retreat had thickened as the battalion caught up with stragglers from division. It was a small but continuous column of lorries, carriers and the odd staff car pushing east at a steady, labouring pace. Some vehicles were clearly struggling and limped along with smoke trailing behind and tailboards hanging open where men had been lifted aboard without ceremony. It was a river of weary motion.

Archer slumped in the cab. The fatigue settled deep in his bones as the Bedford bounced across the desert floor. His head rested against the door frame, and he felt the warm metal beneath the dust. Ahead, the road shimmered in the heat, nothing but glare and distance.

A flicker of movement caught his attention. Off to the right, a small group of soldiers were gathered around a stalled Morris. Two men were bent over the open bonnet, spanners flashing in the light. The rest hovered nearby, offering advice that was neither wanted nor helpful. It was the sort of sight he had seen a hundred times in France and now again in Libya: soldiers clustered by a troubled engine, everyone certain they knew the cause.

But something changed. One by one the loitering figures stopped talking. Their heads turned, not towards the work, but upwards. Another man followed suit. Then another. Soon most of them were staring into the sky, shading their eyes, arms lifting to point at something beyond the heat.

Archer straightened slowly in his seat. Whatever they had seen was enough to silence a pack of bored men. He lifted his hand to signal the driver. "Hold on. Stop!"

The Bedford lurched to a halt. Archer pushed the door open before the engine had even settled, and he dropped down into the sand. He moved around the front of the lorry, eyes narrowed against the glare, trying to fix on what the others had seen.

Something was coming.

And not from the front.

Capitano Vittorio De Luca held the Breda steady in the shimmering heat. The desert spread out below, its surface shaped into long, wind-scored ridges of pale sand. The Breda Ba.65's squat wings cut through the air with a steady tremor, and the engine's deep growl rose as he trimmed the nose a fraction lower. The canopy shook with the vibration of the radial engine: the whole machine was alive under him, built for speed and brute work close to the ground.

The other Ba.65 aircraft kept tight behind him, four of them in a shallow V. Their stubby silhouettes flickered in the haze like hunting dogs crouched and waiting for the word.

He checked the altimeter. They had levelled at three hundred metres, a safe height for the run-in. Below, the road cut through the sand like a pale scar. He adjusted his grip on the stick. Sweat trickled down between his shoulder blades and trapped under the heavy leather of his flight jacket. The cockpit reeked of fuel, oil, and the faint metallic tang hovering through the cockpit.

He tapped the bomb selector with two fingers. All four were set to ripple. One pull. Four drops. A neat line across whatever poor victims were still on that road.

"Sezione uno, chiudete," he said into the throat mic with a calm voice. First section, tighten up.

Two acknowledgements crackled back. Short. Professional. His men were good. Not reckless, but sharp. The sort of pilots who kept formation even when the desert tried to throw them around like scraps in the wind.

The road came into view ahead, a pale ribbon cutting across the emptiness. De Luca eased the stick to the left, letting the Breda tilt just enough for him to study the ground below. Beneath the wing, the desert opened harsh and bright, and every movement became clear. He could see a short column of vehicles running parallel to the road, maybe two hundred metres from it. A few trucks, a carrier, and a small portee carrying guns kicked a sharp line of dust as it fought the ground. From this height, he could only make out dark shapes, but their movement was deliberate and ordered.

Further along, on the road itself, he saw the last stretch of a larger column crawled east. Lorries ran in loose pairs and threes. Dust lifted from their wheels in long pale streaks. A carrier limped in their wake, its track line uneven on the surface. Near the ditch, a stalled truck was tilted slightly with its bonnet open, and a small knot of figures moved around it in hurried, uncertain bursts. The whole rear of the British column looked strained and stretched, a line on the edge of coming apart.

Retreating. British, without question.

A cold satisfaction settled in his chest. He raised his hand from the throttle long enough to give a sharp signal: two fingers forwards and then down towards the road. In close formation, the others would see it at once.

He clicked the throat mic. "Sezione uno, alla strada. Tagliate la colonna." First section to the road. Cut the column.

He dipped his wing, nose sliding towards the off-road trucks. That broken little group would be his. Faster to hit. Harder to escape. The other three Ba.65s would take the road ahead and carve through the tail of the main column.

For a heartbeat, he steadied the Breda at three hundred metres, letting the picture settle satisfyingly below him. Then he pushed the nose down. The altimeter numbers began to unwind as the aircraft slipped into a shallow angled dive. Two hundred and fifty metres. Two hundred. The desert pulled closer. Its heat haze flattened into hard lines of vehicle shapes, dust plumes, and movement.

He eased the dive a little steeper, wanting to get the angle that let him see the trucks cleanly through the canopy frame. His height fell quickly. One hundred and fifty metres. One hundred. The off-road column filled his forwards view now, and he saw the line of lorries with the carrier and the mounted gun clearly.

He dipped the nose, and the reflector sight glimmered faintly. The thin illuminated ring settled over the cluster of vehicles below. Nothing clever, only a marked cross on the canopy, and his own judgement of angle, range and nerve.

He meant to open fire first, all four wing guns together: the pair of 12.7 mm and the lighter 7.7 mm guns on each wing ready to chatter as he flew down onto the column. Once he was over the line of vehicles, he would pull out of the dive and then release his four fifty-kilogram bombs with just enough height beneath him for the fuses to arm before they struck the ground.

Archer's breath caught. The angle of their descent told him everything. They were not scouting. They were coming straight for them. Immediately, he turned to his driver.

"Aircraft! Move!"

The driver crunched the gears and began to pull away. Archer was still on foot but already running. He swung his arm hard to the next truck in line and barked, "Right! Take it right!"

He sprinted on, waving to the next and pointing left. "Spread out! Move! Head over there!"

Drivers reacted at once. Engines growled, gears slammed home, and the neat column erupted into a twisting chain of movement. Lorries hauled themselves across the broken ground, some slewing left, others biting away to the right. Canvas tilts shuddered as the men inside grabbed at anything that would hold them steady.

Dust boiled up under the tyres, hanging thick and yellow in the heat as Archer ran between the vehicles, arms swinging, voice raw above the rising howl of engines and the approaching shriek from the sky.

The first bursts walked the ground behind the column, spitting up hard jets of sand. Archer flinched as the tracer carved towards them, bright red sparks stitching the desert in a rising line.

Then the guns found a lorry.

The rounds struck the Bedford's cab in a flashing spray of splinters and steel. The driver jerked once, hands flying from the wheel, and the vehicle slewed violently to the left. A man in the back twisted like a rag doll as a 12.7 mm round punched through him, flinging him against a tilt and out over the side. Another burst tore through the engine block. Flames licked up at once, thin and bright, and then they billowed as the cab caught. The truck rolled to a halt and started to burn fiercely. Men tumbled clear of the back and threw themselves into the sand.

Archer staggered as another stream of fire ripped past him, rounds hammering the ground so close he felt the sting of grit ricocheting against his neck.

"Keep moving!" he shouted, though his voice was lost in the roar. "Drive, damn you!"

The next lorry in line shuddered as shots ripped through the rear boards. One man collapsed in the open bed, legs kicking uselessly. Another was hit square in the chest and pitched forwards over the side, screaming as he struck the ground. The vehicle kept moving with its boards splintering and men crouching low, clinging on as more rounds snapped through the space above them.

A third truck, a Bedford this time, took a burst through its bonnet. Steam and fluid erupted in a white cloud, the radiator blowing apart. The Bedford lurched, slowed, then ground to a halt as the driver bailed out, clutching a bloody arm.

Above them, the first aircraft pulled out of its dive. It climbed hard and banked away to give space for the drop. The bombs tumbled cleanly from the underside in pairs. Each one caught the slipstream and settled into a straight, stabilised fall. The tail fins kept them vertical, the nose fuses pointing down towards the earth.

There was a sharp, rising whistle, and then a single, crushing detonation that rolled across the ground. The blasts landed so close together that it felt like one vast impact rather than four separate explosions.

The first burst tore into a Bedford on the far side of the spread. The rounds smashed through the open bed, flinging men off their feet in a spray of splinters and torn webbing. One soldier crumpled instantly; another spun sideways as a heavy round caught his shoulder, sending him tumbling into the sand.

The lorry lurched wildly as its driver slumped over the wheel, blood spattering the windscreen from inside. It veered across the churned ground before sliding to a halt, its rear wheels digging in.

The aircraft pressed on, guns hammering. A burst scythed across the towing lorry. The near-side tyre exploded, the bonnet flew open, and the whole vehicle juddered to a stop. Immediately, the gun crew leapt clear as steaming fluid poured from the shattered radiator.

A second burst clipped the carrier. Rounds hammered its armour plate in a hard metallic rattle, one glancing off the shield and showering sparks into the dust. The driver and crew were already flat to the hull, trying to slither themselves into the ground.

The aircraft climbed sharply, engine howling. Archer saw the bombs drop from the racks beneath the fuselage.

"Bombs!" someone shouted, the words torn away by the general panic as men threw themselves prone, clutching at the sand and praying the danger would pass.

Two dark shapes fell cleanly, tumbling once before the fins steadied them. They plunged fast, slicing through the air with a hard whistle.

The dark shapes fell cleanly, tumbling once before the fins steadied them. They plunged fast, slicing through the air with a hard whistle.

The first blast tore into the line, throwing dust and flame high into the air. The second followed almost at once, the shockwave punching through Archer before the world drowned in noise and grit.

CHAPTER 19

For several long seconds, Archer heard nothing at all. No shouting. No engines. No gunfire. Only the dull, rolling echo of the blast drifting away across the desert. The sound flattened out as though the land itself were giving a long, weary groan. Archer attempted to push himself up from the sand, but one hand sank wrist-deep into the warm, shifting grains. As he continued to push up, every movement sent a fresh rush of grit into his mouth and nose. He coughed hard, spitting dry sand from his lips. The air was thick with dust, and a fine yellow haze drifted in slow, ghostly sheets, hanging and swirling like smoke caught in a beam of light.

Relentlessly, heat pressed down on him from above. The blast had stirred the desert into a choking cloud, and the rising sun shone through it like a blurred furnace, turning every shape into a wavering silhouette.

A burning lorry crackled somewhere behind him. The flames hissed and snapped as they chewed through the wreckage of the burning vehicles, steel warping and popping in the heat. Black, greasy smoke coiled upwards, mixing with the dust and drifting low across the ground like a creeping fog. Heat pulsed from it in slow, heavy waves, bending the air until the sand around the wreck seemed to warp. Every gust of wind sent sparks spiralling upwards and drove the smoke sideways, rolling it along the ground in dirty billows that clung to boots and kit.

Somewhere within the twisted frame of the lorry, something collapsed with a dull, hollow clatter. It was followed by the sharp hiss of fuel catching and flaring again. A loose tailboard banged against warped metal, opening and slamming shut as if the lorry were breathing its last. Chains rattled in short bursts, jerked by the heat and the shifting air. Their thin metallic clink cut harshly through the muffled stillness.

Archer could feel the thick stench of burning rubber and scorched canvas in the back of his throat. It mingled with the gritty dust that drifted past him, dry as ash and warm against his cheeks. The smoke crawled over the sand, hugging the earth, swallowing the shapes of scattered kit and twisting the wreck into a dark, crouched silhouette against the pulsating haze. "Sir...?"

Jacks' voice reached him at last. Hoarse and uncertain as if it had been scraped raw.

Archer blinked grit from his lashes. Shapes began to form through the murk. Men lay scattered across the open ground: some sprawled, some curled in tight, instinctive knots as though trying to hide from further blasts. A few were moving, dragging themselves an inch at a time, hands clawing weakly at the sand.

One of the Bedfords lay on its side. Its wheels still turned lazily before swaying to a stop with a faint creak. Another had been blown sideways, its bonnet twisted back on shattered hinges, and steam and smoke rose together in a thin, wavering plume. The towing lorry had simply come apart. Its engine bay was peeled open like a burst tin. The radiator hung by a single pipe with steam hissing as it met the desert air.

The ground itself felt wrong. Uneven. Pocked with fresh craters and gouged trails where lorries had skidded or been hurled sideways. A shallow depression still trembled faintly beneath Archer's palm with the last echo of the blast.

The ground was littered with kit of every kind. Some pieces were smouldering while others had split open. The contents of water tins were darkening the sand in strange, irregular patches. A rifle lay snapped clean in two. A gas cape hung and fluttered uselessly from a broken tailboard. Empty ammunition boxes were overturned and splintered, their wooden fragments scattered and half-buried in the sand like a handful of thrown coins.

Somewhere to Archer's left, a raw, wavering cry from an injured man rose and fell before dissolving into the wind.

Archer staggered to his feet. His knees threatened to buckle as the ground swayed beneath him. He steadied himself while constantly blinking against the harsh, brutal reality of what had happened. He forced his voice through the dryness in his throat. "Jacks? Where are you?"

"Here, Sir!" There was a cough, then a dark shape moved through the dust. "I'm here. Christ, what a mess..."

Archer scanned the devastation. His heartbeat was heavy and loud in his ears. The ringing had not stopped and had faded to a persistent, distant whine.

The air smelt of burning oil, hot metal, burnt powder and scorched rubber. A gritty tang continued to cling to the back of his tongue.

He turned slowly. The enormity of what they'd just experienced was threatening to consume him as he took in the shattered line of what had been his column. The trucks lay scattered across barely a hundred yards, flung in every direction. Archer took in the jumble of wrecked, broken shapes.

Archer swallowed hard.

"Start checking for survivors," he said quietly to Jacks and his voice barely carried. "Anyone who can move. Start helping the wounded. Jacks, get the ones near the burning lorry out of there before it goes up again."

The wind shifted and a fresh wave of darkness rolled past him, thick with smoke. Beneath it, he heard the faint clink of metal, followed by another groan. More shapes were moving. Some crawled. Others simply lay where they had fallen.

A figure staggered out of the drifting murk to Archer's right, one arm clamped tight against his ribs. Kingsley. His sleeve was ripped open to the elbow, and the whole arm hung red and slick, a dark line of blood running down to his fingertips. He limped the last few paces, dragging his boots through the sand. His face was sheet-white under the dirt.

"Sir..." He drew in a ragged breath. "Three dead. Three wounded. Bedford took a direct strafe. I... I don't know if the wounded will last."

Archer put a hand on his good shoulder. "You're hurt."

Kingsley gave a short, humourless laugh. "I've had worse shaving, Sir."

He swayed slightly, caught himself, and then nodded back towards the wrecks. "I saw McBain dragging some poor soul clear of the Morris. Don't know how either of them are standing."

Before Archer could reply, another man pushed through the haze. He stooped, coughing and brushing ash from the front of his tunic. General Fortescue. His cap was gone, and the edge of his trousers had been singed showing a blackened strip, down one leg. He straightened, squinting through the swirling smoke, pipe still clamped in one soot-marked hand.

"Archer!" he barked, voice rougher than usual.

The lieutenant looked up from rummaging in his satchel, where he had finally found a dressing. Kingsley's breathing was coming hard and fast now. Each breath was a strained hiss. The swagger was gone as the pain pushing through.

"General!" Archer answered, gruff but still respectful, though his attention never left Kingsley. He pressed the soft dressing to the open gash along the man's upper arm. Blood seeped up at once. As Archer shifted Kingsley's sleeve aside, he saw the truth of it. It wasn't a clean break, but a mess. The bone beneath was shattered into splinters.

"Christ, Kingsley... sit down before you fall down," Archer muttered and eased him to his knees, then to the sand, supporting him with one hand while holding the dressing firm with the other.

Kingsley tried a smile, the ghost of one, but his eyes were already dimming. "Still here, Sir... just... winded..."

"You're done standing," Archer said quietly. "That's an order."

He glanced up at the general, who watched with his pipe still in hand and soot stained down one side of his face.

"Sir," Archer said, sharper this time, "I need something straight. Wood, crate slat, anything we can split. His arm's gone in two places. I've got to brace it."

Taken aback for half a heartbeat, Fortescue blinked and then nodded. "Right... yes, of course." He turned and strode towards the nearest wreckage, calling for men to search.

Archer worked fast, binding the dressing in place. Kingsley's expression was tight with the effort of hiding the pain he was clearly suffering. His head lolled once, then again. His skin was turning grey beneath the dust. "Stay with me," Archer murmured.

Kingsley tried to answer but only a faint breath escaped. His eyes fluttered, unfocused, then rolled back as the pain claimed him. He slumped sideways into Archer's arm.

Archer lowered him gently to the ground, checked his pulse and then set about holding the broken limb steady until Fortescue returned.

Fortescue returned at pace. Two splintered lengths of crate were under his arm and a torn strap of webbing hung from his hand. His face was still streaked with soot and sweat stained his shirt either side of his Sam Browne belt. He slowed as he reached them, taking in Kingsley's limp form. For a moment, his expression tightened as if he feared the worst. Archer shook his head before the general could speak.

"He's passed out, Sir. I'm amazed he didn't sooner. Probably for the best."

Fortescue nodded once, handing over the makeshift splints.

"What do you need?"

"Just hold his shoulder steady." Archer positioned the broken arm carefully, feeling the looseness in the bone beneath the skin. Kingsley groaned faintly, a low sound somewhere between pain and unconscious reflex.

"Easy... easy..." Archer murmured to himself. He slid the first piece of wood along the outside of the arm, the second along the inside, aligning them as best as the shattered limb allowed. Then, with quick, practised movements, he tore another strip from Kingsley's already ruined sleeve and bound the splints tight.

Each pull drew another pained groan from the unconscious man, but the arm began to hold a straighter shape.

Fortescue steadied the shoulder, watching Archer work.

"Good lad," he muttered under his breath.

Archer cinched the final knot, checked the limb once more and then used the webbing strap the general had scavenged to tie Kingsley's arm to his torso to restrict its movement.

"That's as good as we're going to get out here," he said quietly.

Fortescue nodded in agreement.

Archer looked up. Smoke still billowed into the sky, but more shapes were beginning to form out of the chaos as men rallied after the shock of the bombing. In the drifting haze, he caught sight of Lockett.

"Lockett! Over here!"

"Sir?" The private's face was ashen. His hands shook slightly, and Archer saw at once he had been through it himself. His lorry had been strafed, and Nobby Briggs, the company signaller and Lockett's closest mate, had been killed beside him.

"Good to see you on your feet. Can you assist the general in getting Mr Kingsley into a lorry?"

Lockett blinked, torn between the order and the fact a general now stood waiting for him. The bemusement was plain on his face.

Archer caught the look and added, "Hope you don't mind, Sir," before moving off towards the rest of the broken company, checking for any other men who needed help.

Fortescue raised an eyebrow at Lockett. The private swallowed hard. The general's tone softened, just a fraction.

"Well, Lockett... looks like we have our orders."

The two men crouched beside Kingsley and began to lift him with all the care they could manage, moving slowly through the dust and heat, doing their best not to jolt the splinted arm.

Archer moved slowly through what remained of the company, the wrecks still radiating the day's heat into the air that was full of the remnants of an explosives' tang. Men were now moving in ones and twos. Some were clearly dazed and some clutched at gaping wounds. All of them looked older than they had an hour before. McBain was already at work near the overturned Bedford, giving firm, steady, and practical orders. He kept his voice low enough to keep the men calm.

"Right, form up lads. This will be a squeeze," he called. "First truck takes all the wounded. Be as careful as you can, but it's going to be tight in there."

Archer joined him a moment later, taking in the scene. McBain moved from the Bedford and walked among the wounded, guiding them towards the vehicles. Steady but brisk, he was getting the company loaded, so they could move again. Though older, he was the subordinate, and he gave a short, courteous nod.

"Tom." It was the closest thing to a salute either man could manage in the moment.

"Ten dead, Sir. Six wounded. Two of them bad, including Phil." His low Scottish brogue stalled briefly as he mentioned his friend's name: the weight of the loss flickered across his face. He pushed on.

"It's going to be tight. Four wagons, one carrier and the portee. We can't get the 2-pounder hitched to the Bedford. Its coupling's twisted to hell." He drew a short breath, finishing the report.

"I've told the gunners to spike it, Sir."

"Good stuff. The sooner we are on the move, the better."

It took longer than it should have. The wounded were lifted and packed into the lead truck, laid out as best they could among torn canvas and splintered boards. The rest of the company found space where they could, clambering aboard whatever vehicle that still ran.

Engines rattled reluctantly at first but quickly fell into a grudging rhythm, each sounding rougher than the last. The column lurched forwards, slow and uneven, gathering itself into something resembling order. Archer walked a few paces alongside the lead lorry before he stepped onto the running board and pulled himself into the cab. The Bedford bounced over the torn ground as he settled into the seat beside the driver.

For the next hour, they moved eastwards at little more than walking pace. The coast road was broken by bomb craters, drifting sand and scattered wreckage. Archer starred in resigned shock at the full ruin of the morning's attack that was being exposed by the rising sun.

Bedfords from other units lay scattered in ones and twos. Some were burnt to their frames while others were belly-up with their wheels pointing at the sky. A Morris truck had dug itself nose-first into a bank, and its roof was peeled open like a tin lid. Scraps of kit littered the road, splintered crates, torn blankets and stray vehicle parts were scattered like abandoned offerings to the desert.

No one spoke. The only sounds were the grinding of gears, the rattle of loose fittings, and the occasional moan of a wounded man. Occasionally, the odd swear word carried from men who were too squeezed in to feel comfort.

Travelling at the rear of the column in the carrier, Jacks turned and gazed at yet another wreck. The heat rose in tides and bent the air above the burnt-out chassis. He watched the last of the embers glowing red along a Bedford's tailgate, the metal twisted and scarred to a chalky white where it had been red hot. Against it lay the grim shape of a poor soul whose final terror was frozen in place: a charred skeleton, bone fused into the steel to form a macabre, half-melted statue.

Jacks was no stranger to such scenes, but it never stopped his stomach turning. Nor did it stop his eyes returning again and again to every blackened, charred death as the carrier crawled past. He didn't know why he kept looking. Perhaps to make sure they were real. Perhaps to fix them in his mind. Or perhaps because one day, he knew, it might be him lying there.

The column pressed on, and engines grumbled in protest as they laboured further eastwards. The heat rose quickly now, flattening the horizon into a rippling band of silver and pale sand. The wounded groaned with each jolt of the wagons.

Kingsley sat motionless against the cab wall, propped up by another wounded soldier who leant into his good arm to steady him. His breath came in thin, shallow pulls, each one catching on a ragged edge of pain. Sweat gathered at his brow and fell in trembling lines down his dust-caked face. Every vibration of the Bedford sent a shudder through his splinted arm. As he fell in and out of pained consciousness, the bone beneath the dressing felt as if it were grinding on itself, sharp fragments pressing and shifting. His jaw was clenched so tightly that the muscles flickered along the side of his face, and when the wagon hit a deeper rut, he sucked in a sharp breath, and a faint, broken sound escaping before he could bite it back.

His eyes stayed half-closed, unfocused, drifting between flashes of the road ahead, and the blur of sand on the horizon. At times, he seemed to slip from the present altogether, and his head dipped forwards as the world tilted away from him. Shapes moved in the corners of his vision, shadows that looked like men one moment and drifting smears of colour the next. For a heartbeat, he couldn't tell whether they were real or simply the heat pressing tricks into his mind.

Every now and then, he was jolted fully awake, and a sharp breath would tear from his throat as another ripple of agony travelled through his shattered arm. The soldier beside Kingsley tried to steady him, murmuring something low and comforting but Kingsley barely heard it. The words seemed to come from a long way off, muffled by the dull roaring in his ears.

His world had narrowed to the throb in his arm. The heat pressed down on him and mingled with the sickening pulse of pain that chased every movement of the wagon. At times, he thought he saw water glinting in the distance: a thin silver pool just beyond the next rise, only for it to shimmer and break apart into sand again.

Then the darkness would take him for a moment, dropping him into a brief, merciful nothingness. But even there, he found no rest. Delirious shapes drifted through his mind, voices he half recognised, faces blurring and breaking apart, his brain trying to make sense of the shock, and the shattered bone beneath the dressing. Each time he surfaced again, the pain was waiting.

Still, he made no complaint. Only the tightening of his jaw, and the faint tremor along his mouth, betrayed how close he was to the edge.

For each of the wounded, every mile felt like an hour. The road ahead dipped and lifted as the surface had been broken by bomb splinters. It was stained black where lorries had burnt. The heat hammered down on them without mercy, baking the metal of the trucks until men recoiled from the touch of it. The engine jangled like tired lungs, labouring under the weight of too many bodies and too little rest.

Now and then, Archer caught sight of a figure, in khaki appear on the roadside. Some of them limped while others staggered along with their heads bowed, and their hands raised to shield their eyes from the glare. Stragglers from the division. Men who had lost their ride or watched it burn. The convoy slowed each time, and men reached down to haul the stranded aboard with whatever strength they had left.

The space in the wagons grew tighter each time. Air grew thicker and sourer with every stop. Shoulders pressed further into one another. Legs were drawn up to make room. No one complained though, not properly, but the strain showed in the set of jaws, the blank stares, and the way some men kept their eyes fixed on the floorboards rather than look at the ruin that they passed by.

Weariness settled over them like a second skin. The kind that went deeper than muscle, deeper than bone. A few men nodded off where they sat, jerking awake only when the Bedford hit a rut. Others stared ahead with the hollow expression of those tallying the losses they had not yet spoken aloud. The knowledge of failure, of being driven back, of leaving friends behind on the sand, hung as heavily as the heat. Morale did not break.

But it visibly bent and showed through in the physicality of the men. And still the column crawled eastwards because there was nothing else to do.

Twenty minutes later, one of the Bedfords gave a deep, metallic rattle and began to lose speed, drifting sideways in the sand. A thin plume of steam hissed out from under the bonnet as the engine coughed twice and died. Archer signalled the column to halt.

McBain and two of his men were already at the front, lifting the bonnet up, and the heat rolled off the engine in fractured rippling waves. They worked in silence for a few moments, checking hoses, tapping the metal casing. Then McBain stepped back, wiping his arm across his brow, and shook his head.

"Radiator's gone, Sir. Split clean through. She won't take another mile."

McBain had barely finished speaking when Fortescue strode over, tunic unbuttoned to his Sam Browne. Archer stepped forwards to meet him. Jacks and Anderson followed a pace behind, all of them streaked with the accustomed sweat and sand.

"What have we got?" Fortescue asked, eyes already on the dead truck.

"Radiator's shot, Sir," McBain repeated. "Split right down the seam. We push her another yard and she'll seize solid."

Fortescue exhaled slowly through his nose. "Can it be patched?"

"Not out here," Anderson said quietly. "We'd need water, a solder, and half a workshop. She's done, Sir."

Archer looked across at the men crammed into the remaining wagons.

"Al, see to it she's put out of action. Anderson, get everyone squared away across the remaining vehicles. Jacks, draw off whatever fuel you can. No point leaving that for Jerry."

"Yes, Sir," Jacks replied at once.

There was no argument.

Men began climbing down from the forlorn Bedford, moving with weary purpose as they set about stripping what they could. Tools clattered against metal as Anderson organised the transfer of kit while Jacks crouched by the fuel tank, working a length of rubber hose into place.

He sucked hard on the end of it, face twisting as the first foul, solvent-tasting splash hit his tongue. The thin stream finally flowed, and he guided it into two empty water tins, coughing once before wiping his mouth with the back of his hand.

Jacks glanced up the road, shading his eyes. "Sir... if we keep losing vehicles, we'll be walking to Tobruk. We're barely making pace as it is."

A brief silence hung between them. It wasn't defeat, just the blunt recognition of a hard truth.

Fortescue's gaze shifted from the ruined Bedford to the thin, weary line of surviving trucks. He gave a brief nod, something in his expression suggesting he was more than satisfied with how Archer had handled the situation. Without further ceremony, he turned to Anderson.

"Sergeant Anderson, make room for a couple in my spot. I shall ride with Lieutenant Archer."

A simple one-word answer was all that was needed. "Sir."

It took the better part of thirty minutes of pushing and shoving before the men were organised as best they could be in the remaining vehicles. Anderson had the able-bodied standing where possible as they took up far less space on the wagon floors than those who needed to sit.

McBain met Archer and confirmed they had run the engine until it seized solid, the metal knocking once before locking in place. Jacks, not one to leave a job half done, had sprinkled a light covering of petrol over the wooden bed. He struck a match, and the vapour caught at once: a brief blue flicker before it flared into a bright, hungry yellow as the dry timbers took hold.

Within moments, the wagon was burning well and smoke curled into the hot morning air.

McBain and Archer parted without ceremony, each heading back to their vehicles. A few shouted orders, a few simply waved men forwards, and soon the small convoy was rolling eastwards once more. Behind them, the ruined Bedford burnt fiercely, flames licking along its frame as they left it to the desert.

It was some time into the renewed drive before any of the men who were squeezed into the lead lorry's cab spoke. The driver, Private Harland, a solid Yorkshireman and one of the older hands in 1st Platoon, kept his eyes fixed on the road. Cynical by nature, never one to volunteer for anything, he was nevertheless dependable to a fault. Finding himself shoulder to shoulder with a general for the first time in his life, he chose to concentrate on the driving and nothing else. Fortescue was the one who finally broke the silence.

"Archer, your fellows are holding together well," he said quietly.

"They are, Sir. I wouldn't expect anything else. They haven't let me down once." Archer kept his gaze on the wavering line of the track ahead. "There have been moments when any one of them could have folded, and no one would have blamed them. Yet they carry on. It still amazes me how steady they are, even now."

Fortescue gave a small nod, the sort that held more weight than any speech. "You have something to do with that," he said quietly.

Archer did not answer at once. The Bedford bounced over a rut, and he steadied himself against the dash. When he finally spoke, his voice was low.

"I am not always sure I deserve their trust, Sir. Today especially. There were moments back there... if I had judged wrong by an inch, half the platoon might be lying in the sand." He shook his head. "Plenty of chances for a better man to have made fewer mistakes."

Fortescue's reply came without hesitation. "Everyone makes mistakes, Archer. The difference is that some men face them, and some hide behind excuses. You don't strike me as the latter."

Archer gave a faint breath of something between a laugh and a sigh. "Feels like I've been learning on the job since France, Sir."

"That's how most of us learnt." Fortescue's eyes stayed on the wavering ribbon of track ahead. "My first command was in France, early in the other war. Nineteen fifteen. None of us knew what we were doing. We were trying to fight machine-guns with tactics that belonged to the century before. Lines of good men walking forwards into bullets."

He paused, jaw tightening at the memory. "I was green then... truth is, we all were. Learning as we went, paying for every mistake in blood. Far too many good men were lost before any of us understood what we were facing."

He drew a slow breath. "And here we are again, learning on the job. All I can hope is that we learn faster than we did last time."

Archer turned slightly, taken aback by the general's frankness, but Fortescue went on in the same quiet tone.

Archer listened in silence. When he finally spoke, his voice was low.

"Thirty-three. That's how many have died under my command."

The older officer regarded him for a moment, then answered quietly. "Remember this, young Archer. You cannot erase the men you lose. You only learn how to carry them better. Loss is part of our trade now. And, if I may say so, your conduct today tells me you are very good at it."

Archer looked ahead, jaw tight.

"It's the men, Sir. I am humbled by what they do."

Fortescue heard Archer's words, yet his expression was that of a seasoned wartime officer. He knew full well that Archer was the reason his men acted as they did. There was no point pressing the matter, so he let the conversation fall away.

Instead, he reached into his tunic and produced a small tobacco pouch and a battered pipe with a dark, worn stem.

Archer, ever alert, noticed the embossed emblem on the leather pouch: the silver crest of the Marylebone Cricket Club.

"Member, Sir?"

Fortescue tamped the tobacco gently into the bowl of his pipe.

"Middlesex, actually," he said. "Joined the Taverners years ago. Keeps an old man honest."

Archer's brow lifted. "Did you catch the last Test before the war, Sir? England and the West Indies?"

Fortescue gave a quiet chuckle. "Lord's, June thirty-nine. Hammond's lot. Edrich batted like a metronome. Lovely, disciplined stuff. And Constantine... well, the crowd would have paid their shillings just to watch him warm up."

Archer smiled faintly. "I read about it, Sir. Never been to a Test myself."

"A pity," Fortescue replied, striking a match. "There's nothing quite like Lord's on a summer morning. The crack of the ball, the murmur from the pavilion... civilised warfare, if you like. And a damn sight gentler than what we get out here."

He puffed once, sending a thin wisp of smoke into the night air.

Fortescue drew on the pipe until the tobacco glowed, the faint scent drifting around the cab. He glanced at Archer, his expression softening. "You follow the game much yourself?"

Archer gave a small nod. "A bit, Sir. Played at school. Reading Grammar. I opened the batting for the First XI... when they would have me."

Fortescue raised an eyebrow. "An opener, you say? Takes a steady head. Not many lads eager to face a new ball on a cold April morning."

Archer allowed himself the hint of a smile. "I enjoyed it, Sir. Never set the world alight, but I could stay in. My master used to say I had more patience than talent."

"A valuable quality," Fortescue murmured, tamping the bowl again. "In cricket... and otherwise."

Archer looked down briefly at the sand between his boots. "I miss the feel of a bat sometimes. The quiet before the bowler runs in. It all seems a very long way from here."

Fortescue gave a soft grunt of agreement. "A different world entirely. But it stays with you, that sort of thing. School colours. Long afternoons. The sound of leather on willow."

The conversation drifted on though it was Fortescue who carried it. He spoke easily of cricket, of schools and old grounds, naming counties, players, and matches with the confidence of long familiarity. Archer listened, impressed by the breadth of it, offering the occasional reply when invited, careful not to overreach himself. A particular summer, long dry and bright. A match abandoned for rain that never quite arrived. Grounds he knew only by name. It was talk from another life and one Archer had only brushed against while Fortescue had clearly lived it.

Spoken now without ceremony, almost casually, as if keeping those things alive required no more than saying them aloud.

Archer found he was grateful for it. The rhythm of the conversation, the normality of it. It steadied him. For a few moments, the desert receded, and with it, the war.

As Fortescue spoke, Archer found his thoughts wandering. Cricket had a way of doing that. It carried him back to green things, to short, cut grass that had been rolled flat, to the hollow sound of leather striking willow. He thought of Reading Grammar, of standing at the crease with the early sun still low, his hands tight on the handle, waiting for the bowler to commit. He remembered the quiet concentration of it. The sense that time narrowed to the space between ball and bat.

From there, his thoughts wandered to Pembroke. Not in any ordered way, just flashes of him as he had been. Pembroke leaning back in a chair, boots hooked round the legs, telling Archer about his plans for an inter-battalion cricket league even before the battalion was back up to strength after France. Pembroke laughing at something stupid Archer had said, quick and unguarded, as if the world were still a place where that sort of thing came easily. Then the faint ache of knowing that Archer's orders for the desert had robbed them of the chance to play together, something both men had assumed would happen one day.

The memory brought a brief tightening in his chest. Archer pushed it aside, unsettled by the sudden weight of it. It wasn't the desert that troubled him, nor the war, but the quiet realisation that Pembroke was no longer beside him. No longer close enough to argue with, laugh with, or plan foolish things with. The absence felt sharper than any thought he cared to examine, so he set it aside and carried on.

Charlotte came to him then, unbidden as she always did when home crept too close. The picture of her face was never quite sharp. It was softened now by time and distance, but the feeling remained. The warmth of her hand. The certainty of her presence. England felt impossibly far away in that moment. Not just in miles, but in kind. A different existence entirely.

The conversation in the cab continued, comfortable and unforced, until it slowed and thinned, the way all such things did. Eventually, even Fortescue fell quiet, his pipe reduced to a dull glow. The day pressed in around them. The desert vast and unreadable

The Bedford rattled on, and the engine laboured steadily as the coast road unwound ahead of them. Dust streamed past the open sides, and the hard light flattened the land into pale sand and scrub. Archer could make out the sea: a distant strip of blue to their left. Archer sat with his helmet braced between his boots, hands resting loosely on his thighs, listening to the familiar sounds of men and machinery moving with purpose around him.

Ahead, the road dipped and straightened. Then the Bedford slowed.

Archer felt it before he saw it, the subtle change in the engine note, the driver easing back. Shapes resolved through the dust: coils of wire that had been dragged across the tarmac. Sandbags were piled low, and a truck was angled across the road. Figures moved into view, rifles slung, faces darkened by sweat and grime. A roadblock.

The Bedford rolled to a halt, brakes hissing. Somewhere ahead, a hand went up, palm out. Voices carried faintly through the dust, clipped and businesslike.

Archer leant forwards slightly, narrowing his eyes and already taking the situation in. The coast road continued beyond the wire, bending west towards Gazala, disappearing into heat and haze. Whatever waited there, they had reached the edge of it now.

CHAPTER 20

They pulled off the coast road where it dipped shallowly towards a broad patch of hard-packed sand. It was the sort of place that had become a headquarters simply because there was room to stop. A handful of vehicles were already drawn up in loose order: staff cars nosed together, and a couple of Bedfords had their bonnets up while dispatch riders crouched beside their machine. Their helmets were off, and they drank from water bottles that were already too warm.

There was no signboard, no perimeter. Just a cluster of men with maps spread across a trestle table knocked together from petrol crates, and a wireless set humming fitfully under a length of canvas rigged against the sun. Someone had scratched grid references into the sand with a bayonet, but the lines were already blurring as boots scuffed through them.

It felt temporary in the way all things out here seemed to. Not a place meant to last more than an hour or two.

Beyond them, near the staff cars, the wounded were being gathered. Some men carried stretchers and moved steadily between vehicles, lifting men out and laying them down with practised care. The worst cases were already being loaded. Archer hesitated only a moment, then crossed towards them. No one stopped him.

There was no need.

He moved between the wounded quietly, stepping aside as a pair of bearers came through at a brisk walk, their burden swaying between them. A man groaned somewhere to Archer's left. Another lay still, his eyes closed, lips cracked with dust.

Archer didn't speak. There was nothing useful to say. His eyes found Kingsley who lay on a stretcher; his sleeve had been cut away entirely. The arm beneath was still dressed in Archer's rough splint, the shape of it looked wrong even through the dressing.

Two stretcher-bearers lifted Kingsley's stretcher and moved on without stopping, their pace steady, practised. Kingsley drifted in and out, eyes half-open, unfocused. As the splint was adjusted, a flicker of pain crossed his face, his jaw tightening before it slipped again. For a moment, Archer stood there, watching.

Kingsley's eyes opened briefly and found him. Recognition came slowly, but it came. He managed the faintest nod. Archer returned it.

A soldier brushed past Archer, forcing him to step aside. The momentary connection with Kingsley broke with it. Archer glanced once more at a man he found himself admiring, then turned and made his way to the general.

Archer was the first to step clear of the shade, followed by Fortescue. The young lieutenant had his helmet tucked under his arm, and the dust had completely settled into the folds of his sleeves. Around them, officers moved with clipped urgency, consulting their watches and murmuring then repeating orders. Engines had been left idling as if no one expected to stay long. There was the sense that things had already been decided with units being pushed on or held back with little ceremony. The moment for discussion or argument had long since passed.

Archer could still see it – the message that had been brought in. The colonel had read it through before Fortescue had pushed back, quietly but firmly. The colonel had only glanced at it again and then shaken his head. Major General Fortescue was to return to headquarters. No discussion. No exceptions.

Both men made their way of to a waiting lorry, neither man spoke. Fortescue broke the silence. "I'll be carrying on to Tobruk." Archer nodded. "Yes, Sir."

"I'm sorry I can't take you and your chaps with me."

Archer gave a short breath through his nose. "I appreciate you trying, Sir."

The general replaced his cap, and his manner shifted, becoming just a shade more formal. "Lieutenant."

Archer recognised the change at once. He straightened instinctively, not quite to attention, but with a stiffness born of respect as he waited. Fortescue's expression softened, just enough.

"Remember," he said quietly, "keep the bat straight and your eye on the ball, and you won't go far wrong."

He raised his hand in salute. Archer returned it without hesitation.

"Good luck, Lieutenant." Then Fortescue turned away and walked towards the waiting staff car before climbing in as the engine coughed into life.

Archer watched the staff car disappear, and then he turned as Sergeant Jacks emerged from between two parked Bedfords, sleeves rolled up, face darkened by the sun, and his sweat-stained shirt clinging to him. A rifle was slung over his shoulder. His eyes searched Archer's face for the answer he already suspected.

McBain arrived a moment later with Anderson close behind him, both men had a cloak of dust and dirt that was now a part of them. They waited silently.

There was a muffled rattle behind them, and the four men drew together in a small circle. Archer's face was set, and his expression was grave as he glanced around at them. No one spoke. Jacks broke the momentary silence. "I've seen that face before."

The young lieutenant's eyes went to him at once, his head tilting slightly in acknowledgement. When he spoke, his voice was low but clear. "There's a general order in place. Everything west of Acroma is to hold."

Jacks frowned. "Hold what, Sir?"

"In our case," Archer replied, "A dried-out wadi. About ten miles west of here."

He produced a small piece of notepaper with a hand-drawn map on it. All three men leant in to study the scrap. It was the simplest map any of them had ever seen: a single line marking the coast road, a few rough scratches for landmarks, and a circled point scored with an exclamation mark. Two names were written beside it – El Adem and Tobruk – each followed by a bearing.

Archer allowed himself a thin smile as he watched his officers puzzle over the rough diagram.

"I'm afraid the brigadier didn't have a map," he said. "So, he took mine. Our orders are the same as before," Archer continued. "Slow them. Confuse them. Make as much noise as we can. Every unit still west of Gazala is being used, as the brigadier put it, to put grit in the machine."

Jacks took it in without speaking. His eyes drifted instinctively towards the coastal road shimmering beyond the low rise. Vehicles were moving through in ones and twos, Morris trailers, carriers, a dispatch rider kicking an engine into life. The whole place hummed with impermanence.

He took off his helmet, ran his fingers through his matted hair, wiped his forehead with his rolled-up sleeve, then settled the helmet back into place.

"Ten miles, you say, Sir?"

Archer nodded.

"We may struggle on fuel. I reckon we've got less than ten miles in us. Any chance of getting more?"

Archer said nothing.

The look on his face was answer enough.

Jacks gave a short, humourless breath. "I won't ask about ammo then, Sir."

"We have what we have, Geoff."

Archer's use of Jacks Christian name said enough. Formality had gone; this was between men now, not ranks.

Jacks shook his head once. "Just once, Sir, I'd like to have half a chance against this mob. Just once."

McBain rested his hands on his hips. His shirt was open wide to the heat, and his chest was visibly browned by weeks in the sun. His eyes flicked briefly between the men in the small huddle.

"Waters short. My lads are down to about a quarter of a canteen each," he said.

Anderson nodded in agreement. "It's much the same across the rest of the company, Sir."

Archer thought for a moment. "See if you can find anything to top them up. Based on our fuel situation, I suspect we may be on foot at some point in the next day or so."

McBain nodded once and stepped away, already calling quietly for one of his corporals to approach. The small huddle loosened. Jacks and Anderson drifted to pass instructions on to their men.

The afternoon heat lay heavy and unmoving. The sun had begun its slow descent, but it offered no mercy yet, only a flatter, more punishing glare that bleached colour from the makeshift camp. Shadows stretched longer beneath the lorries and tents, forming dark strips of shade that men instinctively gravitated towards.

A Bedford croaked nearby. It failed and then started again with a reluctant growl. Archer watched as the driver leant against the wing for a moment with his head bowed, gathering himself before climbing back in. Beyond him, the coastal road lay in the distance, a pale ribbon bleached into the landscape. Dust drifted over it in thin veils, stirred by traffic too far away to see.

Archer lingered. He took in the light, the ground, the distance still to cover. He was sure much of it would have to be done on foot. They were some forty miles west of Tobruk. If they were lucky, the trucks might carry them halfway, but the rest would be a march all the same.

He stood by the lead vehicle, the door open, one hand resting on the sun-warmed metal. He glanced along the column. "Let's go. I want us in position before night."

The last of his words were lost beneath the splutter and grind of gears as engines were coaxed into life across the company.

It was a slow ten-mile trek, but they reached the wadi just before the light began to fail. It was little more than a dry, winding, shallow scar in the ground. Its banks were cut low and uneven by long-forgotten rains. Not much to look at, but enough. Enough to break the line of sight from the road. Enough to give the men somewhere to fold themselves into.

Archer walked it slowly, and his boots scuffed on hard-packed sand. He lifted his repeatedly to the rim. The ground fell away well enough for rifles and bodies, but the 2-pounder was another matter. The crevice might hide the gun, but only just.

Judging angles, he crouched, hand on his stubbled chin, and then he shook his head. "Exposed," he muttered.

Jacks and McBain came up beside him. Archer was still studying the ground when a slight bend in the wadi to his south caught his eye.

"Jacks, get the gunners to sight the gun back another ten yards. Tuck it behind that bend. Dig it in," he said, firm now. "Deep as you can. When this goes off, they'll be the centre of attention."

He turned to Lieutenant McBain and pointed further to their south. "Al, get the vehicles behind that rise over there. Have them facing east. When we run, I don't want us faffing about. We'll need to be gone quickly."

The orders went down the line. Picks and entrenching tools came out, and their metal rang dully against stone. Men worked in short bursts, swapping places without being told, sweat darkening their collars even as the evening air began to cool. Sand was piled low and wide, shaped by hands and boots rather than care.

As the sun finally slipped away, the desert changed its mood. Heat drained out of the ground, leaving a creeping chill in its place. Breath began to show. Jackets were pulled on. Helmets were loosened and scarves were drawn up around necks. By full dark, the wadi had taken them in.

The 2-pounder sat lower now. Its shape was broken, and the gun shield had been dulled with dust and shadow. Rifles lay ready along the bank. Men settled into their scrapes, backs against earth, packs under heads.

There was little talk. Only the quiet sounds of a night position being made: a last shovel stroke, a buckle tightened, the soft click of a bolt eased home.

Everything was slower now. Men worked without urgency, without waste, the day's toll beginning to show. Each movement was measured as if anything more would cost them.

No one spoke of the day. There was no need. It sat between them, the fighting, the dead, the retreat. It carried in the silence, in the way they moved, in the looks they shared without speaking.

Archer moved along the line once more, exchanging nods, a word here, or a hand on a shoulder there. The men were tired, yet comfortable in the way soldiers became when the work was done, and the night had not yet turned hostile.

Above them, the stars appeared one by one.

The cold would come later.

The cold never arrived all at once.

It crept in, low and patient, seeping up through the soles of their boots and into the small of the back where a man sat too long without moving. The sand that had burnt through trousers only hours before would soon draw warmth out of bone and muscle with quiet insistence.

Someone coughed down the line. Not loudly. The sound was swallowed by the wadi almost at once.

Archer paused near the bend, listening. Nothing else followed. He waited a few seconds more, just to be sure, then moved on.

Along the bank, trench coats were unrolled and shaken out, their stiff folds crackling softly in the dark. Men shrugged into them, buttoning up with fingers that were already clumsy. Scarves were pulled high with the ends tucked awkwardly into collars. Others improvised. A spare pair of socks became mittens that had been cut so the thumb and trigger finger were exposed. A strip of towel, tied with string, formed a crude lining beneath a tin hat. One man had cut up a shirt and tied it around his head with a knot under the chin like a housewife back home. It looked ridiculous, but it would keep the wind off his ears.

Helmets were loosened, some set aside entirely to rest against knees or left hanging from straps. The metal had grown too cold to tolerate for long.

Archer stopped beside a Bren team who were crouched low behind the bank. The gun lay cradled between them. Its outline was barely visible. The number two was rubbing his hands together, breath puffing faintly in front of his face.

"Everything settled?" Archer asked quietly.

"Yes, Sir."

Archer nodded and moved on. He didn't ask if they were warm. The answer was obvious.

A little further along, he found Jacks squatting near a shallow scrape. His helmet was off, and a scarf was wound tight around his neck. He was supervising his men without appearing to with eyes that constantly moved, taking in small details.

"Men are asking about a brew," Jacks said softly, before Archer could speak. "I've told them no, for now."

Archer looked along the line. Men shifted their weight, stamping their feet softly, and flexing their fingers inside gloves that did little good. Breath hung pale in the dark.

"What's the water situation?" Archer asked.

Jacks hesitated. "If we're careful, Sir, enough for tomorrow. Not generous."

It was night, and they had to be careful with the light. Archer paused, weighing it. He could feel the cold working its way into his own hands now, the rifle sling stiff against his palm. The night was still young. The worst of it was yet to come.

"Right. One burner per platoon. Keep it sharp. Minimal light. Quarter mugs only."

Jacks looked at him, searching his face for a moment. "Right, Sir."

"And tell them to drink it while it's hot."

Jacks' mouth moved, just slightly. "Aye, Sir."

The word went quietly down the line. Stoves were coaxed into life in the shelter of the bank, shielded with coats and packs. Small blue flames flickered, barely visible. The smell of burning fuel drifted through the wadi, thin but unmistakable.

Men gathered close, crouching, hands extended over mugs that steamed faintly in the cold air. There was no chatter, only murmurs. Someone swore softly as he burnt his fingers and passed the mug on too quickly. Another man blew on his, then blew again, impatient despite himself.

Lockett appeared with an enamel cup. It was a quarter full, and the tea steamed in the cold air. Gratefully, Archer took the mug and held it close, feeling the heat through the tin.

He tilted his head, studying Lockett for a moment, and then he reached into his satchel and drew out his flask. He added a careful splash of whiskey to the tea, no more than that, and passed the flask back without hesitation, motioning for Lockett to take a sip.

Lockett took it and, in an instant, lifted it to his lips. Head tipped back, he swallowed once and handed it straight back. Then he offered Archer his closed hand and dropped something into Archer's palm.

Archer glanced down. A boiled sweet. Its paper was twisted tight at the ends. He gave the barest smile, unwrapped it with his teeth, and let it dissolve on his tongue as he drank. The sweetness cut through the whiskey and the sugary taste was sharp and welcome. Lockett was already gone.

The brew didn't last long. It never did. But while it was there, the men's shoulders eased. Breathing slowed. Men leant back against the bank with the mugs cradled between palms, and their eyes were half-closed as warmth spread briefly through their chest and belly.

When the mugs were empty, they were shaken of any contents and placed away. The stoves were extinguished. The night closed in again. Time stretched.

The desert at night had its own sounds, and they were never quite what a man expected. The wind shifted constantly, whispering along the wadi, then falling away to nothing. Somewhere to the south, stone clicked as it cooled. Now and then, a faint rustle betrayed something small moving across the sand, unseen.

Archer settled himself near the bend of the wadi with his back against the bank, and his rifle across his knees. He checked his watch by touch, then didn't look at it again. His thoughts drifted, unbidden, to Charlotte as it always did in these moments.

A flare shot up far to the east. Its pale white arc bloomed briefly against the stars before drifting down and dying. Heads lifted along the line. A few men stiffened.

Archer waited. No follow-up. No engine noise. No answering flare. "Stand easy," came the murmured call from the NCOs.

Later, there was the distinct sound of engines. Very distant but again, the men stiffened. It was a low, steady sound that might have been wind, or might not. It came and went, teasing the ear. Men leant forwards, listening hard, then eased back again when it faded.

The waiting was worse than the heat had been. In the day, discomfort had been obvious, shared. Almost a companion. At night, each man sat with it alone.

One man was quietly relieved when his teeth began to chatter too loudly. Another flexed his fingers repeatedly, careful not to scrape metal against stone. Somewhere near the centre of the line, someone sneezed softly, and then all was still.

Halfway through the night, Archer moved along the line, slow and deliberate. He paused to murmur a word to a corporal whose greatcoat had stiffened with sweat and dust, the fabric creaking as the man shifted. He crouched briefly beside a rifleman whose hands shook violently, Archer waited until the tremor eased, saying nothing at all except a gentle tap the man on his shoulder.

Close by, Corporal Matthews stood with his rifle grounded, and his hands resting on the sling. His helmet was pulled low. As Archer approached, he straightened and then relaxed again at the small nod that told him not to bother.

"Cold enough for you?"

"Just enough to keep me awake, Sir."

Archer nodded. "You still glad you transferred?"

Matthews shrugged. "Ask me again when my fingers work properly."

Archer smiled and placed a hand briefly on the corporal's shoulder. "I'm sure they'll be fine when you need them."

"Aye, Sir."

Archer moved on without another word.

He trusted Matthews. The man had proved himself under fire more than once: calm where others rushed, careful where others guessed. A sapper by trade, a demolition man who had chosen to stay on with Archer and the few who had come back from France, when he might just as easily have gone elsewhere. That had earnt Archer's trust. It mattered. Archer didn't say it aloud, but it mattered.

A little further along, he settled with his back to the bank standing but at rest with his rifle pitched against the wadi wall, and his helmet tipped forwards to cut the glare of the stars. His eyes closed for a moment. It wasn't sleep. Not quite. It was just enough to let the cold settle where it would, so he could feel it properly and be ready when it asked for more.

The stars were sharp and unforgiving above the men: a sky too full of light for any comfort. The moon had not yet risen. When it did, he knew, it would betray them all.

Sometime after midnight, the cold deepened. It seemed to sink into the wadi itself, settling there like water. Men shifted, stamping feet more certainly but careful not to disturb the sand. Breath fogged in front of their faces more heavily now. The cold metal of their weapons bit through gloves.

As the hours wore on, men began to nod where they sat with their heads dipping. They would suddenly snap back up again as discomfort set in. Archer allowed it, within reason. A few minutes here and there, they needed that. But he made sure no one slept too deeply. He made sure no one was left alone for too long.

Just before the first hint of false dawn touched the horizon, Archer found himself alone again, standing near the bend, looking east. The cold had settled fully into his bones now. He could feel it in his knees, his wrists, the base of his spine.

He thought of Fortescue who was already well on his way to Tobruk. The headlights would be hooded, and the convoy would be moving steadily through the dark. He thought of Tobruk, still so distant. He thought of the men around him, folded into the earth, quiet and small.

There would be movement soon.

He could feel it, the way a man felt the weather changing.

He turned back towards the line, drawing his coat tighter around him.

"Stand to," he said softly, the words passing from mouth to mouth, from shoulder to shoulder.

Men stirred. Rifles were brought up. Hands steadied.
The night loosened its grip slightly as the horizon paled, but the cold remained. And the waiting had only just begun.

CHAPTER 21

Dawn crept higher, the light strengthening but it was still colourless, and the desert was washed flat beneath a pale sky. The wadi lay in shadow. Its edges were soft and indistinct while beyond it, the coast road emerged slowly from the grey to form a hard line cut across the sand.

Archer had not moved. He leant into the rock with his binoculars braced, and his elbows sunk into the grit. For a long time, there was nothing. Then, at the far edge of his vision: movement. As Archer kept watch, a dark shape resolved itself, then another, sliding along the road from the west. Lorries, perhaps. Too far yet for him to be sure. The heat shimmer had not returned, but distance played its own tricks, stretching and blurring outlines until nothing quite held its shape. More shapes followed. It formed an unevenly spaced cluster. One of the shapes sat lower than the rest, its profile squat and purposeful.

Another flashed briefly as it crossed a patch of pale ground, its metal catching the light. Staff cars, maybe? Possibly armour?

Archer held his glasses steady, willing the picture to settle. When his eyes had focused as much as they could, he lowered them briefly and glanced along the line. They were ready. His men were still. Heads down. Rifles laid ready. The 2-pounder crouched back from the rim, its crew hunched and waiting. McBain was beside them, ever watchful.

Archer raised the binoculars again and focused in on the column. It was closer now, the shapes firmer. He caught the tell-tale angles of enemy lorries, the spacing wrong for British movement. Their pace was measured and deliberate. Advancing and alert. He felt the familiar tightening in his chest, the urge to act before the moment slipped away.

For a split second, his mind flicked back to the bridge in France. The memory had been stirred by what he was seeing now. Two armoured cars led the column: one light, the other heavier with its squat turret marking it out as something more dangerous. Behind them came a handful of lorries, and a pair of motorcycles ranging ahead and to the flanks. He could imagine the men riding, alert, eager for action in the back of the lorries.

Archer's mind was fixed on the moment, when to give the order. Too early and they would scatter. Too late and the window would close altogether. He counted silently, watching the lead vehicle roll towards a point in the road he had chosen, waiting until the bulk of the convoy was within range, close enough that the first burst would catch them all. The column moved at a steady pace, engines labouring as the ground rose and fell. Dust lifted behind each vehicle in low veils, the spacing deliberate and unchanged.

He eased the glasses down and started to lift his hand slightly, ready to give the order.

The lead vehicle reached the point Archer had marked. Its wheels crunched on the hard edge of the road as it rolled into the open ground beyond. The column followed, stretching out in an orderly routine. They were close enough now that Archer could see faces in the lorry beds, helmets bobbing with the road's rise and fall.

Archer let the seconds' run.

One more vehicle.

Then another.

He raised his arm.

The movement was slow and deliberate, but it rippled instantly along the line. Rifles tightened into shoulders. Breath was held. The 2-pounder's crew leant in. The gun was already laid, its barrel steady on the road below.

McBain crouched beside the shield. His eyes flicked between the sight and the target. The lead vehicle was fully clear now, and the second one closed behind it, the spacing just right.

"On!" McBain shouted.

The 2-pounder spoke with a flat, cracking report that slapped back off the wadi walls. McBain saw the solid shot strike short and spark once as it clipped the metalled road before it skipped away in a hard, ugly ricochet. No pause.

The gun leapt, the breech slammed open, hands already moving. Another round was rammed home, and the trail kicked back into line. The second shot struck hard and true.

The lead vehicle lurched, slewed across the road, and then collapsed in a burst of dust and metal, its front axle folding beneath it.

As the first shell had left the 2-pounder, Anderson's voice cut through the moment. "Fire!"

Rifles cracked in disciplined sequence. Bolts worked fast and clean as the Brens opened up, their steady hammering stitching the road. Men fired without hurry. Each shot was placed: each movement had been drilled into them long before this moment.

Jacks moved among the sections, low and urgent, pointing out targets, shifting fire where it was needed, keeping the line tight.

Anderson was already beside Webb's Bren, crouched close with his hand chopping the air. "That one. Short bursts. Good. Again. Now right, ten yards. Take him."

Webb adjusted smoothly, the Bren barking in controlled bursts.

Meanwhile, Pritchard was already switching targets. He picked up one of the motorcycle riders and fired once. The man pitched sideways and vanished into the dust. Saunders, just a few feet away, stared for a fraction of a second, then worked his bolt and fired again.

Saunders had been tight before it started. His jaw had been clenched, and his breath was shallow. The waiting was always worse than anything that followed. Now, with the firing underway, the edge had gone. He worked his rifle steadily with movements that were small and precise. The world reduced to sight picture and trigger squeeze. The noise no longer mattered. Nor the shouting. Each shot brought him back into himself. The fear settled into something usable, a low, steady focus that carried him through the drill as if it had been waiting there all along.

He was fixed on one lorry and stayed with it. He watched the men in the back rather than the vehicle itself. Picking a figure, he fired, worked the bolt, and fired again. Pritchard's example was in his mind, not as something to match, but something to aim towards. He forced himself to slow, to make each shot count, and his breathing settled as the rhythm took hold. The fear did not vanish, but it narrowed and was drawn into the sights, into the simple determination to hit something every time he squeezed the trigger.

Further along the line, Evans stayed anchored to his scrape. His boots were braced, and his body was angled just enough to work the bolt without lifting his cheek from the stock. His rifle cracked again and again, steady and unhurried, the bolt cycling almost without thought. It was the drill beaten into them long before France, long before the desert, when speed and accuracy were the same thing. Shot, bolt, sight, shot. The rhythm never broke. Men dropped where he aimed. Others flinched and froze under the weight of it as if the fire were coming from more than just Evans' rifle.

To Archer, watching from the corner of his eye, it was second nature made visible: a trained infantryman falling into a drill as natural as walking. The only pause in Evans' rhythm came when he fed another charger into the steel guides and pressed five more rounds into the magazine before carrying on.

Archer observed the change before he felt it. The initial onslaught was spent, and the shouting on the road took on shape. It was no longer a cacophony of individuals but carried by one voice that others answered. Returning fire began to come back with purpose. Not wild but aimed, snapping in along the line. The air cracked above his head as rounds ricocheted off stone close by rather than vanishing harmlessly into the sand.

The answering fire found them at last. A burst snapped in hard and close, and stone flew as a Bren gunner collapsed without a sound. The gun dipped and fell silent. Evans was already moving. He came up out from his scrape and crossed the short gap at a crouch, his boots skidding on stone as rounds cracking overhead. He dragged the gunner clear by his webbing without stopping to look, dropped behind the gun, and brought it back into line. The Bren opened again in his hands, steady and controlled.

Finally, the armoured car's gun spoke, and a flat, hammering crack cut through the rifle fire and tore at the ground around the 2-pounder. The first burst fell short, skipping and ripping through the shallow scrapes either side of them. Stone and sand exploded upwards. A man screamed and dropped. Another was flung back hard, his rifle spinning from his hands as he hit the ground. The line buckled for a moment, heads driven down as the shock of it ran through them.

The armoured car had them now. McBain saw the tracer snap past the shield and bite into the ground behind it. It was close enough to feel the concussion through the soles of his boots.

"They've seen us," he shouted, ducking instinctively as another burst cracked overhead. "Get that bastard silenced. Now."

He dropped to a knee beside the gun. One hand was braced against the trail as the crew worked, the noise of the twenty-millimetre hammering closer with each burst.

The armoured car edged forwards: not charging yet deliberate. Its engine note changed pitch as the driver eased it on. Sand fanned out from its wheels in short bursts, then settled again. It had found their gun. McBain could feel it in the way its turret turned: not sweeping but stopping, selecting its spot.

The first burst came in low. The twenty-millimetre cracked and the ground in front of the 2-pounder erupted, stone and sand slapping hard against the shield. A man cried out. Another ducked instinctively, too late to stop a splinter cutting his cheek. McBain felt the shock through his boots and tasted grit. He didn't think in terms of armour or calibre, only that the thing in front of him was hunting them.

"On him!" he shouted, voice hoarse. "Kill that bastard."

The gun crew worked with sudden, savage focus. The traverse was nudged by inches, not yards. Elevation corrected, then corrected again. The barrel seemed to breathe as the gunner held it steady, waiting for the armoured car to commit. It was close enough now that McBain could see the markings on the side of a closed turret: black on white cross seeming to magnify with each passing moment.

Another burst snapped out. Higher this time. Three explosions raked across the front of the 2-pounder, stone fragments blasting outwards in hard, stinging clouds. The armoured car was forcing its fire in. Burst by burst, adjusting under pressure. The turret swung as the driver edged it round. It did not linger. It was trying to finish the job before their gun could speak again. "Now," McBain said, not loud, but certain.

The 2-pounder spoke again. The recoil slammed back. The shield shuddered, and the shot cracked across the flat ground. For a fraction of a second, it looked wrong, too low, too far left. Then it struck. The solid round hit the sloped armour beneath the turret ring and skidded away, thrown off by the angle with a shriek of metal. The armoured car lurched hard, slewing sideways in a grinding spray of dust, but it did not stop.

The turret snapped round at once. The twenty-millimetre answered, and the ground beside McBain exploded. He was thrown flat, ears ringing, mouth full of dust. When he looked up, the shield was peppered white, and the gun crew were gathering themselves. One man was on his hands and knees trying to regain his breath, another was dragging a dropped round back towards the breech. Someone swore. Someone else shouted that he was hit. The gun sat silent for a heartbeat longer than it should have.

McBain hauled himself upright, spitting grit from his mouth, and he turned to the sergeant.

“Sergeant, if you don’t mind, kill that bloody thing.”

The crew were already moving. The breech clanged, a round slammed home, hands slick with sweat and grit. The second shot punched straight through the armoured car’s hull. It shuddered, slowed, then slewed to the right as flames licked inside, brief and violent.

A third round went in, low and solid. Fire filled the vehicle. Black smoke rolled upwards, climbing steadily into the hard blue sky. A figure clawed at the turret edge and vanished back inside. The armoured car burnt where it stood. Ammunition inside cooked off with dull cracks, sharp enough to make a few men flinch.

For a few seconds, the noise ebbed. Rifle fire slackened, becoming scattered rather than constant. Men lifted their heads cautiously, blinking through smoke and dust. Someone laughed, short and breathless, more of a release than humour. Another voice called out, asking if anyone had a light. A wounded man was dragged back into cover, his boots leaving a dark trail in the dust. The smell of burning fuel and scorched metal hung thick in the air.

Archer took it in without comment. They had held so far. The gun was still working. For the briefest moment, it felt as though they had broken the counterattack.

Then a round came in without warning. There was no whine, no time to flinch, just a sudden thump somewhere beyond the line, and a column of dust rose and collapsed again as quickly as it had appeared. A few men looked up instinctively, puzzled more than alarmed. The second round landed further out. It was longer this time, bursting beyond the wadi lip. Someone laughed again, nervously, and then stopped when the third round came down short, but close enough to be felt through the ground.

Archer knew what it was before anyone said it. He dropped his head and shouted along the line: the words were half lost in the noise. "Mortars. Keep down."

The next bombs began to fall in a loose pattern, not yet settled. Some were long, some short. The Germans were feeling for them. The bursts were smaller than artillery but sharper: a violent crack followed by a hammering rush of fragments. Sand and stone pattered down into the scrapes, stinging exposed skin, filling mouths and eyes. Men pressed themselves flatter, fingers clawing into the dirt as if they could sink through it.

Evans felt the ground lift beneath him and slam back down. Something struck his shoulder hard enough to spin him, knocking the breath from his lungs. He lay still for a moment, stunned, listening to the dull ringing in his ears before he forced himself to move again. His arm burnt hot and wet, but he kept the Bren up, firing short bursts whenever he glimpsed movement through the dust.

A round burst just behind Saunders' scrape. The shockwave threw him forwards. He crawled back on his elbows, breathing fast, eyes wide, trying to work out where he was. His helmet lay a few feet away, split clean along the rim. He didn't notice at first that his hands were shaking, the shock of it still running through his body.

The fire began to creep closer. The Germans had the line now, and they were adjusting. The bombs were walking in methodically. A scrape to Archer's left vanished in a rush of dust and noise. When it cleared, Archer could see one man sitting upright, dazed, with blood running freely from his scalp. The other man did not get up at all.

The 2-pounder was useless against this. The crew crouched low beside it, their hands over their heads, waiting out the storm. Each burst made the gun ring and twitch, the shield chiming as fragments struck it. McBain stayed with the crew. His jaw was clenched as he counted the seconds between rounds, knowing that moving now would only draw the fire tighter.

Along the line, rifles fell silent. The Brens fired only in brief, angry bursts when the dust thinned enough to show shapes moving beyond the wadi. The mortars owned the ground now. They didn't kill cleanly, but they broke rhythm and confidence, turning cover into a trap and every pause into a gamble.

Archer felt the position shrinking under him. Men were still with him, still fighting, but the ground itself had turned hostile. He could feel it in the way heads stayed down for longer, in the way orders had to be shouted twice, and in the way even the bravest men began to measure time in seconds between explosions.

The mortars did not stop, but they loosened their grip. The bursts became less regular, drifting back and forth across the wadi as the Germans shifted focus. In the gaps between explosions, movement began to show itself around Archer.

The mortars had done what they were meant to do. Men stayed pressed into the dirt, counting the seconds between bursts, waiting for the next one to come closer.

The Germans used the space it gave them. It wasn't a rush, not yet. It was just movement where there had been hesitation before. Short bounds. Pauses. Their shapes resolved briefly through the dust before sinking back into cover.

Archer raised his head and shouted, low but hard.

"They're coming on. Infantry. Get firing."

Men forced themselves up, blinking grit from their eyes, rifles quickly moving back onto shoulders by habit rather than comfort. A few shots cracked out, then more. Uneven at first, but they slowly found their rhythm as sections remembered their arcs and fields of fire.

The German machine-guns opened up almost at once. Not a single roaring sweep but overlapping bursts that pinned heads back down and stitched the edges of their position. The fire came from multiple directions. It was hard to fix, snapping in from the flanks as well as the front. It was covering fire: disciplined and deliberate, buying ground for the men moving forwards.

Jacks was already on his feet, moving at a crouch between scrapes. "Steady," he called. "Pick them when they break cover. Don't rush it."

The Brens answered first. Evans fired in short, vicious bursts, and the gun chattered and then fell silent as he shifted aim. Dirt kicked up around the advancing figures. One man went down and stayed down. Another dragged him back by the webbing and disappeared into dead ground.

Along the line, rifles joined in, the sound changing at once. The sharper crack of single shots gave way to rhythm. Bolts worked fast and clean, men firing as they had been trained: not wildly, but with intent. The 'mad minute' kicked in, rifles working at speed, each man driving his bolt and firing as fast as he could aim, not as a drill but as a pressure instinctively understood. Fire, work the bolt, fire again. The line found its pace.

Saunders forced himself to breathe and settled into the moment. He chose a patch of ground where the Germans had to cross open sand and held his sights there, waiting. When a helmet broke the line, he fired, felt the recoil, worked the bolt without thinking, and fired again. The fear shrank, pulled inwards by the need to hit what was in front of him.

The Germans advanced in short bounds. One group moved while another lay down and fired. When they halted, the covering fire lifted, and the next group came on. They made use of every piece of possible cover. Shallow folds and scrub. The smoking wreck of the armoured car had even become a landmark to use as cover as much as it was an obstacle. Men slipped behind it, firing from its far side before moving again.

Machine-gun fire intensified on their left. Archer saw one section who were forced flat, pinned by bursts that chewed at the lip of their cover. Jacks was there in seconds, moving between scrapes, touching shoulders as he went. "That's it lads," he said. "Keep up the fire. Hold them."

The two Brens opened together, raking the ground beyond the wreck. The German fire faltered just long enough. Rifle shots snapped in behind it, precise and unforgiving. A German machine-gun team was silenced. The pressure eased.

The Germans were even closer. Close enough that Archer could see facial features when the dust thinned. He could make out the way they moved, low and practised with their rifles tucked in tight. They were not rushing. They were trying to prise the position open, piece by piece.

Without warning, mortar rounds fell again. Fewer this time but placed to herd them rather than to destroy. One burst drove a section sideways into ground they would rather not have occupied. Another fell behind the line, cutting off easy movement between scrapes. Their position felt smaller with every minute.

The 2-pounder was silent. Its crew were pressed low with their rifles in hand. It was no longer a weapon here, just another shape drawing fire. McBain stayed with it, eyes scanning, knowing its time had passed.

Meanwhile, Evans fired until the Bren's barrel smoked, and then he changed position by inches, dragging the gun with him. He didn't look back at the man he had pulled clear earlier. There was no room to think about him now. When the Germans rose again, Evans met them with fire.

Suddenly, a German section made a push on the right, moving faster, sensing an opening. Archer saw it at once.
"Right side!" he shouted. "Now."

Fire snapped out in answer. Pritchard's rifle cracked, and a man pitching forwards broke the rush. Beside him, Saunders fired again, and again, working the bolt hard, his shoulder aching. The advance faltered and then collapsed back into cover.

The Germans tried again elsewhere. This time on the left and again they were met with a brutal answer. Repeatedly, they probed, adjusted, and shifted their weight along the line. Each time they rose, they were met by rifle fire that came too fast, too accurately. The British sections were fighting independently now, but they were still connected, still aware of one another's fields of fire.

Jacks moved constantly: encouraging, correcting, dragging a man back into cover here, shouting ammunition counts there. He was everywhere Archer needed him to be without being asked.

A German machine-gun opened up from close range, its fire slashing across the wadi floor. A Bren answered at once. The two weapons hammered back and forth. The German gun fell silent. A cheer started and then died as another burst of mortar fire landed nearby.

Minutes dragged. Not quieter, but different. The rush of the attack slowed and was replaced by something more deliberate. German movement became measured again. Less frequent this time. Each bound was covered properly before the next began. They were no longer testing the line. They were settling into it.

Archer felt the change as a tightening rather than a release, the fight no longer ebbing but closing in again as the enemy settled and began to press. This was the dangerous moment, when the enemy stopped spending men and started spending time.

Rifle fire continued, but it came in shorter bursts now, purposeful rather than frantic. Mortar rounds still fell but further out, obviously herding rather than smashing. Beyond the wadi, figures slipped back into dead ground, reappearing somewhere else minutes later. The pressure never lifted. It shifted.

Archer stayed low and moved along the line. He found Jacks first, crouched behind a scrape, face grey with dust. "They're not going to stop," Archer said.

Jacks nodded at once. "Aye. They're a determined bunch."

Archer moved on to McBain who was still with the 2-pounder. The gun was silent now, and its crew were crouched close. He shook his head before Archer spoke.

"She'll deal with vehicles," he said. "But against infantry, with solid shot, she's bloody near useless."

Archer glanced past him towards the wadi.

"Maybe," he said. "But she's keeping their heads down. And she's giving them something to think about."

Archer found Anderson last. The sergeant was propped against the side of a scrape, helmet off, leg stretched out awkwardly. Blood darkened his trouser below the knee had already stiffened with dirt. He grinned when he saw Archer as if to make light of it. "Nothing clever," Anderson said. "Caught it early."

Archer crouched beside him, keeping his voice low. The fire still cracked along the wadi rim, close enough that neither of them had to look to know the pressure hadn't eased.

"We can't stay," Archer said.

Anderson nodded at once. He shifted his bad leg an inch and stopped, breath tightening before he spoke again.

"No."

Archer waited a beat.

"We won't make the lorries if we try to carry everyone."

Anderson met his eye. There was no surprise there.

"You won't carry me," he said. "And you shouldn't try."

Archer's mouth tightened. There was a flicker of relief that Anderson understood that there was no getting him out, and he knew it. The young lieutenant nodded once and put a hand briefly on the sergeant's shoulder.

"I'll keep them steady," Anderson added.

"I know," Archer said.

Archer straightened just enough to be heard.

"Jacks. McBain. We're leaving."

Archer didn't raise his voice when he gave the order. He didn't need to.

Jacks was already moving, passing the word along the line in fragments and gestures. Men shifted without question, rifles still facing forwards, fire thinning and thickening as sections began to peel back from the rim. It was not a retreat yet. It was preparation. The Germans were still there: their fire probing and patient, but the rhythm had changed. The British line loosened, and then re-formed further back, one scrape at a time.

McBain didn't waste words, telling the crew. "We're moving."

The gun crew went to work without being told. Someone brought the sledge down hard on the breech. Once, twice. Metal rang flat and ugly. Sand was kicked into the open block. Thirty seconds later, the gun was just iron and dust, and they were running.

They didn't look back. They moved at a crouch. Rifles were slung awkwardly as they disappeared into the shallow folds that led back towards the transport. McBain stayed a moment longer. His eyes remained focused on the wadi, and then he followed them, leaving the gun squatting uselessly behind its shield.

The Germans fired as the movement became clearer. Machine-gun bursts snapped in, raking the ground the men had just left. Mortars fell again. Not close enough to stop the withdrawal but close enough to hurry it Archer lay low at the edge of the wadi, watching the sections pull back down the far slope towards the vehicles below. The ground broke unevenly there, shallow dips and folds cutting the descent. Men dropped into them and disappeared from sight, then rose again a few yards further on, faces flashing into view before vanishing once more.

They arrived in twos and threes, to the vehicles below, breathless and dust-caked, some bleeding, but all still armed.

At the transport area, engines coughed into life and settled into a rough idle. Men were still dropping in from the line, rifles slung and hands shaking as they clambered into cabs or hauled themselves over tailboards. Drivers were hunched forwards, glancing back over their shoulders, waiting for the word to go. Jacks dropped in beside Archer.

"I've got Evans and Webb on Brens. Saunders and Pritchard in support." He glanced back along the wadi. "Left a few behind. No choice."

Archer nodded once. He trusted Jacks' judgement without question. The four men who were left to cover their retreat were exactly the four he would have chosen. "Get them moving," Archer said.

The line contracted further. Fire lifted and fell as men moved. The soundscape changed as distance grew. The Germans pressed a little harder now, sensing the shift. Their machine-guns snapped more insistently, bullets cracking overhead and thudding into sand where the British had been moments before. But the covering fire of Evans, Webb, Saunders and Pritchard held them. The Brens spoke in short, vicious bursts, and then they fell silent as the rifles answered, keeping the enemy's heads down just long enough.

Evans lay behind the Bren with the gun braced, and his body was angled into the wadi wall. The barrel smoked faintly. Webb was a few yards to his right. His own Bren answered in controlled bursts. The two weapons worked together without need for words. Saunders and Pritchard lay slightly back, rifles trained forwards, bolts working fast and clean as they fed shots into the gaps between the Brens' bursts, the crack of their fire almost keeping pace. Jacks dropped in beside them.

"Right," he said firmly. "Pairs. Webb with Saunders. Then Pritchard and Evans. I'll move with the second."

Evans' Bren opened up, and Webb was already moving, running low, boots slipping on sand before he dropped hard behind a fold in the ground. Saunders was with him, half a step back, rifle tight to his hand. Webb rolled the gun into line and fired. Saunders followed at once, bolt flashing as he fed shots at the Germans.

Evans kept the Bren working: short, deliberate bursts, the recoil steady against his shoulder. Pritchard fired beside him, faster than felt comfortable. Rounds snapped out as German fire answered, cracking into the dirt around them. Jacks stayed low between them, watching the ground, counting the seconds. "Up."

Evans rose and ran. His Bren was held close. Pritchard ran with him. They dropped beside Webb and Saunders and immediately turned back onto the wadi. Fire came at them almost before they were settled. The drill closed around them again. Breathe. Fire. Lift. Watch. They did it once more.

Gradually, the Germans moved closer. Shapes held longer through the dust. A machine-gun opened from the far side of the wadi. Its fire slashed in, stitching the ground Evans had crossed moments earlier. Mortar rounds fell further back, the dull thumps meaning to cut them off rather than stop them.

Jacks shifted, already reading it.

"Again," he said. "Same pairs."

Webb and Saunders moved first. Evans covered, Pritchard firing beside him. Jacks stayed low with them, working his rifle as he judged the moment. They held the ground just long enough, then moved again. Only one more bound to the lorries now. They were close.

Evans rose for his bound. Time stopped as Jacks watched Evans fall mid-step.

There was no cry.

No stumble.

One moment he was upright, the next his body folded.

Hard and wrong.

The Bren skidded from his hands.

He did not move again.

For half a second, nothing happened.

No one moved.

Then Webb was firing, his Bren hammering furiously as Pritchard went for Evans, dragging him back by the webbing, hauling him into cover without looking at his face. "Leave him," Jacks said, sharp and final. "Move."

Pritchard swallowed hard and released the webbing. He didn't look back. He couldn't.

They moved the last distance together.

Running hard now.

No longer bounding but moving as one.

The enemy fire snapped in behind them: too late, too scattered. A round cracked into the dirt beside Webb and showered him with grit His head dipped instinctively, shoulders tightening against the strike. He did not slow.

They reached the last Bedford in a rush. Their breath tore at their chests. Hands grabbed out at them, hauling them in over the tailboard, and they were dragged unceremoniously onto the wooden bed, falling among boots and knees as men pulled them clear.

Already in the back waiting for them, Archer banged on the cab roof.

"Go! Go! Go!"

The engines revved. Lorries lurched forwards as men clambered aboard, hauling one another up by webbing and sleeves. German fire followed them, snapping and ineffective now. A few rounds cracked into tailboards while others zipped past without finding flesh.

The lorries pulled away in a staggered line with their engines labouring as they bounced across the rough ground. Dust rose behind them, thick and blinding. Archer looked back once, just once, towards the wadi.

The Germans were still there, small and distant now, their fire fading as the range opened. The 2-pounder stood abandoned where it had been left: a useless shape against the sand. Beyond it, somewhere closer, a body lay where it had fallen, already becoming part of the desert.

An anonymous voice said, "What? Evans?" The tone was disbelieving.

Pritchard turned back, eyes fixed on where Evans had fallen. For a moment, he didn't move. The pull to get out of the lorry and go to him hit even harder: he forced it down.

Jacks closed in beside him. "Dave, he's gone. You know that." He gripped his arm briefly. "Come on."

Archer had seen Evans go down. He had taken it in without drama, registered it as fact in motion. As he sat with Pritchard and Jacks, he thought about Evans for a moment, but then realised he couldn't let Evans' death become anything more. There was no time for that now. He turned forwards and braced himself against the lurch of the vehicle, numbness spreading through his body. They were moving.

CHAPTER 22

The lorries kept going for a while longer than Archer expected. That, more than anything, gave the lie to hope. Engines droned steadily, and tyres thumped over hard ground. The men were slumped where they stood or sat, packed tight against one another, backs against wooden sides, heads bowed, and rifles held loosely between their knees. There was no room to stretch, no space left unused. The closeness left no room for anything else, each man with his own thoughts, but held there together. Someone slept with his mouth open, chin on chest. Another man quietly laughed once, at nothing in particular, but quickly went silent again.

The desert slid past in dull bands of colour. Sand, stone, and scrub, all bleached to the same flat shade beneath the rising sun. The light was already harsh, and the early cool had drained away, replaced by the familiar pressure that pressed down on shoulders and temples alike.

Archer rode in the second lorry, standing at first because there was nowhere else for him to be. One hand was braced against the tilt as he scanned ahead and behind without really seeing either. After a while, Archer managed a crouch, leaning against the back of the cab. He opened his notebook and ran a thumb down the page, flicking his eyes over names and numbers that had already fixed themselves in his mind.

He braced the notebook against his knee, his pencil paused, then he wrote Evans' name. His gaze on the name was broken by the shifting of men and the sound of the engine. He continued with a few notes then closed the notebook and slipped it back into his satchel.

The coast road lay some five miles off to their left: a pale line he could have turned for if he chose. He did not.

The Germans would be on the road: forward elements, patrols, and vehicles moving with purpose. Archer had no appetite for meeting them head-on with tired men and nothing left to stop them.

Out in the open desert, contact would come early or not at all. He would keep them off the road and let the ground decide the rest.

They had put distance between themselves and the wadi. The firing had fallen away. For the moment, at least, they were unobserved. What mattered now was fuel and how far it would take them. With this thought, Archer heard the lead lorry cough.

It was nothing dramatic. Just a brief hesitation in the engine note. A slight unevenness that most of the men ignored. The driver leant forwards with his foot on the throttle, trying to coax it through. The vehicle carried on, its pace unaltered.

Five minutes later, it happened again. This time, the lorry slowed, only fractionally, but enough that the second lorry closed the gap. The driver glanced back as if looking for reassurance before he looked forwards again, his jaw tightening. The second lorry followed suit a moment later. Its brakes squealed briefly before settling into silence. The sudden quiet was jarring. Idling engines dropped away one by one as the drivers of the other lorries killed them, saving what little fuel remained. It was habit more than hope. Men looked up.

The driver climbed down from the lead vehicle and crouched by the front wheel, lifting the bonnet. Heat washed up around him in a hazy curtain. He stared down into the engine bay for a long moment. He straightened and shook his head once.

Another man tried the starter again. The engine turned over, caught for half a second, then died. He swore under his breath and didn't try again.

Archer stepped down from the lorry and walked forwards, feeling the effort in every step as his boots sank softly into the sand. Each stride dragged at him, heavier than it should have been. He did not hurry. There was no point.

"How much fuel?"

The driver wiped his hands on his trousers. The man glanced back at the lorry, then shrugged. "She's now empty, Sir."

Archer nodded.

He had expected no other answer.

Slowly, the men dismounted, stretching stiff limbs and slinging rifles. Some men sat on the tailboards with their boots planted in the dust. A few looked west without quite knowing why as if something might still come after them. It did not.

Jacks appeared at Archer's side. His helmet was pushed back, and his face was even darker with layers of dust and sweat. He did not ask. He had already worked it out.

"We'll have to walk," he said quietly.

"Yes." Jacks looked past Archer at the lorries, then down the line of men. "Water?"

"Check it."

At once, Jacks turned away, already calling out to the section leaders. The usual voices returned. Canteens were checked and rechecked: stoppers twisted free, water sloshed and weighed in the hand. A few men shook theirs hopefully as if something might appear that hadn't been there before.

Ammunition came next. Pouches felt and counted. The figures were not encouraging. Enough for a skirmish, perhaps. Not enough for a fight.

Someone asked about fuel again as if the answer might change if voiced aloud. No one replied.

The heat was building. The sun climbed higher, and the air already began to shimmer close to the ground. Jackets were loosened, sleeves rolled down despite the warmth as men instinctively protected their skin. They knew they would pay for exposure later.

Archer gathered all the platoon commanders around him in the thin strip of shade thrown by the second lorry. There was no map to spread out. None was needed.

"We go on foot," he said. "Same order. We keep it tight and steady. Keep close. We halt little and often. We move before the worst of the heat if we can." No one argued.

Archer turned to McBain.

"Mr McBain, you'll bring up the rear. Keep them closed up. No stragglers. We've come too far to lose anyone now."

McBain nodded once. "Understood, Sir."

They broke up without ceremony. Packs were adjusted, straps tightened, anything unnecessary was discarded to the desert without comment. A man removed a spare shirt from his pack, tossed his helmet away, and tied the shirt around his head.

Another left behind a battered mess tin that was dented beyond use.

Before they moved off, Archer walked back down the line one last time. Seventy-four men all told. They stood in a rough line beside the trucks, dust-caked and tired, some bandaged, others moving carefully, all worn by the past days' fighting, but not yet spent.

There were no wounded with them who could not walk. The others had been left further back, with what little water Archer could spare and promises no one had voiced aloud. Archer did not look west again. He had done all the looking he was going to do. "Right," he said.

The men formed up without being told, falling into a loose column that would tighten and loosen again as the ground demanded. Rifles were slung. Packs settled into familiar places on tired shoulders.

Archer stepped off first, aiming eastwards. He forced his boots to find their rhythm on the hard-packed sand.

They walked for a time without speaking, conserving their energy.

Relentlessly, the sun climbed higher as though pushing down on each man. Sweat ran freely, darkening collars and soaking into webbing. Short breaths settled into a steady pattern, each man finding his own pace within the group. The desert stretched ahead of them, flat and unforgiving, the horizon a pale blur. No one gave voice to what lay ahead. The march went on.

After half an hour, Archer called a halt. Men dropped where they had stood, sitting or crouching, but grateful for even the briefest pause. Water bottles were passed along, mouths wet rather than filled. No one complained. It took too much effort. When they moved again, the column was smaller.

It was then, somewhere between one halt and the next, that the absence finally asserted itself.

Not in any single moment.

Not with a name spoken aloud.

Just in the way a space opened where it should not have been. Webb noticed it first. He looked up from his boots and scanned the line ahead, brow furrowing slightly before he glanced back. His mouth opened as if to say something, then he closed it again. He adjusted the Bren on his shoulder and kept walking.

Jacks saw it next.

His stride faltered for half a step before he corrected it. He shifted left, closing a gap without comment. His eyes briefly met Archer's. Archer felt it last.

A count that came up short without needing to be made. A weight that was no longer where it should have been.

He did not stop. He did not turn. Their numbers were thinning. Those still on their feet had to keep moving. There was nothing else to be done. They walked on.

The desert offered nothing in the way of distraction. No cover, no variation, just distance measured in steps and short breaths. The heat pressed down. Relentless, it drew water from their skin and strength from their limbs with equal indifference.

At the next halt, Archer redistributed weight. A pack was lightened, a spare ammunition pouch passed forwards, a rifle carried for a man whose shoulder had begun to fail. No one remarked on the absence of familiar hands. They moved again.

Somewhere behind them, a lorry creaked as the wind caught its canvas. Archer did not look back to see which one.

Almost imperceptibly, the ground began to rise into a long, shallow incline that sapped strength without offering any sense of progress as they attempted to climb it. Men leant into it with their heads down. Their boots dragged slightly now, the rhythm slowing despite themselves.

Archer kept the pace deliberately measured as they climbed. Fast enough to make ground Slow enough to hold what remained together.

When they halted again, a man stumbled and went down on one knee, hands pressed into the sand. He stayed there for a moment longer than he should have, breathing hard. Jacks was beside him at once with his hand on the man's shoulder, murmuring something Archer could not hear.

The man got up.

They moved on together.

There was no talk of Tobruk now.

No one pointed east.

No one spoke of distance or time.

Tobruk existed only as a direction, not a destination.

After another mile, Archer halted them again. He checked water once more. Their water was almost gone.

Opening his notebook, he nodded and quickly closed it before slipping it away. They stepped off for the last time that day.

The sun was lowering when Archer finally raised his hand and brought them to a stop. The light had softened slightly, and shadows had lengthened, but the heat still clung stubbornly to the ground.

He had made up his mind.

They would rest while they could.
When darkness came, they would move again.

The men sank down where they stood. Some sat. Some lay flat on their backs, staring up at a sky that was already beginning to pale towards evening. Packs were eased off shoulders and used as pillows. No fires were lit. There was nothing to cook and no reason to draw attention. Archer stood for a while longer, looking east.

In that quiet moment, he thought of Evans. Not as a man falling or a body left behind, but as a place in the platoon that would not be filled again. A standard that would have to be carried without him.

There was no anger in the thought. No self-reproach. Just the steady acceptance of a fact that had been forming since the wadi. He turned back to the men.

"We'll move out in two hours," he said quietly. "Get what rest you can." No one replied.

Archer sat down at last, with his back against his pack, and his rifle across his knees. The desert cooled quickly as the heat drained away almost as fast as it had come. Breath misted faintly in the air. Around him, the company lay scattered and diminished: a loose collection of shapes in the gathering dusk.

Fewer than there should have been. More than there might have been. He did not know which thought weighed heavier.

When the light finally vanished, they lay in silence, and the desert took them in.

AUTHOR'S NOTE

Under Fire and Sun is set during the early stages of the North African campaign, centred around the British offensive known as Operation Compass in late 1940.

What began as a limited operation quickly developed into a sweeping advance as British and Commonwealth forces drove Italian units back across Egypt and into Libya. For many soldiers, this period was marked by rapid movement, uncertain intelligence, and the constant challenge of adapting to desert warfare for the first time.

The conditions were as much an enemy as any opposing force. Heat, dust, distance, and mechanical strain shaped every decision, and units were often required to operate independently across vast and unforgiving terrain.

While the Greenmoor Light Infantry and its characters are fictional, their experiences are intended to reflect those of the men who fought in this campaign. Equipment, tactics, and conditions have been portrayed as accurately as possible, though any errors remain my own.

As the campaign progressed, the nature of the war in North Africa would began to change, setting the stage for the battles that followed.

This story is written with respect for those who served.

THANK YOU FOR READING

If *Under Fire and Sun* held your attention to the end, I'd be grateful if you considered leaving a review on Amazon. Even a short review makes a real difference, helping other readers discover the series and allowing me to continue writing.

To keep up with the series and what's coming next, visit www.richardabasquill.com

Thank you for your support. It truly means a great deal.

Richard A. Basquill

CONTINUE THE TOM ARCHER SERIES

Follow Lieutenant Tom Archer's journey through the Second World War:

Under Fire, Under Command

Under Fire and Fury

Under Fire and Sun

The desert has not finished with them yet.

www.ingramcontent.com/pod-product-compliance
Lightning Source LLC
LaVergne TN
LVHW010635110826
845149LV00014B/2845

* 9 7 8 1 0 6 8 1 5 0 2 1 0 *